PADD
YOUR WEALTH

KEITH FEVURLY

FOREWORD TO "PADD YOUR WEALTH"

By Willis G. Ashby, CFP®
Integra Financial, Inc.
Greenwood Village, Colorado

It is my pleasure to write this foreword to the book, "PADD Your Wealth", by my friend and associate, Keith Fevurly, MBA, JD, Esq., LLM (Taxation), CFP®. I have my own very successful financial planning firm, Integra Financial, Inc., in Greenwood Village, Colorado and currently have some forty million dollars of assets under management. My firm, Integra Financial, addresses and solves the financial planning issues discussed by Keith in his book every day. Integra Financial, Inc is a Fee Based Registered Investment Advisor that has been in business since 1990. Our clients, upper middle and upper class families all have the needs addressed in this book. Keith's expertise from teaching me financial planning in my CFP® classes to analyzing complex investment, retirement and estate tax issues is unsurpassed. He boils down complex issues and explains them in terms our clients and you can understand.

In this book, Keith describes a novel way of analyzing and putting into place the personal financial planning process, which he entitles the P.A.D.D. process. The first step in this process is: Protecting Yourself, Your Family, and Your Property, thus the initial "P" in the title of the book. Next comes: Accumulating Wealth (the "A" in the book title), a section that will likely be of the most interest to a broad range of consumers and those who are engaged in financial planning to achieve financial independence. Third,

Keith looks at the Defense of accumulated wealth (the first "D" in the book title), notably discussing income tax planning, with taxes being one of the two great "usurpers" of wealth (the other being the impact of inflation). Finally, Keith takes up the "fun" part of the financial planning process: the Distribution of accumulated wealth (the second "D" in the title) during an individual's lifetime, notably retirement, as well as at death, the date of focus for most estate planning techniques. While there are no guarantees in life, particularly in today's volatile economic marketplace, if you follow the process outlined in this book, you will have a more-likely-than-not chance of accumulating and preserving wealth during your lifetime.

Finally, this book should give you a level of comfort about your financial future. I like to say that my retired and debt free clients live not only in different neighborhoods but on different planets! Using this book with or without a good advisor can help you to live on a different planet with the few others who actually achieve financial success. That is a rare feat in today's marketplace!!

CONTENTS

SECTION I

THE FINANCIAL PLANNING PROCESS

CHAPTER 1

UNDERSTANDING THE CHALLENGE/THE NEED TO BEGIN

WEALTH AND THE PADD APPROACH

We need to understand one thing up front: This is *not* a book about how to get rich quick (although if you follow the advice given in these pages, you may very well become rich). Rather, this is a book about slowly and consistently becoming *wealthy*.

Wealthy, as defined by Webster, is the state of "having wealth" or becoming "extremely affluent." There is no mention of actual money in this definition, but most people can't become wealthy without also being rich. In other words, the amount of dollars you have (either in your pocket or invested in financial or real assets) is equivalent to wealth. This book attempts to go *beyond* the standard definition of monetary accumulation (or what most people think of when they hear the word "rich") to characterize wealth as a process of achievement involving not only financial independence, but also an emotional and psychological state of looking forward to and being comfortable with the future. Indeed, when we substitute the word "successful" for "wealthy," we see that what most individuals want is a successful and fulfilling future which involves much more than purely monetary riches!

So how do we achieve wealth? There is both a hard (monetary) and a soft (psychological) answer to this question, but certainly if your financial affairs are not in order, it complicates the summative belief that you've achieved a wealthy life. Thus, implementing a financial plan to manage the future is very important. If you have not assembled such a plan, or even if you have not thought about how best to manage the future, don't worry—*you're not alone*! Americans are notoriously *bad* planners (and notoriously *good* procrastinators), but the important point to understand is that financial planning and wealth accumulation are a *journey* and *not a destination*.

You need to *begin* the financial planning process and then (hopefully) continue it as best as possible, with or without professional assistance. This book is designed to help you to do both—that is, as a do-it-yourself planner, as many individuals are inclined to be (either by conscious decision or by default of circumstances), or by becoming an educated consumer when seeking the help of a financial planner. In addition, the book will introduce you to a simple way of thinking about the financial planning process: the PADD approach to achieving lifetime wealth. The steps in this approach are as follows:

- *Protect* your assets.
- *Accumulate* monetary wealth.
- *Defend* your wealth.
- *Distribute* this wealth during your lifetime for the benefit of yourself and your family (and for the benefit of your heirs after your death).

Let's begin!

THE STEPS IN THE FINANCIAL PLANNING PROCESS

As put forward in the Certified Financial Planner Board of Standards *Financial Planning Practice Standards*, there are six steps in the personal financial planning process:

1. Establishing and defining the relationship with the financial planning client
2. Gathering client data and determining goals and expectations
3. Determining the client's financial status by analyzing and evaluating client information
4. Developing and presenting the financial plan
5. Implementing the financial plan
6. Monitoring the financial plan

While these steps are intended for the professional Certified Financial Planner(CFP) certificant, there are several tasks that you, as an individual intent on beginning the financial planning process, should also undertake.

The first task is to gather your financial and personal records. A formal, very detailed data-gathering form and personal financial planning questionnaire are included in appendix A. Keeping good personal records has one very obvious advantage: it lets you know where and how you are currently spending your money. In turn, these records will assist you in constructing a budget for monthly income and expenses—a critical money-management tool for most individuals. (We will talk about budgets shortly.) Record keeping also assists you in determining where you are financially today. You can't begin the journey of personal financial planning without knowing your starting point.

What type of financial and personal records should you keep and for how long should you keep them? In most instances, there is no single answer to these questions, since the type and amount of records you'll need really depends on personal preference. Some of us keep everything (for as far back as one can imagine), while others try to rid ourselves of paper almost as soon as we receive it. However, such documents as copies of insurance policies, brokerage account statements, mortgage statements, deeds and leases, notes receivable, and current statements of vested amounts in 401(k) plans or other company-sponsored retirement plans should be kept indefinitely. In addition, it is important to keep personal income tax returns for at least three years.

There is likely no single document that can tell you more about your financial life than your annual income tax return. Think about it: this return forces you to not only disclose the *amount* of your income, but also to identify the *source* of that income—an extremely important part of the budgeting and financial planning process. Under law, you are required to keep (unless you're committing fraud) your income tax return and supporting details for only three years from April 15 of any given year. However, because of the wealth of information provided by the return and its importance as a guide to your financial past, you may wish to consider retaining it for much longer.

Once you have determined what type of financial and personal records you should keep, the next step is to determine where to keep them. Again, there is no single answer to this, but I tell my estate planning clients (there will be more on wills and estate planning documents later) to keep these documents somewhere in their home where they can easily be obtained in the event of an emergency. The reason that I advise them this way is to get them to consider the *disadvantages* of a safe-deposit box. In addition to often high fees charged for safe-deposit box rentals, many individuals make the mistake of listing only their name as a signatory for access to the box. In the event of an unanticipated injury or death, no other individual can access the important documents stored within it. You should consider instead a locked desk or fireproof case kept in your house or apartment for all important records.

Another critically important task to launch you on the path toward financial independence is to specify *in writing* your long-term (more than ten years), medium-term (five to ten years), and short-term (one to five years) financial goals. Be as specific as you can with respect to these goals. For example, "to become wealthy" is not only hard to quantify for most people but, as mentioned previously, it may not even mean the accumulation of actual dollars. If monetary wealth is important to you (as it is for most people), determine how many dollars you need to accumulate in order to satisfy your written financial goals.

Here are some of the most common financial goals that are mentioned to financial planners:

- To retire early or at normal retirement age with an adequate level of income
- To fund a child's (or children's) college education
- To buy a house or vacation home
- To make home improvements
- To take a dream vacation
- To reduce debt service (for example, to pay off credit cards with an outstanding balance)
- To buy a luxury car
- To minimize income or transfer (estate) taxes
- To start my own business

You may add additional objectives to this list, depending on your own personal and financial situation, but it is important to recognize that the goals on this list should be quantified and monitored. In other words, you should establish a plan to meet these goals and then *track how you are doing*. As with determining an investor's "time horizon," it is important to match your goals to a specified time frame and categorize them according to a long-term, medium-term, or short-term planning period.

What about the possibility that your goals cannot be achieved with your current financial resources? In that event, you have one of three (or combination of three) choices:

1. You can prioritize away the meeting of some financial goals (in other words, recognize that only some, but not all, of your specified financial goals are achievable in the specified time frame).
2. Attempt to increase cash inflows (your income potential).
3. Reduce your cash outflows (adjust your standard of living).

Until you have determined your financial goals and specified a time frame for their achievement, you will likely not know how to begin planning, which may keep you from planning at all!

DETERMINE WHERE YOU ARE NOW

One of the primary assumptions of the financial-planning and wealth-building process is that your *net worth* (assets minus liabilities) should experience a steady increase as you continue to invest. There is no benchmark percentage increase (or dollar amount) by which your net worth should grow annually, only the suggestion that you should strive for as great a percentage increase as possible given your current financial resources. For example, if you are in your peak wage-earning years (typically age forty-five to fifty-five), you should establish a goal of at least a 10 percent increase in net worth annually. When we apply the **Rule of 72** to this increase (seventy-two divided by ten), your net worth will double in a period of only 7.2 years.

You should monitor and track the increase (or decrease) in your net worth at least once a year. (Many individuals calculate this number at year-end). How does one go about tracking and determining this very important number? By preparing the first of two personal financial statements that you should keep among your important financial records: the *statement of personal financial position*, commonly referred to as the personal balance sheet.

An example of a statement of personal financial position is produced below. Before you examine it closely, there are a couple of considerations that you should keep in mind when preparing and interpreting such a statement:

1. Be sure to list all assets at their current fair market value without reducing them to reflect any outstanding indebtedness; for example, list your personal residence at the value you believe it will sell for in the local market *without* taking into account the mortgage balance you may currently owe.

2. Break down your assets into cash equivalents, investments, and use assets. Cash equivalents are those assets that you can access quickly to pay ongoing expenses (bills) or in the event of a financial emergency without fear that they may be worth less than when you purchased them. Alternatively, investments are longer-term assets (greater than one year in maturity or holding period) that may experience a fluctuation in daily value.

3. List liabilities at their current balance or what you owe to the creditor as of that given point in time.

There are no right or wrong answers when preparing the statement of financial position. Certainly, as you proceed along the path of wealth building, the objective is that the value of your assets will exceed the balance of your liabilities (thereby increasing your net worth), but do not become too judgmental of yourself as you construct your first statement. The danger is that you will become discouraged (or even give up), which will run counter to why you are preparing the statement in the first place—as a tool to help you assess your current financial situation and what you want to see happen in the future.

Statement of Personal Financial Position
(As of 12/31/XXXX)

ASSETS		LIABILITIES AND NET WORTH	
Cash Equivalents		*Liabilities*	
Cash on Hand	$_____	Primary Residence Mortgage	$_____
Checking Account	$_____	Vacation Home Mortgage	$_____
Savings Account	$_____	Real Estate Investment	
Money Market Accounts		Mortgage	$_____
or Funds	$_____	Auto Loans Balance	$_____
Certificates of Deposit	$_____	Personal Loans	$_____
(less than one year maturity)	$_____	Student Loans	$_____
Cash Value of Life		401(k) Loans	$_____
Insurance	$_____	Credit Card Balances	$_____
Total Cash Equivalents	$_____	Rent	$_____
		Other (for example, alimony	
Investments		or child support)	$_____
Stocks	$_____	*Total Liabilities*	$_____
Bonds	$_____		
Mutual Funds Balance	$_____		
Certificates of Deposit			
(one year or more maturity)	$_____		
Real Estate Investments	$_____		
Vested Employer Pension			
Benefits	$_____		
Participant IRAs	$_____		
Rollover IRAs	$_____		
401(k) Account	$_____		
Other	$_____		
Total Investment	$_____	*Net Worth (Assets –Liabilities)*	$_____
Use Assets			
Primary Residence	$_____		
Vacation Home	$_____		
Automobiles	$_____		
Home Furnishings	$_____		
Jewelry	$_____		
Artwork	$_____		
Total use Assets	$_____	*Total Liabilities and Net Worth*	$_____
Total Assets			

When planning your estate, it is helpful to identify how each asset is titled. For example, if your primary residence is held in joint tenancy with right of survivorship between you and your spouse, place a (JT) for joint tenancy next to Primary Residence. Note, however, that retirement accounts such as individual retirement accounts (IRA) may only be owned *individually*, even in community property states such as California.

In addition to preparing a statement of personal financial position, you need to track your ongoing expenses and sources of income. A second reference document, the *personal cash flow statement* or *worksheet*, should be completed at least once a year (better done monthly, if possible). Here are the reasons why:

- The cash flow statement lets you see where you are actually spending your money (it will tell you whether you are living within or beyond your means).
- It gives you an idea of your ability to save.
- It pinpoints your financial strengths and weakness with respect to your current standard of living.
- It can serve as a practice document before preparing a budget for future cash flow management (the cash flow statement reviews past financial performance or *looks backward*, whereas the budget *looks forward*).

Just as the statement of personal financial position has three general categories (cash equivalents, investments, and use assets), so does the personal cash flow statement. On the cash flow statement, you should separately identify cash *inflows* (sources of income), cash *outflows* (ongoing expenses), and any resulting cash *surplus* or cash *deficit*. A cash surplus or deficit is merely the difference between your cash inflows and cash outflows. Of course, what you want at the end of the year (or month) is a cash surplus, sometimes known as discretionary income, since that amount will be available for saving. A little mental trick to help you to save: Include a fixed savings amount or percentage of income on the first line of the cash outflows column. In other words, *pay yourself first* and treat the savings amount the same as any other fixed expense.

An ongoing issue with respect to preparation of the cash flow statement is whether to show income and social security taxes as a separate expense or cash outflow (alternatively, you would show the after-tax amount among your cash inflows since your paychecks reflect this). The better practice is to list these taxes as a cash outflow, since (again) one of the purposes of the cash flow statement is to show you how you are spending your money. If you include a separate line item for income and social security taxes among the cash outflows, it forces you to account for what may be an otherwise invisible expense.

On the following page is an example of a properly prepared personal cash flow statement.

Personal Cash Flow Statement
(For Period XXXX)

CASH INFLOWS

Salaries	$_____
Bonuses	$_____
Self-Employment Income	$_____
Interest Received	$_____
Dividends Received	$_____
Capital Gains (from sale of assets)	$_____
Rents and Royalties	$_____
Pension and Annuities	$_____
Social Security	$_____
Other Income	$_____
Total Cash Inflows	$_____

CASH OUTFLOWS

Savings	$_____
Rent/Mortgage Payments	$_____
Repairs, Maintenance, Improvements	$_____
Utilities	$_____
Auto Loan Payments	$_____
Credit Card Payments	$_____
Food	$_____
Clothing	$_____
Insurance Premiums:	
Life	$_____
Health	$_____
Long Term Care	$_____
Disability	$_____
Auto	$_____
Homeowners (if not included in mortgage payment)	$_____
Umbrella Liability	$_____
Total Insurance Premiums	$_____
Medical Expenses	$_____
Property Taxes (if not included in mortgage Payment)	$_____
Income Taxes	$_____
Social Security and Medicare Taxes	$_____
Child Care Expenses	$_____
Recreation and Entertainment	$_____
Other Expenses	$_____
Total Cash Outflows	$_____

CASH SURPLUS (OR DEFICIT) $_____

You may be wondering how both statements (the statement of personal financial position and the personal cash flow statement) tie together. A cash surplus from the cash flow statement at the end of the year (or for whatever period you choose to list your income and expenses) *increases* your net worth, as reflected on the statement of personal position. Conversely, a cash deficit *decreases* your net worth. Increasing net worth is a financial *strength*, while decreasing net worth (particularly if the decrease continues over a long period of time) is a financial *weakness*. In other words, if a cash deficit continues (you are spending more than you are earning), you need to do something to reverse the situation. If not, your financial goal of future wealth accumulation is impossible.

Budgeting

For many people, putting together and sticking to a budget is one of life's little burdens. Sometimes the thought of limiting your spending (and therefore your lifestyle) is so threatening that people refuse to even think about preparing a budget. I have heard it said, "What budget? I spend what I make, so that's my budget!" Living without a budget will damage your long-term financial health. Look at a budget as an opportunity to prove your own financial self-discipline. You could even pay yourself (and add to your savings) if you come in under budget each month and show that you can live within your means. Over time, that practice will significantly increase your net worth.

As mentioned, a budget *looks forward* and is a benchmark for what you plan to spend. It may take you a few months to get it right, but get it right you must! If you are just starting to prepare (and comply with) a budget, be conservative in the assumptions you make. For example, an underlying assumption of any budget is that your current employment is secure; if it is not (if you anticipate a job change or layoff), you will likely need to set aside *even more* savings and (hopefully) spend *even less*. This will help you build up an emergency or contingency fund—another financial planning practice that is critical to long-term financial well being.

Normally, a budget is developed in several steps. First, it is very helpful to have determined your financial goals and the amount of savings necessary to accomplish them. Next, be as realistic as you can when estimating your future income and forecasting your anticipated expenses for the budget period. Finally, a well-developed budget should contain the flexibility to accommodate financial emergencies or one-time major expenses (hence the need for the emergency fund).

A sample of a very detailed budget is included in appendix B, but take this to heart: *A budget only has value if you intend to use it.* If you do not use it, you are likely better off attempting to meet your short- and long-term financial goals by focusing on some other planning technique (say, by hoping to win the lottery).

CASH FLOW AND DEBT MANAGEMENT

As a matter of financial prudence, you should maintain an emergency or contingency fund for unanticipated expenses. This fund should be kept in *liquid assets* (those that may be converted quickly to cash without a significant loss in value) and equal in amount to three to six months of expenses. (For example, if your monthly expenses average $5,000, you should have a contingency fund of at least $15,000—$5,000 times three—in a checking, savings, or money market account or mutual fund.) The size of this fund will vary depending on the nature of your employment and the constancy (or variability) of your income. A self-employed individual who has no employer to provide benefits that serve as a safety net (such as sick or personal days) should consider an even larger fund to compensate for lost income.

There is an investment trade-off, however, when establishing a contingency fund. This trade-off is a *lower* investment rate of return from money kept in more conservative cash equivalents. For this reason, you may wish to consider establishing an unsecured line of credit with a bank or a home equity line of credit to substitute as emergency fund assets. Be careful: If you do this, you must arrange for the credit line *before* the financial emergency occurs. For example, if you lose your job (for whatever reason), the bank is unlikely to extend you any credit. Plus, if you are using a credit line as your emergency fund and you need to access the line once you have lost your job, you will incur even more debt—likely the last thing you need once you are no longer employed.

Let's move on to a great tragedy or success story (depending on how you look at it)—the amount of debt carried by the average consumer.

We read a great deal in the media about the negative savings rate of many Americans. Is that bad? It depends. There is both good and bad debt. *Good* debt is generally any debt incurred for the purchase of an asset that is likely to *appreciate*—for example, your home or real estate in some parts of this country. More specifically, good debt is any interest rate assumed on an obligation where you are paying less than what you can make, in terms of investment return, on the asset for which you have borrowed the money. Another example (in a rising stock market) is the margin interest incurred on the purchase of an individual stock or mutual fund from which you can potentially earn a far greater return than what you must pay the broker to make the purchase.

Bad debt is any debt incurred on an asset that is likely to *depreciate* in value, such as a new car or automobile. Another type of bad debt is credit card debt, which not only carries extremely high rates of interest (18 to 21 percent annually, on average), but also "revolves" from month to month so that it is very difficult to completely satisfy the obligation. Both automobile and credit card debt share the income tax disadvantage that they are considered as personal or consumer debt, so that the interest paid is generally *not* deductible in reducing your annual income tax liability.

So how does one go about reducing bad debt? The obvious answer is not to incur it in the first place (by paying cash for a new car, for example), but oftentimes this is impractical. Here are some tried-and-true debt reduction techniques:

- Focus on one type of bad debt to the exclusion of others. For instance, adopt a payment schedule and amount to pay off on your credit card debt—and stick to it! Consider it another form of paying yourself: If the interest rate on the card is 18 percent annually, it is similar to earning 18 percent on an investment. (That does not mean, however, that credit cards are a good investment.)
- Consolidate or restructure your debt. The most common example of this is a college or graduate student who consolidates several smaller loans into one larger loan. While this does not eliminate the debt, it often reduces the total amount of debt service (interest).
- Borrow from your cash value life insurance or 401(k) plan. The advantage of these alternatives is that you are, in essence, borrowing from yourself. But be careful: You need to repay this money in a timely manner or you will reduce the amount of your life insurance coverage and retirement plan benefits payable in the future.
- Switch to debit cards. Debit cards work much like ATM machines, since the money comes out of your checking account immediately. Although a debit card does not stop you from excessive spending, it does make you reckon with the cash flow consequences much more quickly than would a traditional credit card.

Finally, it cannot be stressed enough that poor cash flow and debt management can put you on the path to financial ruin. Fortunately, credit counselors and some financial planners (not all planners offer this service) can assist you in reducing your debt load. If you think you have a problem with debt, you probably do! If you can't solve the problem, the wealth-building techniques discussed in this book will take much longer to work for you—if they work at all.

MONITOR YOUR PROGRESS AND LIFE-CYCLE PLANNING

How often you review your financial progress depends on your age and the time frame you have specified to meet your financial goals. In most cases, an annual review is sufficient. This may be done with or without the assistance of a professional financial planner. (The question of whether you need a financial planner will be addressed in the next chapter.) If you go it alone, ask yourself the following questions:

- What life cycle or life stage are you in? Are your short- and long-term goals representative of peers in the same financial planning cycle or stage? In other words, are your financial goals realistic?
- Have these goals remained the same throughout the review period?
- Are you living at or below your means?
- How much money did you save during the review period?
- With respect to your savings, are you earning the investment rates of return you need to meet your goals?
- Has anything changed in your personal and financial situation that may cause you to reconsider either the priority of the financial goals you established or the time frame in which you anticipate meeting them?

It is generally agreed that there are four financial planning life cycles. While there are no hard-and-fast ages at which an individual will transition from one life cycle to the next, during each, certain financial goals are typically more important than others.

The first of these stages is the *accumulation stage* (between ages twenty-five and forty-five for most consumers). In this stage, individuals are usually in the early-to-middle years of their employment career and, if married, are raising young children.

Typically, their net worth is relatively small and their debt load may be excessive, normally due to student or personal loan obligations. Their major financial goals are likely to be reducing their debt, buying a house, and beginning the financing of their children's education.

The next of the financial planning life cycles is the *consolidation stage* (ages forty-five to sixty-two or other retirement age). In this stage, individuals are typically past the midpoint of their careers and are likely approaching their peak wage-earning years. Most, if not all, of their debts have been paid off and their net worth is growing rapidly. Their children are in college or graduate school and those expenses have also been satisfied or are in the course of payment. Financial goals for individuals in the consolidation stage of life are likely to include making home improvements, taking a dream vacation, buying a luxury car or vacation home, and minimizing income taxes.

The third life-cycle stage, the *spending phase* (ages sixty-two to eighty-five), is sometimes combined with the fourth phase, or the *gifting phase*. The spending phase is characterized by the individual's approaching retirement or the early years of retirement. In this phase, his or her peak earning years have likely concluded and, from an investment perspective, the focus turns from growth to income. The individual's children have likely begun their own careers and have moved from the family home. Financial goals for individuals in the spending stage shift to early retirement, retirement with adequate income, and, perhaps, the starting of their own business.

Finally, the fourth and final life-cycle phase, the *gifting phase*, is synonymous with an individual's retirement years. Excess assets, if any, may be used to benefit family members during life or in the event of the individual's death. Estate planning becomes very important in this phase, and as such a primary financial goal is minimization of transfer (estate and gift) taxes. Also characteristic of this phase is a very conservative investment approach and withdrawal rate, due to the fear of outliving the amount of retirement monies the individual has saved.

Now, let's proceed to an often asked question: do I need a professional financial planner to help me get control of my financial life or can I do it myself? The answer to this question is the focus of the next chapter.

CHAPTER 2

DO YOU NEED A
FINANCIAL PLANNER?

A WORD ABOUT SELF-HELP

Now that you know about the basics of the financial planning process, do you think you can do it yourself? Only you can answer that question, but here are several important factors to consider as you attempt to do so:

* Financial planning is a lot like doing your own income tax return. As a matter of fact, income-tax planning is one of the subjects covered by the certified financial planner (CFP) certification examination, so CFP certificants must demonstrate competence in that area. Like income-tax planning, financial planning is a *dynamic* process requiring the planner to stay abreast of many laws and regulations that may impact the planning result.
* Retirement income (and other) computations require knowledge and application of **time value of money** (present and future value) principles. While you can learn how to apply these principles with use of a financial function calculator or computer software program, there is still a learning curve involved for the average consumer.
* Certain financial planners, like CFPs, must comply with a professional code of ethics that requires them to act at

all times in your exclusive best interest. Of course, you will not hesitate to act at all at times in your own best interest, but without extensive knowledge of the economic, legal, and regulatory environment in which we all live and work, you may not be aware of what your best interest actually is.

- Finally, like a New Year's resolution, many individuals vow to get their financial life in order, but due to common, everyday pressures, fail to actually do it. Will you be the exception to the rule?

Assuming you have made the decision to seek the assistance of a professional financial planner, the question now becomes a matter of *when* you should you seek the assistance. That question, like so many others in financial planning, has no definitive answer, but one determining factor is the complexity of your financial life. Generally, the *more money* that people make, the *more complicated* is their financial life. This is certainly true of corporate executives and self-employed individuals. In addition, higher net-worth individuals (such as business owners) are likely to recognize the need to have a financial planner as part of their advisory team.

Beyond all that, middle-income America is quickly appreciating the need for more detailed guidance with respect to their financial lives. As we shall learn, the two biggest obstacles to a lifetime of wealth accumulation and distribution are: 1) inflation and 2) taxes. While the former is a fact of economic life that the average Joe (or Jane) can do very little to prevent, a financial planner can help to minimize the deteriorating effect of inflation on your overall portfolio return. The latter (income taxes) can be managed, if not avoided in large part, with the assistance of a skilled professional.

One significant warning: *The seeking of professional assistance does not absolve you of responsibility for your own financial future.* It is *your* financial life and the goals you establish are *your* financial goals. While a financial planner can hopefully direct you on a path to wealth (in the fullest sense of the term), you must still make the necessary decisions with respect to your financial well being.

TYPES OF FINANCIAL PLANNERS

You'll want to seek a financial planner you trust and with whom you will establish a rapport. From a compensation standpoint, there are three types of planners in today's marketplace.

The first type of planner is paid solely by commission from the sale of financial products. These products include insurance (usually life insurance), mutual funds, stocks and bonds, and fixed and variable annuities. Typically, the commission received by the planner is taken off the top of these products and, at least to you, it is invisible. However, it does add to the cost of the product you are buying. Commission-only planners are prevalent at banks, broker/dealers (securities firms), and insurance agencies.

There is a great deal of controversy within the financial planning profession with respect to whether a commission-only planner can be objective. In other words, does the planner have an inherent conflict of interest? For example, the more he or she sells of a particular product, regardless of whether it is actually suitable for your needs, the more money he or she makes. There is no definitive answer to this question (inherently, just because a planner is paid by commission only, it does not automatically mean that the planner is not acting in your best interests), but it is something to consider as you decide what type of planner to work with.

The second type of planner is a fee-and-commission planner, sometimes referred to as a fee-based planner. These planners are paid in two ways. First, for their planning activities (an example would be the preparation of a statement of personal financial position), the planner charges an hourly or fixed fee. In addition, they receive a commission for any products you buy from them; for example, mutual funds with a service charge or "load." Some fee-and-commission planners now offer investment advisory services based on a percentage of the amount of money they manage for you. This fee, known as a wrap fee or advisory fee in the trade, typically ranges from 1 percent to 2.5 percent of the money managed annually. While arguably the fee is not a commission at all, since it is paid by you to the planner and does not come off the top like a product sale, you will likely think of it as constituting a commission all the same.

The third (and rapidly growing) type of planner is a fee-only planner. These planners typically do business independently and accept no commissions. Rather, they charge an hourly fee for financial planning advice and, usually, a fixed fee for developing a comprehensive financial plan. Like fee-based planners, they also charge an annual percentage fee for assets under management (again, 1 to 2.5 percent annually), but they do not sell securities and are not normally employed by or associated with a broker/ dealer. As such, the fee-only planner works only for the client. Historically, this type of planner has tended to work primarily with high-net-worth or higher-income clients, but recently these planners are reaching out to more middle-income clients.

As you will see in the list of questions to ask a financial planner provided later in the chapter, one of the things you will want to know before engaging the services of a planner is how he or she is paid. However, more important than this is your level of comfort with the planner and defining the scope or range of services that he or she will provide. Many a professional engagement or relationship has been made more difficult by not reaching a clear initial understanding of the respective responsibilities of the client and the planner. Remember, this is *your* financial life and future, so use the planner as an advisor and not as a substitute decision-maker.

CERTIFIED FINANCIAL PLANNER PROFESSIONAL AND OTHER FINANCIAL PLANNING DESIGNATIONS

While there are other financial planners who have distinguished themselves in today's marketplace with one or more professional designations, likely the most well known financial planning credential is the CFP certificant. Individuals who have achieved this credential are subject to a mandatory Code of Ethics and Professional Responsibility enforced by the Board of Professional Review, a subsidiary of CFP Board of Standards that is responsible for awarding the CFP license. As a part of this code, the planner must agree to assume a fiduciary duty under law, meaning that he or she must act at all times in the exclusive and best interest of the client. In addition, a planner who achieves this credential must participate in mandatory continuing education in the specified subject areas of financial planning, as well as complete a separate refresher course in the principles and rules of the ethics code. CFP planners must also have graduated from college, have at least three years of financial planning experience, complete a formal education program covering specified financial planning topics, and successfully pass a rigorous, comprehensive, ten-hour examination in these topics.

Another meaningful credential for a financial planner is the chartered financial consultant, or ChFC. This designation is awarded by the American College in Bryn Mawr, Pennsylvania, to individuals who have completed their eight-course curriculum, some of which can substitute for the CFP educational program requirement. The American College was first originated and funded by the life insurance industry, so their education tends to emphasize insurance matters more than broad-based financial planning. However, the designation is well respected among financial planners generally.

A third highly recognized financial planning professional designation is one available only to certified public accountants (CPAs) and is offered by the American Institute of Certified Public Accountants (AICPA). A CPA who also holds the designation of Personal Financial Specialist (PFS) has passed a written examination covering personal financial planning subject matter and also has practical experience in the area. Currently, there are only approximately ten thousand CPAs with this designation, although personal financial planning is a much-sought-after service requested by clients of CPAs.

In addition to these three broad-based financial planning credentials, there are a number of other specialized credentials in today's marketplace. These other credentials indicate that the financial planner has completed some particular course of instruction and commands some specialized experience, such as in retirement or estate planning.

You may wish to consider including a CFP certificant or other financial planning professional among a team of financial advisors. (High-net-worth individuals and small business owners have been doing this for years.) Specifically, financial advising teams have traditionally consisted of a financial planner, a life insurance or property and casualty insurance agent, an accountant (usually a CPA), an estate planning attorney, and, sometimes, a bank trust officer. Each fulfills the following roles:

- The financial planner: Typically, this individual has the broadest knowledge of your financial life and as such is often considered the quarterback of the financial advising team. He or she often prepares paperwork and financial documents used by other members of the team in properly advising you, the client.
- The life insurance or property and casualty agent: Actually, since separate state licenses are required to sell life insurance and homeowners/automobile insurance policies, you will often need to contact two different professionals to buy each respective policy. The life insurance agent or broker can obtain needed life insurance protection, and the property/casualty agent can do the same with respect to protecting your important property. Sometimes, insurance agents have both state licenses, but not often.
- The accountant: Normally, the accountant performs income-tax-related tasks, including the preparation of your annual income tax return. However, this professional can also work closely with your financial planner in advising

how best to organize and operate a small business and when it may be most appropriate to sell assets (such as appreciated **stock** and **mutual funds**).

- The estate planning attorney: The role that this professional fulfills as a member of the financial advising team is in his or her title. The estate planning attorney is responsible for the proper drafting of wills, trusts, and power-of-attorney documents with respect to your financial life, as well as certain business planning documents, if you are also a small business owner.

- The bank trust officer: This member of the financial advising team is generally only involved in the event that you (a) have drafted a **trust** with the assistance of the estate planning attorney/team member and (b) have elected to use a professional **trustee** to manage and distribute the trust assets. However, you may also be the **beneficiary** of a trust established by someone else and might interact with the bank trust officer in this manner.

It is possible (and practically even probable) that any of these professionals may perform several roles. For example, many accountants may not only advise you with respect to taxes, but also have broadened their services to include traditional financial planning advice. To provide both services, they must hold and maintain not only the CPA state license, but also the CFP professional credential.

QUESTIONS TO ASK A FINANCIAL PLANNER

As you can likely appreciate by now, if you choose to work with a financial planner, the selection of the planner is not an easy task. This is complicated by the fact that, unlike doctors and lawyers, there is no formal licensing (and accompanying regulation) of financial planners. Right now, anyone can call themselves a financial planner—even a taxicab driver in New York City! If you work with an unqualified advisor, your financial future may be at risk.

How do you protect yourself against this possibility? One answer is to work only with someone who demonstrates considerable financial services experience and expertise, such as an individual with an advanced business degree or a well-respected financial planning designation. However, in addition to this preliminary screen, you should also ask the planner or advisor certain basic questions, such as those listed below from the Financial Planning Association (FPA), the major professional association of personal financial planners. The FPA's website is www.fpanet.org.

The FPA suggests that you ask the following ten questions of any prospective financial planner with whom you are considering working. I have added commentary to each to assist you even further in deciding which planner might be best for you.

1. *What experience do you have?* Experience in any industry or profession is important, but in the rapidly changing world of financial services, such experience may be considered invaluable. If the planner does not have at least five years of advising and working with clients, you may wish to keep searching until you find a planner who does.

2. *What are your qualifications?* Qualifications mean educational and professional designations that you can trust with respect to expertise in the financial planning process.

3. *What services do you offer?* In most instances, a financial planner offers investment advisory services as part of implementing the financial plan for a client. Therefore, they must have a Series 65 or Series 66 Financial Industry Regulatory Association (FINRA) license. In addition, most planners offer additional services that require state or federal licensing (and accompanying regulation).

4. *Can I have your engagement agreement in writing?* The first step in the personal financial planning process for the professional planner is to establish and define the client–planner relationship. As a part of this step, the planner should offer to define for you in writing the scope of the

engagement, which is the universe of services that the planner and client agree is necessary and appropriate, and that the planner is qualified and willing to provide. In mutually defining this scope, the client and planner may agree to only parts of the financial planning process (segmented financial planning or goal-specific planning) or the completion of a comprehensive financial plan.

5. *What is your approach to financial planning?* This question will usually involve a discussion of the planner's investment approach (for example, does he or she adopt or more conservative or aggressive approach when investing a client's money?), but some planners adopt more of a financial life planning approach than others. Financial life planning is difficult to define, but generally tries to anticipate life events and prepare for them at a point much earlier in time than does traditional financial planning. Financial life planning also explores more fully the psychology of money and attempts to compliment more completely the merging of an individual's financial goals with his or her lifestyle needs.

6. *Will you be the only person working with me?* Like any professional, the practicing financial planner will usually have staff that work in the same office. These individuals may or may not have the same expertise as the planner, not to mention his or her same rapport with you. If this is a concern to you, you should ask the planner how much time he or she will personally spend on your particular case file. In addition, if the planner works as a member of a financial planning advisory team (see the earlier discussion), you may wish to ask for the names of the other team members and investigate their qualifications and background.

7. *How much do you typically charge?* The total amount that the financial planner will charge for his or her services depends on the nature and extent of those services, but the planner should be able to provide you with an hourly fee (if he or she charges in that manner) or flat fee or the

percentage of commissions or investment assets under management that is standard for their practice.

8. *How are you paid?* As discussed, financial planners are paid on a commission-only, fee-and-commission, or fee-only basis. As a part of the written engagement letter that the planner should provide at the beginning of the relationship, the planner should explain how he or she is paid. Some will also give you an estimate of the total amount of fees or commissions that will be due.

9. *Have you ever been publicly disciplined for any unlawful or unethical actions in your professional career?* This is a very important question to ask. While public discipline of a planner is a matter of record, you will likely not know where to find such information. If you know (or ask) what licenses are maintained by the planner, you can check the records of those particular regulatory bodies or agencies, but it is better to have a simple conversation with the planner about any past disciplinary problems. If the planner objects to this conversation, it may be because he or she has, indeed, incurred regulatory sanctions.

   If the planner provides investment advice and is registered as an investment advisor with the Securities and Exchange Commission (SEC) or the state securities commission, under securities law, he or she *must* provide you with a disclosure form entitled SEC Form ADV Part II or the state equivalent. If the planner is employed by a securities firm that is registered as an investment advisor, the firm's disclosure form must be given to you.

10. *Can anyone other than me benefit from your recommendations?* (Stated another way: *Do you have any potential or current conflicts of interest?*) Another big question! This is maybe even more important than the public discipline inquiry. If a planner has a current conflict of interest (for example, if he or she is on the board of directors of a company

whose stock you are considering purchasing), it should be disclosed to you initially—preferably, in writing. In addition, if during the course of the engagement, a potential conflict of interest arises for the planner, it should be disclosed to you as well. An advantage of working with a CFP certificant is that, under their applicable code of ethics, both current (real) and potential conflicts of interest *must* be disclosed to you in writing. It is then your decision whether you wish to begin working with (or continue working with) the CFP certificant.

In addition to these questions, I would ask two more:

11. *What is the typical net worth and annual income level of your clients?* Unfortunately, many financial planners and investment advisors prefer to work with individuals who have already made money or accumulated assets and want to increase their net worth even further. If this is not you, do not despair. More and more planners are focusing on middle-income Americans and their need for financial security.

When searching for a financial planner, ask the candidates you are considering to draw you a mental picture of their clients with respect to income level and net worth. You may want to ask about the financial goals and life-cycle status of a typical client and compare his or her situation to yours. If there is a great disparity, or you feel condescended to in some manner, you may wish to consider another planner.

12. *Do you construct an investment risk profile for your clients and, if so, can you explain to me in simple terms how you evaluate and use this profile?* It is likely that among the first issues you will address with the planner is how to build your wealth through investment in real or financial assets or both. To properly analyze this issue, it is necessary to determine your tolerance to assume investment risk (your *risk tolerance*). This is a complicated determination for many individuals. Many people consider themselves to be

conservative investors and expect their investment advisor to know what this means. Skilled financial planners and investment advisors know how to probe for the real meaning of the term *conservative* (and its polar opposite, aggressive) by providing real examples of investment situations and asking how you would react if these situations happened to you.

For example, consider this question: "If you had $50,000 invested in the stock market, how much of this amount could you tolerate losing and over what time period—and still sleep at night?" If the answer is none or a very small amount, you are likely a conservative investor. However, be aware that this answer means that your *investment return* (reward for risk) is also likely to be very small. Generally, as we age, we become more conservative in our investment outlook, although as we shall learn later, this does not mean that we should avoid investment risk altogether. Indeed, there are many forms of investment risk and just because we may avoid the risk of loss to the principal of an investment, we may instead assume the loss of future purchasing power due to inflation. A skilled financial planner can assist you in determining what level of investment risk you are comfortable with and, accordingly, how well you can sleep at night.

In the recent severe decline in the stock market (or bear market, to use the most common description) beginning in October 2007, many investors have come to more properly appreciate their assumed level of risk. Until October 2007, many younger investors had never experienced a market in which a consistent decline in the market value of securities is the norm. As a result, many are reevaluating the allocation of their portfolio and moving into financial assets that are deemed to be safer (defined in the investor's mind as U.S. government securities). As such, we now have the somewhat illogical result of investing in securities whose nominal or stated rate of interest is *less than* the accompanying inflation rate. In normal circumstances, this is not a prudent rule of investing, but such is the behavior of individuals who fear for the future value of their portfolio and the ability to satisfy their financial goals.

CHAPTER 3

ELEMENTS OF PERSONAL FINANCIAL PLANNING AND THE WEALTH MANAGEMENT PROCESS

Academic studies have shown that following a financial plan will help you build wealth more rapidly than is possible without a financial plan. This is because a financial plan enforces self-discipline, the key to any future accumulation of wealth. People earning between $20,000 and $100,000 per year who follow a financial plan typically have up to twice as much savings as those in the same income bracket with no financial plan. For those earning more than $100,000 per year and following a financial plan, the savings rate is some 60 percent greater than that of their peers. Clearly, people who adhere to some form of financial plan—either in writing or informally by matching their savings practice to a predetermined set of financial goals—have a significant advantage. Bottom line: *you have to convince yourself of reasons to save or you will likely not do it.* One of the purposes of this book is to provide you with those reasons.

PERSONAL FINANCIAL PLANNING AND WEALTH MANAGEMENT

The general areas of personal financial planning are

- Insurance and risk management
- Employment benefits (often simply referred to as fringe benefits)

- Investments
- Income tax planning and management
- Planning for retirement
- Estate planning

I suggest that you use these general categories to examine and review your own financial life.

There are numerous issues that need to be addressed within each of these areas. Determining your own status in each category may help you begin the process of record keeping. A professional financial planner will orient his or her work around each of these areas, and some will demonstrate a specialty in one or more of the subjects.

The concept of personal financial planning has had an interesting and somewhat complicated past. While financial planning has always been about a process of determining whether and how an individual can meet his or her financial goals through the proper management of financial resources, planners have occasionally been sidetracked and focused too much on the *resources* component of the definition instead of the *process* component. In other words, financial *products*—such as an attractive stock or the newest insurance product—that are necessary to implement the process had become predominant. Alternatively, some financial planners prefer to think of themselves as *wealth builders* or *wealth managers*" to differentiate themselves from the product side of the business.

There is likely no subject in the personal financial planning process that is more important than the others, but planners who think of themselves as primarily wealth builders tend to place a large amount of emphasis on investment selection and investment management. As a result, those planners prefer to work only with high-net-worth clients and specify a minimum amount of investable assets (usually in the high six figures or even in the low seven figures) consisting of money that can immediately be put to work in the capital market. But wealth managers and financial planners are really beginning at the same place: the client's financial goals. It is only the amount of financial resources a client can bring to bear in accomplishing these goals that distinguishes a financial planner from a wealth builder or wealth manager.

Is there any importance to the order in which I have listed the general areas of financial planning? In terms of thinking about your financial life, there is. Your employment status will determine whether you have any employment benefits to consider, but think of these benefits as really nothing more than a temporary safety net that you can use to protect your financial well being. When you change jobs, these benefits may or may not be portable (likely, they will *not* be). This is why it is much better to build a permanent safety net constructed from individual life insurance and other benefits that you purchase on your own that are intended to remain with you throughout your lifetime, regardless of your employment status. Since both temporary and permanent benefits are primarily secured so as to provide protection against possible future financial loss, this is why, sequentially, they should be thought of *first* in the financial planning process.

The PADD approach to building and managing wealth places the general categories of personal financial planning in a real-life context that can be used as a blueprint to financial independence:

- *Protect* yourself against the risk of catastrophic financial loss.
- *Accumulate* wealth through investments.
- *Defend* that wealth through prudent income tax planning and management.
- *Distribute* that wealth for your retirement and as part of your estate at death.

First, however, because of their importance in the overall financial planning process as the "engine" in generating substantial wealth, we need to spend some time discussing investments and investment strategies. This begins with the need for a well-thought-out investment policy statement.

THE NEED FOR AN INVESTMENT POLICY STATEMENT

Many planners refer to the investment policy statement as the third mandatory personal financial statement (in addition to the statement of personal financial position and the cash flow statement discussed earlier). The investment policy statement helps the investor specify realistic investment goals while also forcing him or her to consider the risks and costs of investing. For example, specifying that you wish to obtain an average 15 percent annual rate of return on an investment in an individual stock begs the question of whether you also expect the stock to increase in price by this same amount consistently every year. If so, you need to engage in a reality check! Such thinking ignores the risk of stock investing since the market price of stocks can fluctuate dramatically from year to year. This is known as **volatility**, which you need to understand and accept thoroughly prior to investing in the stock market.

There are four basic sections of any well-developed investment policy statement. With allowances for the specific wording of any customized statement, these sections are

1. Statement of the Investor's Objectives: The formulation and statement of these objectives are your primary input to the statement and should explain your investment goals in terms of investment risk and return. A careful analysis of your risk tolerance should precede any discussion of return objectives. As we have discussed, typically, you will not know how to adequately define your risk tolerance; accordingly, this is one of the benefits of using a financial planner, who will help assess and clearly specify the amount of risk you are willing to assume.

   A person's return objectives may be stated in terms of a percentage, but they may also be stated in words. For example, *capital preservation* means that investors seek to maintain the purchasing power of their investment— therefore, the necessary return must be no less than the rate of annual inflation. Alternatively, *capital appreciation* is an appropriate objective when the investor wants to achieve growth of their investment through capital gains (a return considerably more than annual inflation). A *current income* objective means that the investor wants the manager to invest in dividend-paying stocks or interest-earning bonds to generate income. Finally, a *total return* strategy implies that the investor seeks to increase the value of investments by taking advantage of both capital gains and reinvesting any current income back into the investment for future growth of principal.

2. Statement of Investment Constraints or Limitations: In this section of the statement, you will need to specify your investment time horizon, or the time period in which you intend to invest. Concomitant to this time period is your need to access the money without a significant loss to principal (also known as liquidity). Investors with longer investment horizons, such as an investor who is saving for retirement, generally require less liquidity and can thus tolerate more investment risk. Investors with shorter time horizons, such as an investor already in retirement, generally seek greater liquidity and less risky investments since losses cannot be overcome nearly as quickly.

Additional factors or limitations that you will typically wish to consider when developing a policy statement are the current and expected state of the overall economy and sectors of the economy in which you may be considering investing (for example, technology). Your current tax status of any previous investments should also be taken into account. For example, an individual who is saving for retirement and is taking advantage of the tax-sheltered nature of an individual retirement account (IRA) may engage in more frequent investment transactions than someone who holds these investments in a taxable portfolio where capital gains must be recognized at the date of sale.

A final, often included limitation covers the unique circumstances or preferences of the investor. Here is where you should state any preference to invest only in socially responsible companies. Similarly, you should give some thought to your current or anticipated cash flow. For example, if one of your goals is to purchase a vacation home during a shorter, specified time period, you will need to be investing in relatively liquid assets. Alternatively, if you expect to receive a large inheritance during the time period (thus providing additional money for investment), you should discuss what you want to do with this money.

3. Meeting the Investor's Objectives and Allocation of Investment Resources: Although the typical investment policy statement does not indicate specific stocks or bonds the investor should purchase or sell, it should provide guidelines with respect to which asset classes to include and the relative percentages of each. In other words, the investment policy statement should provide an *asset allocation strategy*.

The assets you may wish to invest in may not be the same as the typical investor based on your risk tolerance level, desired rate of return, and investment time horizon. However, most investment policy statements use only three categories or classes of investment assets:

- Stocks
- Bonds
- Cash or cash equivalents (savings accounts, short-term certificates of deposit, money market funds, and any asset that is relatively liquid)

Investment percentages are assigned to each class.

There are many methods used to allocate the investment percentages, including some involving computer software. There are also a few rules of thumb. For example, one commonly cited rule is that you should subtract your age from one hundred to determine the percentage amount that should be devoted to stock or stock mutual fund investments. The rest should be split between bonds and cash or cash equivalents, with only a relatively small percentage allocated to cash given its lack of relative return. Here are four sample asset allocation scenarios for a young, mid-life, pre-retiree, and retired investor of moderate risk tolerance:

i. Young investor (aged twenty-five to forty-five): 75 percent stocks; 20 percent bonds; 5 percent cash or cash equivalents
ii. Mid-life investor (aged forty-six to fifty-five): 60 percent stocks; 30 percent bonds; 10 percent cash percent cash equivalents
iii. Pre-retiree investor (aged fifty-six to sixty-four): 50 percent stocks; 35 percent bonds; 15 percent cash or cash equivalents
iv. Retired investor (age sixty-five plus): 40 percent stocks; 40 percent bonds; 20 percent cash or cash equivalents

Once the asset allocation process has been determined, you should consider a mix of assets that have the highest probability of meeting your financial goals at a level of risk with which you are comfortable. As you get closer to meeting your financial goal, you should adjust this asset mix. For example, if you are several years away from meeting your goal, *safety* of principal should become more important to you than *growth* of that principal; accordingly, you should be adjusting the percentage of asset mix *toward* short-term bonds and cash equivalents and *away from* stocks.

Asset allocation generates **portfolio diversification,** which is the key to reducing your investment risk. We will talk more about diversification shortly, but for now you should understand that a well-thought-out asset allocation strategy is the foundation of any effective investment policy statement.

4) Monitoring the Performance of the Investment Plan: The drafting of a policy statement will assist you in judging the performance of your investment manager. Typically, the statement should include a model or *benchmark portfolio* against which the performance of the manager may be judged. For example, if you choose to invest in *large cap stocks* (companies that have a large amount of outstanding public stock), you will likely want to compare the performance of the manager against the benchmark annual return of Standard & Poor's Index of five hundred stocks. Alternatively, if you choose to invest in smaller capitalization stocks, a benchmark portfolio of similar stocks, such as the Russell 2000 Index, should be used. Because benchmark portfolios set an objective performance standard, the investment policy statement acts as a starting point for periodic portfolio review and assessment of investment manager performance.

THE BASICS OF A DIVERSIFIED PORTFOLIO

A diversified portfolio should be diversified in two respects: *between* asset classes and *within* asset classes. Therefore, in addition to allocating your assets among stocks, bonds, and cash equivalents, you will need to mix your investments within each of these three asset classes. The key to doing this successfully is to identify investments that may perform differently under different market conditions. For example, you will want to locate a stock that does not go down (or does not go down much) in a declining or *bear* market. The search for a stock that behaves in this manner, also known as *correlation*, is not easy; in essence, finding such a stock is how a portfolio manager earns his or her money. Investment textbooks available at public libraries can tell you how this can be done. A word of advice, however: leave this to the pros! If you choose to go about trying to select lower positively correlated or negatively correlated stocks on your own, you will quickly expend a lot of research time and possibly money and will still likely not pick the stocks correctly.

Because achieving effective diversification is not easy, you may prefer to purchase a number of mutual funds. Mutual funds are a type of professionally managed asset regulated by an investment company that pools money from many investors and invests in stocks, bonds, and financial assets. Such a fund makes it easy for the individual investor to own a small portion of a great number of investments. Be careful: a mutual fund investment does *not* necessarily guarantee instant diversification. For example, the mutual fund may be investing only in stocks issued by companies involved in the same industry (called a sector fund). Thus, if you purchase a sector mutual fund, you have diversified *between* asset classes but not *within* asset classes. A mutual fund investing only in the stocks of technology companies is not participating in the broader market that includes the stocks of many more types of companies and industries.

There are also ways to purchase mutual funds that are automatically diversified based on your age and life stage. A life-cycle fund is a diversified mutual fund that automatically shifts toward a more conservative mix of investments (more bonds, less stocks) as it approaches a particular year in the future, known as its target date. Given a considerable boost by pension plan legislation passed in 2006, life-cycle funds are frequently used by investors who prefer to use a prepackaged number of investments to meet their financial goal—usually, saving for retirement. The managers of life-cycle funds make all decisions with respect to the asset allocation, diversification, and rebalancing of the fund. Such funds are easy to recognize since they usually have a target retirement date (the year 2015, 2020, 2025, etc.) included in their name.

THE BASICS OF REBALANCING

Rebalancing is a necessary aspect of the initial asset allocation decision and is necessary to bring your portfolio back to its original asset mix or percentages. Why is this necessary? Over time, some of your investments and asset classes will grow faster (or decline more) than other classes, thus deviating from the original percentages you specified as a part of the investment policy statement.

Let's say that the stock market had a good year (a year in which the asset values of the majority of stocks increased in price). As a result, your initial stock allocation of 60 percent has now increased to be 75 percent of your total portfolio. (This also means that your percentage allocation to bonds and cash equivalents has decreased.) You are faced with either selling off some of your stock investments or purchasing more investments from the bonds and cash or cash equivalents asset classes, assuming that you wish to remain true to the **asset allocation** you established when the investment policy statement was prepared. This is not a bad thing. One of the steps in the financial planning process that is often not done well is step six, or the monitoring part of the plan. Portfolio rebalancing is an automatic trigger that will assist you in the practical accomplishment of this step.

How often should you rebalance your portfolio? Like many other questions in financial planning and wealth building, this one has no definitive answer. If you have engaged the services of an investment advisor or professional financial planner, and a separate account has been established to hold your assets, the advisor will notify you when it is time to rebalance. Alternatively, if you are proceeding on your own, this decision is yours to make, although an annual review is likely prudent. Whatever the time frame, before you rebalance your portfolio, consider any transaction fees or income tax consequences that may result from the rebalancing.

If you've invested in a taxable account and you have experienced a loss on the value of your stocks or bonds, consider selling those assets now and using the loss against your income taxes. When doing so, you will also be avoiding one of the biggest mistakes of the average investor: refusing to let go. Some securities will never return to their original value. Even if they do, think of what you could have made with your money in the meantime. The opportunity cost of what you could have done with your money— but did not—is rarely considered by the average investor.

INVESTMENT STRATEGIES

The number of investment strategies that may be pursued to build your wealth is likely limited only by the constraints of your own imagination and securities law, but let's talk about a few of the most common strategies.

Dollar-Cost Averaging and Share Averaging

Dollar-cost averaging is sometimes euphemistically referred to as the poor man's method of saving. Using dollar-cost averaging, an investor purchases additional shares of stock in a mutual fund at regular intervals, usually in equal amounts, regardless of market conditions. Often, this is done through the use of an automatic withdrawal plan offered by the stock issuer or mutual fund company. When you are having withdrawals made from your paycheck to make **401(k) plan** contributions, you are essentially pursuing a dollar-cost averaging strategy.

The practical result of dollar-cost averaging is to gradually increase the number of mutual fund shares that you own over a long period of time. In the event that the current price of the fund is less than or below that of its previous price, you have succeeded in purchasing *more shares* of the investment. Because more shares are acquired when the price of the fund declines, this has the effect of *reducing* the average cost per share. Subsequently, if the price of the fund rises, you will now earn more profits on lower-priced shares, thereby increasing your overall rate of percentage return.

For example, assume that you purchased a share of $5,000 in ABC mutual fund in January 2011, when its share price was $20. You purchased a total of 250 shares ($5,000 divided by $20). Now, instead, assume that you made five separate purchases of ABC mutual fund during 2011 using this same $5,000, but in $1,000 increments, when the price of the fund fluctuated as follows:

Month	Share Price	# of Shares Purchased
March 2011	$22.00	45.45
May 2011	$19.50	51.28
July 2011	$18.00	55.55
September 2011	$17.50	57.14
December 2011	$20.25	49.38
		Total: 258.80

Now, further assume that you plan to sell all of the separately purchased ABC shares in January 2013, when ABC's per share price will be $24. Your total sale price will be $6,211.20 ($24 times 258.80 shares) and you will have **recognized** a gain of $1,211.20 ($6,211.20 less $5,000). What if you had sold your original January 2011 shares? Your gain would have been only $1,000 ($6,000 less $5,000). Using dollar-cost averaging, you increased your annual compounded rate of return by almost 2 percent (from 9.54 percent to 11.46 percent).

As the example illustrates, dollar-cost averaging works best when markets are declining or fluctuating. It does not work well when the market is steadily increasing; in that event, you are better off buying as many shares as possible, as soon as possible, when the price per share is lower. If an experienced investor learns one lesson throughout his or her years of investing, it is that markets rarely go straight up or straight down. Rather, fluctuation in share values is the rule and not the exception. Therefore, dollar-cost averaging should be a valuable wealth-building strategy for you, as it has been for millions of other investors.

A variation of the dollar-cost averaging technique is share averaging. When an investor *dollar-cost averages*, the amount of dollars spent on the stock or mutual fund purchase at regular intervals is held constant, but the number of shares purchased with these dollars varies. Conversely, when an investor *share averages*, the number of shares purchased remains constant, but the amount of dollars spent to make those purchases varies. With share averaging, the investor purchases a *fixed* number of shares regardless of how low the price falls; thus, he or she does not obtain the reduction in the average cost of the shares to the same extent as is possible with dollar-cost averaging. This is why, as a wealth-building technique, more investors implement dollar-cost averaging than share averaging.

Averaging Down

As may be seen from our example involving dollar-cost averaging, an investor can leverage his or her gain by buying more shares when the share price *declines* (so long as the price eventually goes back up before the investor sells). Is there a strategy that results in buying additional shares only when the price goes down? Yes. It is referred to as *averaging down*. In our example, you would have bought ABC shares only in May 2011, July 2011, and September 2011, when the share price fell below the original $200 purchase price, and not in March 2011 and December 2011, when the price was more than $20.

Is pursuing this strategy a good idea? The answer depends on whether you are more interested in purchasing the stock or in the company issuing the stock.

If you are interested only in the *stock*, share averaging may not be a good strategy since (like dollar-cost averaging) the ability to make a profit ultimately depends on the share price increasing. If the share price does not increase, you will have purchased more shares of a stock that you likely should have considered selling in the first place. In other words, you will now have more shares of a losing stock.

Alternatively, if you are purchasing the *company issuing the stock*, presumably you have researched the prospects of that company and the industry in which it does business. Accordingly, you should have a greater confidence in the possibility for an increase in the price of that company's stock, as well as reasonable assurance that a decline in price is only temporary. Therefore, if using the strategy in this manner, averaging down may make more sense as a long-term investment technique.

In any event, proceed carefully. Unless you are an experienced investor, averaging down is an investment strategy you should not try without the help of a professional.

DIVIDEND REINVESTMENT PROGRAMS

Unlike averaging down, which is only for experienced investors, stocks that offer a dividend reinvestment program (DRIP) should be considered by *any* investor. With a DRIP, dividends declared are automatically reinvested in the stock, adding to the investor's overall ownership share. If you want to build an ownership percentage in a company, this is the way to do it.

What are some other advantages of a DRIPs? If the dividends are reinvested instead of paid directly to the shareholder, the investor purchases the additional shares of company stock *without* having to incur a broker's commission. Also, since the company tracks your purchases and keeps records of the purchase price, it can easily provide you with cost **basis** information in the event that you want to sell.

Many mutual funds may have similar programs. If you are working with an investment advisor or financial planner who has positioned your holdings in some form of advisory account, ask him or her about whether you can opt to reinvest any capital gain or dividend distributions (or both) into the purchase of additional shares of the fund. If this option is available, consider taking advantage of a DRIP as an easy way to save and build wealth.

LADDERING

You can go about laddering or staggering the maturity of fixed income investments, such as **bonds** or certificates of deposit, in a number of ways. The most popular is to figure out the longest and shortest term maturities you want to assume and then sequence your purchases between those maturity dates.

For example, if you have $50,000 to invest and you want to invest in bonds with a maturity of no longer than ten years and no shorter than one year, consider ten purchases of bonds in $5,000 increments with a maturity date each year from the end of year one to the end of year ten. This has the effect of minimizing the impact of the price changes in the bonds due to interest rate fluctuations, also known as interest rate risk. In addition, as the short-term bonds mature, their principal may subsequently be invested at potentially *higher* market interest rates.

You can adopt the same approach with respect to bank certificates of deposit and also obtain the advantage of Federal Deposit Insurance Corporation (FDIC) insurance on each certificate so long as the total ownership in each bank and certificate does not exceed $250,000 per depositor.

BUY AND HOLD

Another phrase that describes the buy-and-hold investment strategy is passive portfolio management. In other words, the investor does not intend to actively trade the stocks, bonds, or other assets in his or her portfolio and instead owns those investments for a relatively long time. Buy and hold, coupled with dollar-cost averaging, is a common strategy of the average investor in building wealth to meet the saving-for-retirement financial planning goal.

The buy-and-hold strategy has several advantages:

- You can minimize your acquisition and trading costs in the trading of securities, leading to considerable savings over time.
- It will assist you in managing your income tax obligations. For example, if you do not sell a security in a given year, you do not need to recognize a capital gain or loss on your income tax return.
- Academic studies have shown that the most significant gains in the securities markets are made during several trading days throughout the year; a buy-and-hold strategy ensures that you will not be out of the market during those days.

A warning: many individuals say they are buy-and-hold investors when in fact they are not. Most of us allow changing market conditions to influence our buy-and-sell trading decisions—that is, we let short-term emotions get in the way of our long-term investment decisions. Mega-investor Warren Buffett has made his investors rich in part by not permitting emotions to dictate his investment philosophy. If you are a pure-buy-and-hold investor, you will remain in the market for a long period of time with little concern for market volatility.

MARKET TIMING

Market timing is the behavioral opposite of the buy-and-hold strategy. It is an attempt to *predict* the overall direction of the securities market and to take advantage of the market's volatility, whether that general direction is up (a bull market) or down (a bear market).

Market timing should not be confused with the rebalancing strategy discussed earlier in the chapter. You should rebalance your portfolio to maintain consistent asset allocation percentages over time. However, when you rebalance, you are responding to rules and conditions that *you* have established; namely, through an asset allocation strategy, included in an investment policy statement, that is intended to culminate in the meeting of your financial goals. Market timing is responding to external market circumstances—rules and conditions that have been established by the *market*—over which you have no control. In essence, portfolio rebalancing is *proactive*, whereas market timing is *reactive*.

Does market timing work? Probably not, largely for the reason mentioned earlier—an investor needs to stay invested in the market all year long to experience the greatest gains. Nevertheless, if done properly, market timing can have some value. For example, as an investor, you should pay attention to reports that indicate whether a large number of market timers are either buying or selling over a period of several weeks. This may give you some perspective with respect to overall market sentiment (and, accordingly, whether the market is likely to go up or down).

VALUE VERSUS GROWTH INVESTING

Value and growth investing are really just different sides of the same investment coin. In this case, the investment coin is the **price to earnings ratio** (P/E ratio) of stocks.

Value investing is an investment strategy that is concerned with the *market price* of stocks; specifically, finding stocks that are currently undervalued by the market. Thus, investors who practice value investing attempt to find stocks with high dividend yields and low P/E ratios. The strategy assumes that the current P/E ratio of the stock is *below* its proper level (or what the ratio should be, given current market conditions) and that an efficient market will soon accommodate this and drive the price of the stock upward.

Growth investing focuses on the potential *earnings* of the company issuing the stock. Growth investors look for growth stocks—stocks of a company that has shown a proven ability to develop products quickly and efficiently with a minimum of marketplace competition. Such stocks usually have a superior rate of earnings growth (typically 15 percent a year or more), low dividend payouts, and an above-average P/E ratio.

There is some practical evidence that in a bull market, a growth investing strategy tends to outperform a value investing approach. Conversely, in a declining or fluctuating market, value investing may be more appropriate. As an investor, you should likely consider *both* strategies as appropriate methods of building wealth.

INVESTING IN REAL ESTATE

Most Americans have made an investment in real estate—whether they realize it or not—in the form of their own home. Is your home a *good investment*? While an answer to this question depends on many factors, not the least of which is the geographical location of your home, studies have shown that the average annual real (after inflation) return on residential real estate historically lags that of stocks and bonds. According to a Fidelity Research Institute report, using data obtained from Global Financial Data and Winans International even before the most recent turndown in the market, the average annual ten-year real (after inflation) rate of return on residential real estate is only 1.62 percent. This compares to an average annual real rate of return of 5.85 percent for stocks and 3.18 percent for bonds over the same period.

Despite this low rate of real return, home ownership is very important in our society because it allows the investor to build equity, which is the difference between the fair market value of his or her home and the amount he or she owes on it. In addition, the financial obligation of making mortgage payments may make the investor or homeowner a better saver than an individual who rents. The ability to save (or, more accurately, the exercise of financial self-discipline) is a very important trait for any effective wealth builder. As a result, studies show that the net worth of homeowners is some *eight times* greater on average than that of renters, regardless of age or income level.

Later, as a part of the *accumulation* step in the PADD approach to wealth, we will talk in more detail about investing in financial versus real assets. However, as noted in the Fidelity Research report, the average investor should be wary of over-investing in real estate. This is especially true when certain financial assets, such as stocks and bonds, have proved their superiority as wealth-building vehicles over time.

SECTION II

PROCTECTING YOURSELF, YOUR FAMILY, AND YOUR PROPERTY

CHAPTER 4

INSURING YOURSELF AND YOUR FAMILY

This section of this book introduces the first step in the PADD approach to accumulating and managing wealth: *protecting* yourself against the risk of catastrophic financial loss. In this chapter, we discuss the most important form of risk management—insuring your life (and the resulting loss of income at death) by purchasing life insurance.

Before we begin, you should keep in mind the following guiding principles with respect to purchasing *any* type of insurance:

1. *Never risk more than you can afford to lose.* In other words, buy only the amount of insurance required to ensure that you and your family will be restored to the before-loss status quo.
2. *Do not buy insurance you don't need.*

Do I need life insurance? How much?

There are few financial questions that are likely to be more troublesome than "Do I need life insurance?" This is in part because it prompts the asker to confront his or her own mortality. In addition, the need for life insurance is a philosophical issue for some individuals. For example, historically, farmers and people who make their living off the land (and intend to pass this land down to their families) do not believe that a financial product such as life insurance can substitute for something God did not create.

Let's accept for a moment that we are all going to die someday. Once you have accepted your mortality, figure out what you want to have happen in the event of your death. Most people with spouses and children want to protect the financial lifestyle of their heirs. In other words, they don't want their families to have to suffer financially because they have lost a source of income.

It makes sense, then, that how much life insurance you need is primarily determined by how much income needs to be replaced after your death. As a rule of thumb, many life insurance agents say that you should purchase a life insurance death benefit to replace between five and seven times your annual gross income. For instance, if your annual gross income is $100,000, you should purchase between $500,000 and $700,000 of life insurance coverage. But, like most rules of thumb (and contrary to the financial planning process that should guide your decision), nowhere in this rule is any consideration given to financial goals or particular individual needs and family circumstances. As such, there are two primary methods used by most financial planners to determine the amount of life insurance that an individual should purchase.

The first of these two methods is the *human life value approach*. This approach estimates the amount of income your family would need, based on the financial loss they would incur, if you were to die today, anticipating the number of possible working years that still remained. This amount is then adjusted downward for what you would have personally consumed or paid in taxes (referred to as the family's share of earnings). Utilizing a rate of return known as a discount rate, the present value of your life to your family is estimated.

For example, let's say you currently make $70,000 per year in salary and have approximately twenty years left in your working career. Your amount of personal consumption and taxes due on this income is $20,000, resulting in a family's share of earnings of $50,000 ($70,000 less $20,000). By applying a rate of return to these earnings of 5 percent annually and using a financial function calculator or software program, we can determine a life insurance need of approximately $625,000.

The human life value approach focuses *only* on your income-earning potential and the income loss to your survivors resulting from your death. As such, it is a relative method that assumes that your life only has value as it impacts the financial life of your survivors. It does not consider the recurring nature of your dependents' expenses or any unusual expenses that may result from your death, such as the future need for college education for minor children. Rather, these expenses are part of the alternative computation known as the *needs approach* to life insurance planning.

The needs approach to determining the optimal amount of life insurance is very sophisticated and usually computed via a computer software program. Very briefly, the approach considers your marital status, whether your spouse is employed outside the home, the size of your family, and any separate income earned by your dependents (children or elderly parents). For example, an individual who is single and has no dependents has little need for life insurance coverage. As a result, life insurance for this person may only be necessary to repay debts and expenses related to his or her death. A married person or single working parent who supports dependents has a need for life insurance to continue the flow of income to these dependents in the event of his or her death. The needs approach is suitable to determine the amount of this need.

Here are some of the typical needs of an insured person and his or her family in the event of death:

- Burial or cremation expenses, including funeral costs
- An adjustment fund, which is a short-term fund intended to cover one-time expenses incurred by the family as it adjusts to the loss of the primary (or other) wage-earner
- An income continuation fund, including an amount for mortgage payoff (if the insured's house is not paid off)

- An educational fund for the college education of minor children
- An amount to provide a lifetime income for the surviving spouse (This need arises if the spouse is unemployed and does not have the necessary skills to enter the workforce or cannot otherwise earn sufficient income to replace the insured's income.)

As the potential insured of a single-income family, you should consider that even if your surviving spouse could potentially generate sufficient income to cover the loss of your earnings, the spouse's entry into the workforce might not be preferable to purchasing additional life insurance for this need. In other words, do you intend to *require* your spouse to work? The answer depends on what you have agreed on with your spouse, but if you do not wish to have this discussion, you should purchase the necessary additional life insurance.

Term versus Cash Value Insurance

Many life insurance companies offer various life insurance policies. All of these policies generally consist of only two basic methods of providing life insurance: **term** (also known as temporary life insurance) and **cash value** (also known as permanent life insurance). Term insurance protects you only for a specific period; if you die during this period and are current in your premium payments, the company will pay your family the contractual death benefit that is due. Cash value insurance protects you for life and also offers a savings component in the form of a cash value buildup. Types of term life insurance policies include annual renewable term, level premium term, and decreasing term insurance. Types of permanent life insurance policies featuring a cash value buildup include traditional whole life, universal life, variable life, and variable universal life (VUL) coverage.

Both of these methods of life insurance can be very valuable in protecting yourself and your family. You should not think of either term or cash value insurance as an all-or-nothing proposition; many thoughtful individuals purchase *both* forms of coverage. But generally, as you age, term insurance coverage will become *more expensive*, whereas the cost of cash value coverage will remain *fixed*. This is because, as part of the policy structure, cash value expenses are "front-loaded" since some of the premium expense beyond the pure mortality cost associated with any life insurance policy goes to build a cash reserve or cash fund that you can potentially access for emergency needs.

Just as in determining the amount of life insurance that may be needed, there are rules of thumb pertaining to whether it is best to purchase term or cash value insurance. One of the most common is to buy term and invest the difference—that is, given the fact that term is at least initially less expensive than cash value (the *younger* you are, the *longer* is your life expectancy and the *less* the mortality cost associated with term insurance), take the savings and invest it in higher yielding financial investments such as mutual funds. While the appeal of this strategy is obvious, permanent insurance advocates counter that the buy-term-and-invest-difference concept depends on several flawed assumptions:

- The difference will always be diligently invested every year that the insured owns term insurance, regardless of the insured's personal financial circumstances or ongoing standard of living.
- The alternative investment will always be financially superior to that of the incremental cash value buildup.
- Somehow the need for insurance will magically disappear as the insured ages.

Ultimately, the final decision with respect to how best meet your life insurance needs is yours. In providing for these needs, you should remember that life insurance should be purchased to *protect yourself and your family*; investments, on the other hand, should be purchased to *accumulate wealth*. While there are some investment characteristics to cash value policies (particularly the newer forms of universal and variable universal life), life insurance is first and foremost a risk management product and *not* a product designed to generate significant investment growth.

Types of Term Insurance

Today, most buyers of term insurance purchase either annual renewable term or level premium term. Historically, decreasing term insurance has been a popular form of temporary protection and has been used as a mortgage payoff vehicle at the insured's death. However, decreasing term has fallen out of favor in recent years, primarily because it does not reduce protection at the same rate as the typical mortgage balance, thus resulting in an unnecessary premium cost to the insured.

With *annual renewable term*, you pay the premium each year and the policy remains in force. As you age, the cost to the insurance company increases and the premium goes up each year. However, the level of protection—the death benefit—afforded your family remains constant.

Level premium term insurance initially costs more per year than annual renewable term, but the premium remains level for a fixed period (generally anywhere from five to twenty years). Thus, as you age, presuming you still want a relatively inexpensive temporary life insurance policy, you should probably consider replacing annual renewable term with level premium term. But beware: as you approach the expiration date of your level term policy, you should begin to set aside some additional funds for premium payments once the policy expires. Typically, depending on your age and the length of your original level term policy, you will experience a significant increase in premiums once you purchase a new term policy.

An attractive feature of some term policies is the ability to convert from term or temporary coverage to cash value or permanent life insurance protection *without* evidence of insurability. This means you can obtain permanent protection without having to pass a medical examination. Accordingly, the opportunity to convert is particularly valuable for insureds whose health may have declined during the term. As such, if your health has changed for the worse and you currently own a term policy, you should probably consider converting to a cash value policy as soon as possible, since it is unlikely that you will be able to qualify for permanent coverage at a later date.

Types of Cash Value Insurance

There are three basic types of cash value policies—traditional whole life, universal life, and variable life. A fourth type, variable universal life (VUL), combines the features of universal and variable policies.

Traditional whole life is the standard form of cash value insurance that has been offered by life insurance companies for many years. It features a fixed premium for the life of the policy as well as a savings component that grows on a tax-deferred basis. The policy is initially very expensive and, unless you continue to make premium payments, will lapse and you may lose coverage. In addition, at your death, your beneficiaries will receive only the death benefit payable from the policy and *not* the accumulated cash value. If you choose to access the cash value or savings portion during your lifetime, you must do so through a policy loan or withdrawal, which in turn reduces the amount of death benefit paid.

Universal life takes the concept of "buy term and invest the difference" in a new direction. Yes, you are able to invest the premium amounts charged in excess of pure term coverage and generate some additional return, but you must do so by investing in what the insurance company chooses for you—which are usually conservative, fixed-income vehicles such as investment-grade bonds. Thus, the return generated by a universal life policy, while higher than that of the traditional whole life policy, still lags that of a variable life policy where equities (stocks) are the primary form of investment.

The primary advantage of a universal life policy is its *flexibility* with respect to premium payments. That is, the policy premium is not fixed or tied to the amount of death benefit protection purchased, except in the first year of the policy. The premiums are then deposited into an accumulation fund from which the insurance company withdraws monthly mortality charges. A minimum payment is required to keep the policy in force only when the accumulation fund is close to zero. The policyholder, subject to his or her continued insurability, may increase the death benefit of a universal life policy.

The third kind of cash value insurance, *variable life insurance*, differs from traditional whole life and universal life in one primary respect: you (and not the insurance company) are in charge of your investment choices. Variable life policies allow you to invest in various combinations of stocks, bonds, and mutual funds and feature subaccounts in which you can allocate your assets (very similar to the variable annuity form of insurance). While the premium payments due on a variable life policy are fixed (as in traditional whole life), the death benefit may increase, as may the underlying cash value accumulated within the policy subaccounts. The *variable universal life* (VUL) policy takes this concept one step further by combining a choice of investments and increasing death benefit protection with the ability to make flexible premium payments.

Which of these cash value life insurance forms is best? It almost invariably depends on your comfort level with assuming investment risk. If you consider yourself to be a moderately aggressive or aggressive investor (remember, a primary advantage of working with a financial planner is that he or she can help you determine your risk tolerance level), a variable or variable universal life policy may be preferable. If you are relatively uncomfortable with assuming investment risk or you do not like making investment decisions, a traditional whole life or universal life policy may be more to your liking.

This summary of the types of term and cash value policies available will help you weigh your options:

Type of Policy	Description	Insurance Need	Death Benefit	Premium Structure	Who Should Buy It?
Annual Renewable Term	Pure life insurance with no cash value	Temporary	Fixed	Increases each year	Insured with limited funds
Level Premium Term	Pure life insurance with no cash value	Temporary	Fixed	Level for period of years; then increases	Insured with limited funds
Traditional Whole Life	Cash value accumulation; predictable maximum cost	Permanent	Fixed	Level for insured's lifetime	Insured with need for predictable savings
Universal Life	Cash value accumulation; flexible cost	Permanent	Adjustable (may increase)	Flexible with minimum payment	Conservative investor
Variable Life	Cash value accumulation based on investment performance	Permanent	Guaranteed minimum (fluctuates)	Level for insured's lifetime	Higher risk tolerance investor
Variable Universal Life (VUL)	Features of both variable and universal life policies	Permanent	Adjustable with guaranteed minimum	Flexible with minimum payment	Higher risk tolerance investor/

Now that we have considered the types of life insurance policies that are available for purchase, let's move on to choosing an insurance company.

INSURANCE COMPANY SELECTION AND RATINGS

Before purchasing any type of life insurance policy, even a term policy, find out the financial strength of the insurance company underwriting (or insuring) it. Remember, the purpose of the policy—to provide for your family members in the event of your death—will not be realized until sometime in the (hopefully) distant future. As such, you'll want the company from whom you buy the policy to be in business when it comes time for the death benefit to be paid. Moreover, should you need to access a portion of the death benefit during your life through one of the popular **accelerated death benefit riders** available today, you'll want to ensure that the company will be there to provide it.

The primary measure that most financial planners use to assess the financial strength of an insurance company is to consult an independent rating service. There are five primary insurance company rating organizations: A.M. Best, Standard & Poor's, Moody's, Fitch Ratings, and Weiss Research. While their rating letters are different, all use A+, or some variation thereof, to rate the *highest* companies and several use F as the *lowest* rating. The table shows the top six ratings from each organization as well as the lowest ratings.

	A.M. Best	Standard & Poor's	Moody's	Fitch Ratings	Weiss Research
Highest Rating	A ++	AAA	Aaa	AAA	A+
2nd highest rating	A+	AA+	Aa1	AA+	A
3rd highest rating	A	AA	Aa2	AA	A-
4th highest rating	A-	AA-	Aa3	AA-	B+
5th highest rating	B++	A+	A1	A+	B
6th highest rating	B+	A	A2	A	B-
Lowest rating	F	D	C	CCC-	F

None of these organizations is any more preferable than the others; they all provide valuable information and basically review the same data on each insurance company. However, it is important to understand which organization's ratings are being cited. For example, a company rated "A" by A.M. Best means the company is of the third highest quality, while the same company rating provided by either Standard & Poor's or Fitch Ratings indicates a level of only the sixth highest quality. Regardless, with the number of many insurance companies in business today, you should likely seek out only those of the highest or second highest rating using any rating measure. Typically, companies that deserve those ratings are very well known and have been conducting business for many years.

One final point to consider: some financial planners and insurance advisors believe that an insurance company's financial strength is not as important with a variable or variable universal life (VUL) cash value policy than as with a traditional whole life or universal life policy. This is because the insurance company uses its general assets to stand behind a claim filed with respect to a traditional whole life or universal life policy. However, this is not the case with the variable forms of life insurance. In these types of policies, the cash value accumulates in a separate subaccount that is *not* subject to the claims of the insurance company's other general creditors. As such, the financial viability of the company to pay your claim on a variable form of life insurance policy may not be quite as critical.

CHAPTER 5

INSURING YOUR HEALTH AND LONG-TERM CARE

The issues of health insurance and health insurance coverage are controversial and politically charged, particularly given individual preferences about national health insurance versus a private payer system.

The potential necessity for long-term care insurance is not nearly as well known or discussed. However, the National Clearinghouse for Long Term Care Information estimates that about 70 percent of Americans over the age of 65 will require some form of long-term care before they die.Candidates for long-term care suffer from chronic or disabling conditions that require nursing home care or other constant supervision. It is estimated that approximately 40 percent of individuals aged sixty-five or over will require long-term care at some point during their lives. The cost of this care can be expensive—even catastrophic—for many individuals and their families. One way to provide for the cost of this care is to purchase long-term care insurance while you are still healthy and young enough to qualify for it.

Let's look first at the factors that should be considered in selecting an individual health insurance policy and the types of policies available in today's marketplace.

Considerations in Selecting a Health Insurance Policy

Here are five general considerations in selecting the right health insurance policy:

1. *Health insurance costs a lot, but not having it costs a great deal more.* Quite by accident, as a result of a recruitment tool used to entice veterans returning from World War II, the United States has an employer-based health insurance system. Accordingly, a majority of Americans are covered through group health insurance policies provided by their employers. However, many self-employed individuals and their employees do not have health insurance, given the prohibitive cost of coverage. The same is true for salaried individuals who are laid off as a result of a weak economy.

When it comes to health care expenses, studies show that if one family member is not covered by health insurance and suffers an accident, the resulting medical bills will have an impact on the future economic health of the entire family. The obligation to pay high medical bills is the number one reason for personal bankruptcy filings today. As such, the need for group and individual coverage is very important.

If you are not covered by an employer or individual health plan, follow these steps as recommended by health care advocates and consultants:

- Get in touch with your state's insurance department to find a list of health care plans that provide coverage in your state. Because of the extensive cost of health care to the uninsured, and the continuing inability of some individuals to qualify for health insurance, many states have established health insurance pools that offer coverage for high-risk individuals.
- Contact the top-ranked plans in your state for details regarding premiums and costs for major medical procedures.
- Find out whether any preexisting conditions are excluded from coverage. If you have previously been covered by a group policy, recent health legislation may assist you in

obtaining individual coverage even if you have a preexisting condition as specified by the insurance carrier.

2. *If your employer offers a group health plan, you are likely better off participating in that plan than purchasing individual health insurance.* This can be a tough lesson to learn if you are young and healthy. As a young person in good health covered by a group plan, you may be *over insured*, given that you are paying for a great deal of coverage that you may never use. You can minimize this cost by selecting as high a deductible and co-payment as the plan will permit. You are still probably ahead cost-wise by participating in the group plan rather than purchasing individual coverage. In addition, you need to establish coverage under a group plan so as to exercise certain legal rights that may be necessary in the event that you change or lose your job (otherwise known as COBRA rights, after the Consolidated Omnibus Budget and Reconciliation Act of 1985 that provided for the same).

3. *Review the co-payment and deductible provisions under health insurance plans carefully.* Under most **managed care plans** (including health maintenance organizations [HMO] or preferred provider organizations [PPO]), the insured pays a fixed charge each time he or she sees a medical doctor or fills a covered prescription. This is known as a *co-payment* and should be distinguished from *co-insurance*, where the plan provider and the insured *share* the cost of covered medical expenses once the plan deductible has been met. Generally, you want the co-payment to be as small as possible, unless you do not anticipate using the insurance policy heavily during the year (if you are young and healthy, for example). In this case, you may want to opt for as high as co-payment as possible, which in turn should reduce your premium cost.

Many health care plans, particularly in recent years as the cost of health insurance has skyrocketed, require each insured to retain a certain portion of the health care expense risk in the form of a *deductible*. This is an out-of-pocket amount that the insured must pay *before* any insurance coverage is afforded. Once the covered medical expenses equal the plan deductible (usually on an individual or family basis), further expenses then qualify for the co-insurance provision. Typically, once the co-insurance provision is triggered, the insured must then pay 20 percent of the expenses until a certain maximum amount is reached (known as a stop-loss), at which point the insurance company pays 100 percent of the excess.

If your employer offers a **flexible spending account** (FSA) to help you with the payment of any deductibles or co-payments associated with its health insurance plan, put as much money into this account as you can afford. An FSA is a special form of employee benefit that allows you to pay for certain medical expenses (such as deductibles and co-payments) with *before-tax* dollars, thus reducing your taxable income. We will talk more about FSAs later, but as a general rule of tax planning (part of the *defending your wealth* step in the PADD process), whenever you can pay for an expense with before-tax rather than after-tax dollars, it will usually prove advantageous.

4. *The more flexibility you have in selecting health care providers, the more the plan will cost you.* Many insureds do not need to concern themselves with this consideration since their employer has already taken this flexibility away from them. For example, employers who offer only health maintenance organization (HMO) enrollment to their employees have substantially restricted the employee's right to choose his or her own primary care physician or specialist. But insureds who participate in other forms of health insurance plans, such as preferred provider organization (PPO) plans, may typically see either an in-network physician or one who

does not participate in the network (an out-of-network provider). This same concept also applies to participating and nonparticipating hospitals. If you want to see an out-of-network doctor or hospital, you will likely pay more for the privilege, but at least your choice is preserved.

As a result, if participating in a PPO managed care plan, one of the questions you should research is whether your preferred doctor or hospital is a member of the plan's network of medical providers. Usually, you can check out the network physicians and hospitals participating in the plan before signing up.

5. *Make sure you know your legal rights if you leave your job (and the employer-provided coverage).* In recent years, two legislative acts—the Consolidated Omnibus Reconciliation Act of 1985 (COBRA) and the Health Insurance Portability and Accountability Act of 1996 (HIPAA)—have gone a long way to ensure continuing health insurance coverage for individuals who once had health insurance protection. Unfortunately, neither of these acts do much to address the ongoing problem of the uninsured or, just as important, the rising cost of health insurance premiums. (Note: See the subsequent discussion of the 2010 Patient Protection and Affordable Care Act, sometimes referred to as Obamacare, which was passed in part to address the problem of the uninsured and rising health care costs.)

We will talk in more detail about both of these acts shortly, but you should be aware that if you once had health insurance coverage but lost or changed jobs, it is relatively easy to continue that coverage for a period of time. Although your share of the health insurance premium may increase (if you exercise your COBRA rights, you will have to incur the portion of the group health insurance previously paid by your employer), it is still much better than going without coverage. As mentioned earlier, there is no single event that can threaten your future economic security or that of your family more than incurring substantial medical bills for which you have no individual, employer-provided, or government-mandated insurance.

PATIENT PROTECTION AND AFFORDABLE CARE ACT OF 2010

On March 23, 2010, President Obama signed into law the Patient Protection and Affordable Care Act (or PPA). The provisions of this act will change health care insurance and protection as we know it, but among its most important provisions are

- A mandate requiring all individuals and certain employers to maintain or offer a minimum essential amount of health care insurance or face a penalty. This mandate is among the more controversial provisions of the PPA and is currently being challenged with respect to its constitutionality. If found to be constitutional, the mandate will go into effect in 2014.
- The requirement of automatic enrollment provisions for all employees covered under group health insurance, subject to certain specified opt-out rights
- The prohibition of waiting periods to be covered under a health insurance policy of more than 90 days
- The prohibition of preexisting condition exclusions
- Extended coverage for dependents up to age twenty-six

The PPA also includes several provisions to help finance health care reform. Among the most important of these is an increase in the threshold for medical expense deductions from 7.5 percent to 10 percent of a taxpayer's adjusted gross income (AGI) and an increase in the Medicare payroll tax from 1.45 percent to 2.35 percent for taxpayers with annual income over $200,000 (single filers) and $250,000 (joint filers). Both of these provisions are scheduled to take effect in 2013.

Types of Health Insurance Policies

Historically, there have been only two basic types of health insurance policies: (1) indemnity or fee-for-service policies, and (2) managed care policies. In recent years, however, a third type of health insurance coverage spurred by Congressional legislation (the health savings account, or HSA) has come onto the scene. The first two types of policies dominate the employer-provided range of coverage, while the HSA represents a new way of looking at the individual health insurance problem. The HSA is designed to make the *individual*—rather than his or her employer—the party responsible for making financial decisions related to health. For this reason, the HSA and its predecessor, the medical savings account (MSA), are part of what is now referred to as consumer-driven health care.

Indemnity (Fee-for-Service) Policies

True indemnity policies do *not* include a deductible or co-payment and as such are sometimes referred to as first-dollar coverage (since they pay from the first dollar of expense). Over time, indemnity policies, which historically have included first-dollar coverage for hospital, surgical, and physician's expenses (often known as basic medical insurance) have evolved into the *comprehensive major medical policy*. The major med policy, as it has come to be called, includes both a deductible and a co-insurance provision, as well as a maximum dollar limitation of coverage, usually at least $1 million in lifetime medical expenses.

As a rule, indemnity policies, including major med, cover only accidents and illnesses and do *not* cover preventative care. In addition, they pay a benefit based only on the usual, customary, and reasonable (UCR) rates in your area, *not* on the actual bill or expenses incurred. Individuals insured under indemnity policies are often billed by their medical providers, submit claims to the insurance company, and are subsequently reimbursed for expenses. Insureds usually have complete freedom with respect to which medical providers they use, thereby driving up costs for both the insured and the employer-sponsor. Primarily because of the cost implications, indemnity policies have largely been replaced by managed care policies in recent years.

Managed Care Policies

In the mid to late 1990s, managed care became the most popular form of health care, and some of its benefits were integrated into major comprehensive medical policies. Notably, managed care introduced the concepts of co-payment (rather than annual deductibles) and the primary care physician, also known as the gatekeeper physician or PCP. Another innovation of managed care is the coverage of routine physical exams and other forms of preventative care, in furtherance of the belief that it is less expensive to treat disease in its early stages of development rather than waiting until more extensive treatment is warranted.

There are three primary forms of managed care approaches: (1) health maintenance organizations (HMOs); (2) preferred provider organizations (PPOs); and (3) point-of-service (POS) plans.

An HMO offers medical services to its subscribers for a monthly fee. The members of the organization must use the on-site doctors of the HMO unless referred to a specialist by their assigned primary care physician. The organization provides all medical services and administrates all medical claims filed by the insured. As such, an HMO is not technically an insurance company, since there is no third party to whom the insurance risk is transferred. Rather, the organization provides only prepaid medical services.

A PPO is most often administered by an insurance company acting as an intermediary between medical care providers and the health care consumer. Generally, the various providers affiliated with the PPO, referred to as in network providers, accept reduced fees in exchange for the insurance company paying their fee more rapidly and for a guaranteed payment. Many PPOs allow consumers to receive care outside the network of preferred providers; however, if an out-of-network provider is used, the insured pays a higher co-payment or deductible.

A POS plan combines attributes of the HMO and PPO. If contracted providers in a POS plan are used, their services are available for a low co-payment or are covered completely (like an HMO). However, if an out-of-network provider is used, the insured pays a higher co-payment, and some preventative care may not be covered (like a PPO). Newly enrolled policyholders are required to choose a primary care physician to direct their medical treatment. This physician becomes the insured's point of service and is chosen from a list of preapproved physicians in the plan's medical care network.

Health Savings Accounts

The health savings account (HSA) that any individual who does not participate in an employer-sponsored plan can establish on his or her own is the latest entry in the health insurance marketplace. An employer may contribute to an HSA established by an employee if it so chooses. Today, many HSAs offer investment options, ranging from money market accounts to mutual funds to individual stocks. Most of these investment options are currently underutilized.

An HSA is set up more or less like an individual retirement account (IRA), except that the tax-deductible contributions made to an HSA may only be used to reimburse the account owner for qualifying medical expenses. If they are not used for this purpose, prior to the owner reaching the age of sixty-five, a 10 percent penalty is imposed. Like the IRA, earnings generated by HSA investments accumulate income-tax-free. Therefore, if the distributions from the HSA are used to pay for qualified medical expenses (including long-term care insurance premiums), the account is *never taxed*—not when contributions are made, not while these contributions are generating earnings, and not when the contributions and earnings are withdrawn.

Generally, an individual below Medicare age (age sixty-five) who is not covered by any group or individual health plan can establish an HSA. There is a high deductible (for example, $1,200 for a single individual and $2,400 for a married couple in 2011) required on the health insurance policy, as well as specified limitations on the annual amount of tax-deductible contributions that may be made to the account. However, unlike the IRA, there are *no* income caps for individuals claiming the HSA deduction, nor is the claiming of the deduction dependent on whether the individual itemizes his or her tax deductions at year end.

Who should implement an HSA? Certainly any younger, healthier individual who is unlikely to have large medical bills in the near future and does not participate in an employer plan should consider the option. In addition, older, self-employed individuals who will not have the advantage of retiree health insurance should look very closely at the savings opportunities presented by the HSA. Upper-income and relatively healthy persons may also find HSAs attractive if they switch to a high-deductible insurance policy and then take advantage of the deduction for contributions to offset their taxable income. An often overlooked benefit of establishing an HSA is that you can roll over money from an IRA to an HSA without incurring income tax and avoid a tax bill altogether if you then use the money for qualifying medical expenses.

CONTINUATION OF HEALTH INSURANCE COVERAGE AFTER YOU HAVE LEFT YOUR JOB

Many health care consumers are not aware that if you lose your job voluntarily or involuntarily, you can continue your previous group health insurance coverage. Under the federal COBRA law, employers with twenty or more employees must let you remain enrolled in their policy at your own expense. Typically, this right must be afforded for a period of up to eighteen months after you leave your job.

While it may require some new cash flow planning to pay not only your previous share of the employer group policy premiums but the employer's share as well, it is still probably wise to pursue your COBRA rights. Most group policies (including those of your potential new employers) have waiting periods before you are entitled to coverage. In some cases, the waiting period may be as long as six months. Taking this into consideration, as well as the possibility that it may take you some time to find another job, flexing your COBRA rights is prudent cash flow management.

Other COBRA qualifying events include the death of a covered spouse, divorce or legal separation that causes an employee's spouse or dependent children to lose coverage, and attaining Medicare age. In these events, the term of coverage afforded under COBRA may be as long as thirty-six months.

PORTABILITY OF HEALTH INSURANCE COVERAGE

The phrase *portability of health insurance coverage* is a bit of a misnomer. It does not mean that you can literally transfer the same group policy from your previous employer to your new employer. However, it does mean that, under the Health Insurance Portability and Accountability Act (HIPAA) of 1996, as long as you have been covered under a group policy for a specified period, an insurance company cannot deny you coverage, even if you have become seriously ill in the meantime.

Specifically, the HIPAA states that there cannot be enforcement of a preexisting medical condition clause by the new insurance company if

- you were covered by a prior employer's health insurance plan for at least twelve months
- less than sixty-three days have elapsed since you lost coverage under the prior employer's plan

How do you know when you lost coverage under the prior employer's plan? Your previous employer must provide you with a certificate of coverage that states the length of your insurance coverage and the date when you lost it. Keep this certificate! Should you enroll in a new group health insurance plan that applies a preexisting condition exclusion, proof of prior coverage often guarantees that you can avoid application of this exclusion. Unfortunately, the HIPAA does not regulate premium costs, so there is no guarantee that you will actually be able to *afford* the new insurance to which you are legally entitled.

MEDICARE AND MEDIGAP

Medicare is a federal government health insurance plan that covers individuals once they reach the age of sixty-five. Historically, Medicare consisted of two major parts—Part A, hospital insurance; and Part B, supplementary medical insurance. In 2003, Congress passed a third major part of Medicare—Part D, prescription drug coverage. Part D became fully effective on January 1, 2006, but unlike Parts A and B of the plan, Part D coverage is not included within the traditional Medicare program. Instead, beneficiaries must elect to enroll in one of many hundreds of Part D plans offered by private insurance companies.

Medicare Part A coverage is provided at no premium cost to eligible participants. It covers four broad categories:

- In-patient hospital care up to ninety days. The patient pays a deductible for the first sixty days and a co-payment after this up to the ninety-day maximum.
- Skilled nursing care benefits
- Home health services
- Care in a hospice for the terminally ill (defined as a person with a life expectancy of six months or less)

Perhaps the most misunderstood part of Medicare Part A coverage (and, for that matter, of any other part of Medicare coverage) is that long-term nursing-home coverage (referred to as custodial care under most long-term care insurance policies) is *not* provided. Rather, a very short-term limited benefit known as the skilled nursing care benefit is available. Notably, this benefit means that the patient must enter a skilled nursing facility at the direction of a medical doctor within thirty days after leaving a hospital where he or she was treated for a serious illness for three or more consecutive days. In addition, the patient's condition must be expected to improve as a result of entering this facility. Many medical diagnoses involving dementia, including Alzheimer's disease, are *not covered* under Part A of Medicare.

This leads to the question of how to financially provide for an aging parent who needs continuing care. We will address this issue when we discuss long-term care alternatives, but, speaking as someone who has personally wrestled with the problem, there are three basic choices: (1) you can attempt to self-fund, either using your own money or that of your parent; (2) you can investigate whether it is still possible for your parent to qualify for coverage under a long-term care insurance policy; and (3) you can attempt to take advantage of the very strict requirements to qualify the parent for Medicaid assistance. The practical problem is that most of us either do not have the money to self-fund the coverage or wait so long that our parent no longer qualifies for or can afford the purchase of a long-term care policy. Thus, the purchase of a long-term care insurance policy for one's self or for aging parents is increasingly becoming a cornerstone of proper wealth management.

In contrast to Part A, Medicare Part B coverage is not free to the participant; it entails the payment of a specified monthly premium by the insured. In addition, there is a deductible that must be paid by the insured as well as co-insurance toward covered expenses in any calendar year. Currently, this co-insurance percentage is coordinated with the percentage share of most indemnity medical plans, or 80 percent on the part of the government and 20 percent by the insured. You can opt out of Medicare Part B coverage, but at the time you qualify for Medicare Part A coverage, you must tell the social security administration (who also administers Medicare) that you do not wish to participate in Part B coverage.

As you can likely appreciate, individuals who are eligible for Medicare may have substantial medical costs for which they are responsible *in excess* of the covered expenses. The reimbursement of these excess expenses is why you (or your parent) should purchase a Medicare supplemental health insurance policy, colloquially referred to as a Medigap policy.

Medigap policies are fourteen supplemental policies that have been standardized by federal legislation and are identified by the letters A through N for the types of benefits provided. (Effective June 1, 2010, Plans E, H, I, and J are no longer sold, although if purchased before this date, they are still valid.) Generally, you must have both Part A and Part B coverage under Medicare before a Medigap policy may be purchased. Under law, seniors (defined here as individuals aged sixty-five or over) may only be sold one Medigap policy at a time. The policy must accept all applicants within the first six months of their qualifying for Medicare, *regardless* of any preexisting conditions. Medigap policies can be obtained through a variety of companies and organizations, including the most popular source, the American Association of Retired Persons (AARP), headquartered in Washington DC.

There is also a second form of Medicare coverage that seniors may wish to consider. This is the Medicare Advantage plan, which is *private* insurance subsidized by the federal government that offers the same basic coverage provided by Medicare but also includes the most important features of Medigap policies. There are two types of Medicare Advantage plans: those that include the attributes of managed care plans, and a second option—private fee-for-service plans (or PFFS plans), which feature open access to health care providers with few restrictions. PFFS plans are currently the fastest growing type of alternative Medicare coverage.

THE IMPORTANCE OF LONG-TERM CARE INSURANCE IN PROTECTING YOUR WEALTH

The need for long-term care can mean a variety of different living situations to different people, but generally it results from any chronic or disabling condition that requires nursing home care or constant medical supervision. Long-term care insurance policy provisions will cover not only care in a nursing home facility, but also nursing care in your own home. Payment for care received in your own home is the number one reason you may want to consider purchasing a long-term care insurance policy for yourself or your parent.

Long-term care is very expensive, no matter where you or your aging parent reside, and most people cannot afford to cover the cost of this care for very long. For example, the average cost of a nursing home in the United States in 2011 was approximately $75,000 per year—and it may be considerably higher depending on the level of care that is received and where the nursing home is located. Fortunately, the average stay in a nursing home is less than three years (2.7 years, to be exact), but this is the *average*—you or your parent may reside in such a home for much longer than three years, sometimes even as long as fifteen to twenty years. You should keep this statistic in mind when deciding how long a benefit period you wish to purchase as a part of a long-term care policy. As a general rule, the *greater* the benefit period, the *higher* the long-term care insurance policy premium.

Since 1996, when the HIPAA legislation was passed, most long-term care policies have been issued as qualified policies. While the primary advantages of a qualified long-term care policy are the accompanying income-tax benefits, another real advantage is the fact that it must be *guaranteed renewable*. This means you have the right to continue the policy as long as the premiums are paid. Thus, the insurance company cannot cancel the policy if your health declines and cannot increase the policy premiums, unless it does so for all members of the same class of insureds covered by the policy. In addition, long-term care policies may be issued on a *non-cancelable* basis, meaning that they must have a fixed, guaranteed level premium throughout your lifetime. However, given the rapidly increasing cost of providing long-term care, no insurance company is currently underwriting a policy where the premiums cannot be increased. Still, check around! They may be beginning to change this practice.

If a long-term care policy is tax-qualified, premiums paid by the policyholder are deductible as itemized medical expenses up to a dollar limit that depends on the policy owner's age. Also, benefits paid from a qualified policy are income-tax-free without limit. If an employer pays for long-term care insurance coverage for its employees (a *group* long-term care policy), the premiums are tax-deductible to the employer and are not considered as taxable income to the employee. (Note: There is also a non-tax-qualified form of long-term care policy that does not provide any tax advantages. However, non-qualified plans permit only "medical necessity" as an acceptable condition to be eligible for benefits, whereas tax-qualified plans require the failure to perform certain activities of daily living, or ADLs, for benefit eligibility.)

From an income tax standpoint, you should be aware that insurance premiums paid on a qualified long-term care policy are deductible as a medical expense; thus, they are deductible only to the extent that they exceed 7.5 percent of your adjusted gross income (AGI) for any given year. This means that you likely will *not* be able to deduct the premium until *after* your entry into a nursing home and the incurring of substantial medical expenses. The primary advantage to you from the policy is the income-tax-free nature of the benefits paid. Remember, though, that most long-term care benefits received are likely to be paid in reimbursement of medical expenses and therefore are not subject to income tax under current law.

There are seven basic types of coverage afforded by a qualified long-term care policy, only a few of which (such as skilled nursing care) are covered under Medicare. Even so, the qualifying conditions under the policy are likely to be much more favorable than those afforded under Medicare law. In addition, as mentioned, the major benefit of custodial care coverage in a long-term care policy is not included among Medicare coverage provisions.

The basic types of long-term coverage (in order of level of care) are

- Skilled nursing care: This is the highest level of medical care available and is provided in traditional nursing homes on a daily basis.
- Intermediate nursing care: This is similar to skilled nursing care, except that the care is provided only occasionally and not on a daily basis.
- Custodial care: This is traditional nursing home care and does not have to be ordered by a physician.
- Assisted living: These are facilities that provide apartment-style housing (often including meals) and support services for individuals who need only intermittent assistance with the tasks of daily living.
- Home health care: This is care that allows the patient to remain at home and receive part-time skilled nursing care or other rehabilitative assistance.
- Hospice care: This is care for terminally ill patients and may be ad ministered daily or less frequently. The care usually occurs at the patient's home, but may also be delivered at a hospice care center.
- Adult day care: This care is provided for persons who need assistance and supervision during the day at home and whose spouse or family members work outside the home.

Most long-term care policies have two criteria that must be met before benefits are payable. The insured must meet *either* one of these two criteria:

1. The insured must be *chronically ill* as defined in the policy. Chronically ill is defined as being unable to perform, without substantial assistance, two of six activities of daily living (ADLs) for at least ninety days. The six ADLs are

- Eating
- Bathing
- Dressing
- Transferring from bed to chair
- Using the toilet
- Maintaining continence

2. Substantial services are required to protect the insured from threats to health and safety because of brain damage resulting from, for example, strokes, dementia, or Alzheimer's disease.

Usually, in proving that you meet either of these criteria, written verification by one of more physicians is required, but there are policies that will pay benefits upon the submission of a claim and an internal investigation (no doctor's letter is required).

Let's address some of the more common exclusions and limitations on benefits you should be aware of before purchasing a long-term care policy. The most important of these are

- Daily benefit amount: Each policy typically guarantees a daily benefit amount or dollar amount payable per day based on the level of care being provided by the facility. A good place to begin in determining what this amount should be is to check the daily rate of nursing homes in your area. You may wish to consider an inflation rider to account for future increases in this rate.
- The elimination or waiting period: This period is the number of days you must wait before benefits are paid under the policy. During this time, you will have to pay for the cost of care you receive out of your own private funds or those of your family. As may be expected, the *shorter* the elimination period, the *higher* the long-term care insurance period. The standard elimination period for most policies is ninety days.

- The benefit period: As mentioned earlier, the average time that is spent in a nursing home facility is 2.7 years. As such, you may wish to consider a three-year benefit period (or less). Since this is the average, so you may also wish to consider a longer period. Policies are available for lifetime benefit, but the *longer* the benefit period, the *higher* the policy premium.
- Preexisting condition limitation: A preexisting condition is a condition for which a physician recommended medical treatment within six months before the effective date of insurance coverage. Some long-term care policies include a preexisting condition limitation. If they do, it means that benefits will *not* be payable for long-term care related to the medical recommendation. (It is possible to find a policy without any preexisting condition limitations, but they are more expensive.)
- Policy exclusions: The most common exclusion is for long-term care that is necessary because of alcohol or drug addiction. Almost uniformly, policies do *not* cover this condition.

ALTERNATIVES TO LONG-TERM CARE INSURANCE

The first question that should come to mind with respect to long-term care insurance alternatives is whether you are likely to require long-term care during your lifetime. For some people, the answer is relatively simple, based on problematic family medical history or current poor health. For others, the answer is much less clear-cut. However, statistics bear out that approximately four out of ten people aged sixty-five or over will require long-term care assistance at some point during their lifetimes. These are relatively good odds! Thus, the question becomes not so much a matter of if, but rather when long-term care will be needed, and how it will be paid for.

Historically, there have been three choices available with respect to paying for long-term care: (1) pay for such care yourself or rely on the financial resources of family members; (2) attempt to qualify for government assistance in the form of Medicaid (as opposed to Medicare); or (3) purchase a long-term care insurance policy. Recently, a fourth method has become available: purchasing an *accelerated death benefits* or *living benefits rider* as part of your life insurance coverage. This rider accelerates payment of the death benefit if the insured contracts a terminal disease or becomes chronically ill—in other words, being certified by a physician as unable to perform, without assistance, certain activities of daily living. There is a difference in the income tax treatment of a policy cashed in using this rider.

If an insured is *terminally ill* (generally defined as being expected to die within twenty-four months from the date of onset of disease), he or she can use the proceeds *for any purpose* during lifetime. Thus, there is *no* taxable gain to an insured that is terminally ill. However, if the insured is only *chronically ill*, he or she must use the proceeds *only for long-term care* to avoid taxation on the gain (defined as the cash value of the policy less any premiums paid to date).

For example, assume you are terminally ill but previously purchased a $250,000 universal life insurance policy with an accelerated benefits rider. To date, you have paid $50,000 in premiums and the policy has accumulated a cash value of $75,000. You have $25,000 ($75,000 less $50,000) of potentially taxable gain (**ordinary income** and *not* **capital gain**). Since you are *terminally ill*, you can use the $75,000 cash value for any purpose free of income tax. However, if you are only *chronically ill*, you must use the cash value of $75,000 only for long-term care expenses if you want to avoid the payment of taxes on the $25,000 gain.

Many individuals—either intentionally or by reason of financial circumstances—choose to self-fund the payment of long-term care. A savings or investment plan may help you do so. However, this option requires financial self-discipline, a trait that some of us do not possess in considerable quantity. You may also rely on accessing the equity in your home, either by downsizing to a less expensive home and using the savings to fund possible long-term care costs, or entering into a *reverse mortgage*, whereby the lender pays you a monthly income based on a percentage of the amount of equity in your home. But, given the vicissitudes of residential real estate markets in many areas of the country, this option entails some risk as well.

Medicaid is a joint federal and state funded program for the poor that provides for both health and long-term care. In order to qualify for coverage, applicants must meet income and asset tests as determined by the state where they live. Some relatively wealthy individuals have attempted to deliberately qualify for long-term Medicaid coverage by "spending down" assets and income to the specified level. However, a series of laws dating back to the 1980s have curtailed this activity, notably through the implementation of a look-back period in which most assets that are gifted to others ("spent down") are ignored. For example, an individual who transfers assets to family members (usually, members other than the spouse) during a period of sixty months prior to applying for Medicaid may find him or herself penalized and prohibited from receiving Medicaid assistance for a significant period of time. Relying on government assistance to help you with long-term care expenses may not be the most prudent planning alternative.

This leads us back to the possible purchase of a long-term care insurance policy. If you believe that family or personal circumstance might warrant purchase of such a policy, here are some factors you should consider:

- When (at what age) should I buy the policy? The guideline is that you should purchase a long-term care policy while you are still relatively healthy and young, but not so young as to pay premiums for an inordinate period of time. Generally, the optimal time to purchase a long-term care insurance policy is around age fifty-five, as you are approaching your retirement years but can still qualify for policy coverage without major health questions.

- What type of long-term care are you likely to need? Certainly, skilled nursing care is not desired by anyone, but payment for home health care services is likely an objective of most prospective purchasers. You may wish to purchase a long-term care insurance policy just to provide for this possibility.
- How much can you afford to pay for long-term care? The answer to this question will usually determine what the elimination period under the policy will be and how long you can make payments before the private insurance coverage becomes effective.
- What is your attitude with respect to leaving an estate for your spouse or children? There is nothing that can decimate the size and distribution of one's accumulated estate to others more quickly than a prolonged stay in a nursing home facility. Accordingly, the purchase of a long-term care insurance policy may be thought of as a stopgap measure to preserve at least some portion of your estate.

In case you must unexpectedly enter a nursing home and have otherwise been attempting to qualify for Medicaid assistance, consider purchasing a long-term care insurance policy to cover the requisite look-back period. This means that the applicable benefit period of the policy will likely have to be at least five years before you apply for Medicaid coverage.

The next chapter deals with another major threat to your ability to become wealthy: the threat of losing your earning power.

CHAPTER 6

INSURING YOUR
EARNING POWER

Ask any financial planner or insurance agent what the most neglected or underinsured financial risk is and he or she is likely to say the risk of losing your ability to earn a living. Most individuals simply do *not* give sufficient attention to this possibility and, if they do, they believe that they are adequately covered. In other words, they believe they will never lose their earning power.

However, according to the **Commissioner's Individual Disability Table A,** one in three working Americans will suffer some form of disability that lasts at least ninety days before they reach the age of sixty-five. In addition, one in seven employees will be disabled for five or more years prior to their retirement. You are two to three times more likely to become disabled during your working career than you are to die during this same period. These are impressive (and somewhat frightening) numbers.

Many individuals believe they are adequately insured against the loss of future earning power because they are covered by a group disability income policy at their place of employment. There are two major flaws in this thinking:

1. Most employer policies only replace 50-60 percent of your monthly income.
2. Once replaced, this benefit is probably income-taxable since the employer paid the cost of the insurance premium while you were working. In turn, this means you will receive

less than the 50-60 percent of monthly income promised to you.

How is this often forgotten risk adequately covered? Most commonly through the purchase of an individual disability income policy.

IS THE LOSS OF YOUR EARNING POWER ALREADY ADEQUATELY COVERED?

There are other forms of insurance that you may rely on to protect your earning power in the event that you are unable to work. Among these is supplemental income insurance, which is designed to pay your living expenses while disabled. The most well known of these policies is issued by American Family Life Assurance Company—better known as AFLAC. Quack, quack!

In addition to supplemental policies, employee benefits from your employer are typically available. For short-term illness, your employer may provide sick leave, short-term disability income protection, or both. All employers are mandated by the state to provide worker's compensation benefits in the event of a serious injury while on the job.

Most employers only provide group long-term disability policies. Benefits from these types of policies begin when short-term benefits, if there are any, stop. Long-term benefits then generally continue until you reach age sixty-five, until your full retirement age under Social Security, or until you return to work. However, group policies include a cap or limitation on the amount they will pay—usually no more than 60 percent of your monthly income. As with most employee benefits, once you leave your current place of employment, the disability income coverage is terminated.

Social Security income protection is a disability benefit provided under the Social Security system, but qualifying for it is not easy (some would say impossible). Specifically, to qualify for a disability benefit under Social Security, you must

- have been disabled for at least five full calendar months
- have a disability expected to last at least twelve months or end in death
- be unable to engage in *any substantial gainful occupation* and not just your own occupation at the time your disability begins

Like funding for possible long-term care needs, many individuals (if they have given any thought to their chances of becoming disabled) attempt to self-fund for disability through investment. To determine what you would need to self-fund, review the basics of what we have discussed so far—most notably, the preparation and analysis of a personal cash flow statement—and see what your monthly expenses are. Then multiply this amount by twelve and determine the amount of your total *annual* expenses; this will give you some idea of the funds needed to take you through one year of disability. Most long-term disabilities last more than a year, so you should now be able to appreciate the actual amount of savings needed to cover the risk of loss to your earning power. Most people cannot afford to self-fund for very long.

Accordingly, that brings us back to considering the purchase of a disability income insurance policy.

DEFINITIONS OF DISABILITY

The most important part of any disability income insurance policy (and the single most important consideration for you) is the language used by the policy to define disability. Fortunately, there are really only three definitions:

1. *Own Occupation (Own Occ)*: This is the *most favorable* definition of disability from the point of view of the insured. The definition states that the insured is considered totally disabled (and therefore eligible for benefits payments) if he

or she is unable to engage in the primary duties of his or her own occupation. For example, a medical surgeon would be unable to engage in his or her own occupation if he or she suffered an injury to the hands. This would be the case even if the surgeon were still able to diagnose illnesses as a general practitioner of medicine.

2. *Any Occupation (Any Occ)*: This is the practical *opposite* of the own occupation definition and requires the insured to be unable to perform the duties relating to any gainful occupation before he or she is considered to be totally disabled. It is not unlike the Social Security definition of disability, except that there is no five-month waiting period and expected length of disability. The any occ definition is usually limited to blue-collar workers, although white-collar workers and professionals may also obtain a policy with this definition. The reason these individuals would want to do so is to achieve premium cost savings.

3. *Modified Any Occupation (Modified Any Occ)*: This definition is slightly less restrictive than the any occupation definition, but not as liberal as the own occupation definition. Modified any occupation defines disability as the insured's inability to engage in any occupation for which he or she is reasonably suited by education or experience and for which he or she could easily become qualified. Applying this definition to the medical surgeon example, if the surgeon could become a general practitioner reasonably easily after the injury to his or her hands, the policy probably would not pay a benefit.

Group long-term disability policies usually use a combination of the own occupation and modified any occupation definitions (called a split definition policy). Split-definition policies permit benefits to be received for a period of months or years under the own occupation criteria and then, after retraining for another position, apply the stricter modified any occupation definition. Why? By design, the split definition encourages the worker to return to work and remain with the company, even though it may be in a new position or occupation.

It is also possible to write an individual disability income policy with a loss of income definition. With this kind of policy, the type of disability is not defined; rather, if, as a result of injury or sickness, the insured suffers a loss of income, benefits based on that loss are payable *regardless* of whether the insured returns to work in the same or a related occupation. Given that it does not usually provide as great a benefit, the loss of income policy is not as popular among professionals or other workers as the own occupation definition, but insurance companies like the loss of income standard because it establishes a simple benchmark from which to measure the amount of benefits payable.

Additional Important Provisions in an Individual Disability Policy

Many of the same provisions that are included in a long-term care insurance policy are found in an individual disability income policy. For example, like long-term care policies, disability insurance has an elimination or waiting period, a benefit period, and a benefit amount.

The *elimination period* in disability insurance essentially works the same way as that included in a long-term care policy. That is, it is the period of time *after* the insured has met the qualifying conditions to collect under the policy but *before* any benefit payments are actually made. In the case of disability insurance, an elimination period of ninety days is probably optimal when considering the trade-off between covering the required payments from personal funds for a number of days and the need for as low an insurance premium as possible. Longer elimination periods naturally reduce policy premiums, but the *longer* this period, the *greater* the need for personal savings or other alternatives to cover the insured's ongoing living expenses.

A somewhat novel and increasingly popular alternative that insurance agents are recommending to cover the elimination period is for the insured to separately purchase a *critical illness* insurance policy. Critical illness insurance is an insurance policy that makes a lump sum cash payment if the insured is diagnosed with one of the critical illnesses listed in the policy and survives a minimum number of days (typically thirty) from the date of diagnosis. Such a policy may be underwritten to require payment for the same illness or condition that prompts the insured to make a claim under his or her disability policy—and to make payment *immediately* rather than some ninety days later.

The maximum number of months or years that a disability income policy will pay a benefit is referred to as the *benefit period*. Most disability policies written today provide benefits until the insured becomes eligible for Medicare or reaches age sixty-five. Nonetheless, some insurance companies will write a policy that ensures disability payments are made throughout the life of the insured. The *longer* the benefit payment period, the *higher* the insurance policy premium. As such, you should think very carefully about whether this trade-off is financially worth it. During retirement, if you are looking for a financial product to make lifetime payments, some form of annuity policy is likely a less expensive way to ensure an income stream, rather than an extremely long disability insurance benefit period.

Finally, what most people are interested in when purchasing a disability income policy is the *benefit amount* that is payable. The general approach in the underwriting of all disability income policies is to pay individuals slightly *less* than their net after-tax income if they were able to work, thus encouraging them to return to work as soon as possible. This typically works out to a benefit payable of somewhere between 50 and 60 percent of monthly gross pay. If you are covered at work by a group long-term disability policy at the time you apply for individual coverage, the amount of new disability insurance that you will be able to obtain will likely be limited because of underwriting restrictions. If this is the case, ask your insurance agent if the company will sell you a rider—an addition to the insurance policy with specified benefits or conditions—that allows you to increase the benefit amount without having to undergo a qualifying medical exam. Or, better yet, purchase and implement an individual disability policy *before* you participate in the group policy; then you can receive *both* benefits in the event that you leave the company.

You should also consider whether and how much of the disability insurance income may be taxable. In other words, how much of this income do you actually get to keep? Fortunately, unless you are self-employed, the answer is relatively simple. If the employer pays the disability income insurance premiums on your behalf, the disability income payments are *taxable*. Alternatively, if you pay the disability insurance premiums, the disability income payments are *income-tax-free*. Therefore, when coupling a group policy with individual disability coverage, the group payments are taxable whereas those payments made from an individual policy are not. In summary, you are now in the same position you would be in if you had been able to continue working and receiving a steady paycheck.

Let's now address two other questions you should be sure and ask before purchasing an individual disability insurance policy. Each of these questions has to do with continuing policy coverage in the future and at what price.

POLICY CONTINUATION PROVISIONS

The first question you will want to ask with respect to policy continuation is whether the policy can ever be canceled. In contrast to group policies, individual disability income policies may be underwritten as *non-cancelable*. This is a guarantee that not only can the insurance company *not* cancel the policy, but it cannot *increase* the policy premiums unless otherwise provided for in your contract. This kind of guarantee does not come cheap, particularly in today's inflationary society, but you want the cash flow protection if you can get it.

The second question to ask with respect to policy continuation is whether the company can raise your premiums. Certainly, if you have been fortunate enough to secure a non-cancelable policy, the answer is no, but what if you cannot or do not want to incur the additional cost of a non-cancelable policy? In that case, you have another option: you can purchase a *guaranteed renewable* policy. A guaranteed renewable policy allows the insurance company to increase the premiums but *not* to change the terms of the policy once written. The company also guarantees that you can renew the policy at the date of expiration as long as you have paid the premiums on a timely basis. In addition, the company cannot single you out for any rate increase; it may only increase the premiums for an entire class of similarly rated insureds.

Guaranteed renewable policies generally have lower premiums than non-cancelable policies. Once issued, insurance companies are loath to increase the premiums on guaranteed renewable policies for fear of creating disgruntled policyholders. As such, it may be possible for you to get essentially the same level of protection with a guaranteed renewable policy as with a non-cancelable policy but at a much *lower* cost.

ADDITIONAL POLICY BENEFITS TO CONSIDER

Many individual disability policies offer additional benefits, usually in the form of a policy rider. Here are some of the more important possible additional benefits:

- Cost of living adjustment (COLA) rider: The most common form of this rider increases the disability benefit paid *after* you start to collect benefits, thus protecting you against inflation. Another form increases the policy benefits by a specified percentage (usually 5 percent) each year *before* you become disabled, thus ensuring your constant purchasing power once you begin to draw benefits.
- Return of premium: This benefit requires the insurance company to refund a portion of your premium if no claims are made for a specified period of time.

- Waiver of premium: This benefit allows you to stop paying the premium on the policy if you are disabled for a period of time, usually ninety days.
- Partial disability rider: This benefit is triggered when you are unable to perform some important duties of your own occupation but are able to perform enough other duties to allow you to return to work part-time. In this event, the policy pays a partial benefit, such as 50 percent, of the total that would otherwise be payable.
- Residual disability rider: This rider provides that if you are able to return to work full-time but at lesser pay than before due to a disability, the policy pays the difference between your former pay and the current pay for the benefit period.
- Guaranteed insurability rider (also known as an increase in benefits rider): This rider guarantees you the opportunity to increase the benefit amount payable under the policy at specified time periods, *regardless* of your physical or mental health at the time. A usual requirement to obtain this rider is that you must have initially purchased a disability policy that is at least 80 percent of the maximum benefit amount that the insurance company would approve.

POLICY EXCLUSIONS

Just as with other insurance contracts, it is important to know what is *not* covered under a disability income policy. These are known as policy exclusions and, with respect to disability income policies, refer to particular injuries or illnesses that may result in the insured not being able to work. Those that are most frequently encountered are disabilities resulting from

- war or an act of war
- pregnancy or complications from childbirth
- the insured committing or attempting to commit a crime
- a period when the insured was incarcerated

- an injury or disease that was self-inflicted, including those related to or caused by drinking alcoholic beverages or the illegal use of drugs

Remember, if your disability results from any one of these exclusions, the policy will likely *not* pay benefits.

QUESTIONS TO ASK BEFORE PURCHASING AN INDIVIDUAL DISABILITY INCOME POLICY

1. What is the definition of disability in my policy?
2. What is the amount of benefit payable from my policy?
3. Do I have to pay taxes on that benefit?
4. How long are my benefits payable?
5. Is my benefit adjusted for inflation (and if so, in what amount)?
6. Is there an elimination or waiting period before I can begin to receive my benefit (and if so, how long is it)?
7. Is there a way I can ensure that payments are made during this waiting period?
8. Can I renew my policy without undergoing a medical examination?
9. Can the company increase my policy premiums?
10. What are the policy exclusions and do they affect me?

This chapter concludes our look at *personal* risk exposures. Now, let's consider a risk exposure that most of us also have: the risk of loss or damage to our *property*.

CHAPTER 7

INSURING YOUR PROPERTY

Typically, an individual's most important possessions are his or her home and automobile. Now that you have learned how to insure your life, health, and earning power, you will want to be sure that your home(s) and automobile(s) are protected against significant financial loss as well.

Unlike homeowner's insurance, which is generally not mandatory unless you are required to purchase it by your mortgage lender, automobile insurance *is* required by many states. Specifically, states require all drivers to be financially responsible for damages or injuries caused to others as a result of automobile ownership. Liability insurance must be carried by every driver. However, insurance reimbursement for damage to your car or property (collision and comprehensive insurance) need *not* be carried. As such, you may choose to drop collision coverage and obtain only comprehensive (also known as *other than collision*) insurance for older automobiles. This is good cash flow planning since it makes little sense to ensure a car worth only $1,500 for collision coverage when the annual premiums for such coverage may be $300 or more after a $500 or more deductible.

WHAT TO CONSIDER WHEN INSURING YOUR HOME

Homeowner's insurance insures your home (commonly referred to as "the dwelling" in the insurance policy) and personal belongings that are in the home. In almost all cases, insurance companies write a package policy, meaning that the policy covers not only damages to the home but also liability for any injuries and property damage you or family members cause others while they are on the premises. There are various types of homeowner policies that insure property based on the kind of dwelling you own, and most include the following general forms of coverage:

- Coverage A: Dwelling
- Coverage B: Other Structures
- Coverage C: Contents (Personal Property)
- Coverage D: Loss of Use
- Coverage E: Personal Liability
- Coverage F: Medical Payments to Others

You should also be aware of damage from natural disasters that are commonly excluded in the standard homeowner's policy. Notably, damages caused to your home by flooding or earthquakes are *not* covered. However, federal flood insurance may be purchased through your property and casualty insurance agent or broker. If the federal policy is insufficient, you should consider buying excess flood coverage from a private insurance company. Similarly, you can insure against earthquake damage by purchasing an earthquake endorsement to your standard homeowner's policy. For example, in the state of California, an earthquake endorsement must at least be offered to the homeowner (though purchase of the endorsement is not required under state law).

Coverage A (Dwelling)

Many homeowners make a huge mistake by only covering the fair market value of their home. Instead, your policy should cover the cost of rebuilding in the event of severe damage or destruction—this is known as insuring your home for its *replacement cost*. To get the full benefit of such coverage, you need to cover your home for at least 80 percent of its replacement cost. Otherwise, you will likely only be paid the *actual cash value* for your home, which is its replacement cost *less* a depreciation charge that the insurance company figures in based on the age and condition of your house. In other words, if actual cash value applies, you will only be paid a percentage of the damage or loss to your home.

Some insurance companies offer an extended policy rather than guaranteed replacement cost coverage. An extended policy pays a certain limit—generally, 20 to 25 percent over and above the fair market value of your home—for the purpose rebuilding. For example, if the fair market value of your home is $500,000, an extended policy would pay to rebuild your home up to a cost of $600,000 ($500,000 times 1.20).

How do you determine the replacement cost of your home? Generally, a local developer or construction expert can provide an estimated rebuilding cost. Sometimes, local property appraisals may help, but be careful: appraisals of your property for property tax purposes may be undervalued or overvalued depending on the need for revenue in your particular community. You can also go online to obtain at estimate of replacement cost at such websites at www.insuretovalue.net. Additionally, as part of the annual insurance checkup that you should be doing with your property and casualty agent, ask the agent what he or she shows as the replacement cost for your home.

Coverage B (Other Structures)

This coverage amounts to 10 percent of the dwelling coverage (Coverage A) and insures outbuildings on your property such as an unattached garage or storage shed. For example, if your dwelling is insured for $500,000, you will see separate structure (sometimes referred to as dwelling extensions) coverage in the policy of $50,000 ($500,000 times 0.10). Typically, this amount is adequate coverage, although if you have built a considerable structure not attached to your home but still on the property, you may wish to consider purchasing a higher amount of coverage.

Coverage C (Contents or Personal Property)

This coverage insures all the personal property included in your home unless the property is specifically excluded or limited in the amount of coverage. Coverage is generally 50 percent of Coverage A and, unless you pay a higher premium and obtain replacement cost for personal property items, the policy will pay you only the actual cash value (or depreciated value) of the property.

Particularly valuable items to insure are usually not adequately covered in a homeowner's policy. For example, jewelry and furs, if stolen, are typically limited to a value of $1,500 per article lost. Anything that is worth more than the limits specified in the policy should be covered with an endorsement to the homeowner's policy or through a separate policy known as a personal articles floater. Typically, personal property items that have a replacement cost in excess of the policy limits should be insured with a **floater**. If you do not know the replacement cost of the personal property but suspect it is considerably more than your current policy limits, have the property appraised before purchasing coverage.

The advantage of a floater is that the listed property is insured at the appraised value for damage or loss, often without any deductible applied. However, once an item is insured via a floater, it is no longer covered under the basic limits. Therefore, for example, if your jewelry is appraised at $10,000 (and "scheduled" for this amount), you would not receive a reimbursement of $11,500 ($10,000 plus $1,500) if the jewelry was stolen; rather, coverage would be limited to only $10,000.

Would you remember all of your personal property items if your home were destroyed by fire? Most people would not. It is very likely time and money well spent to record your belongings and separately store the video footage on a personal computer. Put this video in a fireproof safe in your home and another copy in a safe-deposit box. You will be glad you did.

Coverage D (Loss of Use)

If your home is damaged by fire or one of the other listed perils in the standard homeowner's policy, this coverage will pay your living expenses during the time required to repair or rebuild your house. Usually, the amount is 30 percent of Coverage A or sometimes Coverage C, depending on the type of policy. You'll typically want the limitation tied to Coverage A, since it will be a much higher reimbursement amount.

Coverage E (Personal Liability)

Coverage E insures certain liability risks, including in the event of an invited guest being injured on your property, whether or not you are at home at the time. If the injured individual was not an invited guest, under most state laws, you are relieved from liability. Regardless, the amount of liability coverage is usually very important. Many people only maintain a maximum of $100,000 per occurrence for personal liability. In today's litigious society, this is usually not enough, particularly if you are a professional, such as a physician or lawyer. To obtain additional supplemental liability coverage (referred to as **umbrella coverage**), many companies require you to maintain underlying liability coverage of at least $300,000 per occurrence in your homeowner and automobile policies.

We will discuss the possibility of obtaining umbrella coverage to protect you and your family shortly.

Coverage F (Medical Payments to Others)

This coverage is designed to pay the medical costs of individuals who are *not* residents of your home but are on the premises with your permission and are injured. Medical costs may also be paid for individuals who reside away from your premises but are injured by the actions of your pets (for example, a dog that has temporarily left the premises). The coverage is usually limited to $1,000 per occurrence, but with today's rising medical costs, it is not unusual to see higher limits (some as high as $5,000 per occurrence).

TYPES OF HOMEOWNER'S POLICIES (AND THE ONE YOU WANT)

While it is important to understand the types of homeowner's policies and what you are insured against (known as a *peril* in insurance language), it is equally important to know what is *not* covered. We have already mentioned the two most common exclusions—damages caused by *flooding* or *earthquakes*. There are six other, very common exclusions (in other words, when your property is *not* covered against potential loss):

1. if your dwelling is condemned or does not comply with local building codes and has to be replaced or destroyed
2. losses resulting from power failure or interruption of power from the utility company
3. losses resulting from neglect by the insured (if you have not reasonably maintained your home and you have a loss because of this, you are not covered)
4. losses caused by war
5. losses resulting from a nuclear hazard
6. any damage resulting from an intentional act of the insured (if you burn down your own house, the insurance company will not cover this loss)

Now, let's mention the perils that *are covered* under the **standard homeowner's (HO) policy**. This is where the types of policies diverge—for example, the standard HO-1 policy covers only specified *basic* perils, whereas the HO-2 policy extends this coverage to additional and specified *broad* perils.

The *basic* perils are losses to your property resulting from

- fire
- lightning
- wind (tornado or hurricane)

- hail
- riot or civil commotion
- aircraft collision
- vehicle collision
- smoke
- vandalism or malicious mischief
- explosion
- theft
- volcanic eruption

To these basic perils, the *broad* form of homeowner's coverage adds losses to your property resulting from:

- falling objects (for example, tree limbs)
- weight of ice, snow, or sleet
- accidental discharge from a sprinkler, heating, or air-conditioning system
- sudden and accidental tearing of a hot water tank or air-conditioning, heating, or sprinkler system
- freezing of a plumbing, heating, air-conditioning, or sprinkler system
- sudden and accidental damage from an artificially generated electrical current (for example, an electrical generator)

As a homeowner, generally, you do not want either an HO-1 or HO-2 policy specifying named perils. Rather, you should ask for an HO-3 type policy that provides for special or *open peril* coverage. Open peril coverage means that you are protected against *all* losses (even from unknown perils) unless the cause of that loss is specifically *excluded* under the terms of the policy. In addition, many companies offer a rider to an HO-3 policy (known as an HO-15 endorsement) whereby you can also provide for open peril coverage on all your personal property included within the dwelling. Still other companies have combined the HO-3 policy and HO-15 endorsement into one standard HO-5 policy. If you can get an HO-5 policy in your state, do so, as it will provide the most protection for each premium dollar expended.

You should also be aware that many insurance companies writing property insurance policies do not call them HO-1, HO-2, etc., but instead market them under their own proprietary names. Nonetheless, all homeowner's policies track the coverage and limitations that have been mentioned. If you are in doubt, ask your insurance agent to enumerate the types of perils or causes of loss against which you are protected, and then check them off from the lists above.

If you rent an apartment or home, you will want to ensure that you have an HO-4 (renter's insurance) policy. If you are an owner of a condominium or co-op property, an HO-6 policy is preferable.

If a centuries-old, historic home is destroyed, insurance coverage is often limited. This is because the cost to rebuild the home using new construction materials and methods will very likely exceed the fair market value. As such, only a modified insurance coverage policy, known as an HO-8 policy, is available in today's marketplace. If you live in a much older home, you should make sure that you have this type of homeowner's policy.

In summary, here are the types of homeowner's policies, categorized by the kind and extent of losses covered (basic, broad, or open peril):

	HO-1	HO-2	HO-3	HO-4	HO-5	HO-6	HO-8
Coverage A: Dwelling	Basic	Broad	Open Peril	N/A	Open Peril	Broad	Basic
Coverage B: Other Structures	Basic	Broad	Open Peril	N/A	Open Peril	N/A	Basic
Coverage C: Personal Property	Basic	Broad	Broad*	Broad	Open Peril	Broad	Basic
Coverage D: Loss of Use	Basic	Broad	Open Peril	Broad	Open Peril	Broad	Basic

* Can be combined with an HO-15 endorsement to provide for open peril coverage on all personal property located within the dwelling.

WHAT TO CONSIDER WHEN INSURING YOUR AUTOMOBILE

Like homeowner's insurance, there are many forms of automobile insurance (four are provided by almost all insurance companies), but most types of coverage derive from a basic form of policy known as the **personal automobile policy (PAP)**. The PAP has four general areas against which it provides protection:

- Coverage A: Personal Liability
- Coverage B: Medical Payments
- Coverage C: Uninsured Motorist Coverage
- Coverage D: Physical Damage or Loss Coverage

Most states have laws that require drivers to have personal liability insurance in a certain amount. Increasingly, however, these amounts are not generally viewed as sufficient. If you have only the state-minimum amount of liability insurance, it is likely that you are *underinsured*. A way to remedy this situation is to purchase additional liability insurance as a part of your current policy, but another, often overlooked solution is to purchase an umbrella liability policy from the same company that insures your car, home, or both.

Coverage A (Personal Liability)

Personal liability limits are quoted on either a *split-liability* limit basis or as a *single-limit liability*. If the liability limit is specified using a *split-liability*, it specifies the maximum amount that will be paid by the insurance company, if you are at fault in an accident, is divided among various benefits. For example, if you are quoted a policy with liability coverage limits of 50/100/25, it means that you have protection of up to $50,000 for injuries to one individual resulting from an automobile accident, up to $100,000 for injuries to all individuals per accident, and up to $25,000 per accident for property damages (damages to the car you hit). Alternatively, if the liability limit is a *single-limit*, one maximum amount applies to all bodily injuries and property damages per accident, without regard to a per person maximum. In either instance, if the injured party has expenses over and above your policy's personal liability limits, generally he or she must sue you and hope that you have sufficient assets to cover those expenses.

A common question about liability insurance concerns whom this personal liability coverage is provided for. For example, is liability coverage provided if someone borrows your car with your permission? Yes, and it applies whether the injured party is related to you or not. For instance, if you lend your car to your employer, who then is involved in an accident, your employer is covered under your policy for damages to another person or property. However, if your employer injures another while using your car as a delivery vehicle (for a business reason), it is likely that the insurance company will *deny* coverage under a prevailing liability exclusion in the personal automobile policy. A commercial liability policy would be required in this instance.

Another frequently asked question about liability coverage concerns what qualifies as a covered automobile for the purposes of liability protection. The standard PAP defines a covered vehicle as follows:

- any vehicle shown in the declaration page of the policy (that is, your car or cars)
- a newly acquired vehicle; however, normally only for a period of thirty days (in other words, you need to let the insurance company know to extend insurance coverage within thirty days of acquiring the new car)
- any trailer owned by the insured owns
- any car that is being used as a temporary substitute automobile (such as a rental car or loaner)

Be careful! Your insurance company may have a different, lesser time period under which they insure a newly acquired vehicle for collision coverage (for example, only fourteen days). As a result, it is good practice to notify your insurance company agent or broker *as soon as* you purchase a new car and to ask them how to optimally insure the car in your state.

Coverage B (Medical Payments)

This coverage pays your medical bills and those of your family or any other occupant of the car if you are hurt in an automobile accident. It also covers any medical expenses that you may incur as a result of being struck by an automobile while you are a pedestrian.

However, any payments that are made to you as a result of the liability coverage of *another* driver who is at fault reduce *your* medical payments coverage. And if you collect under your employer's group or individual health insurance policy, it may reduce pro rata the amount of benefits you can collect under Coverage B.

Coverage C (Uninsured Motorist's Coverage)

Uninsured motorist's insurance is an agreement that pays the amount that the insured could have collected from the insurance company of a negligent driver if the driver had maintained automobile insurance. Logically, given state laws *requiring* personal liability insurance on the part of all drivers, uninsured motorist's coverage makes little sense. Nevertheless, practically, such coverage is necessary for your or your family's adequate protection. The persons insured under uninsured motorist's coverage might be you, any family member, and other occupant of your vehicle at the time of an accident.

Like Coverage A of the PAP, the *higher* the bodily injury limits under Coverage C, the *better*. As a recommended limit, if you are quoted a split-liability policy, you should have at least $250,000 per individual and $500,000 per accident of uninsured motorist's coverage. If quoted a single liability policy, the higher limit of $500,000 is preferable. Given the fact that uninsured motorist's coverage essentially acts as a secondary liability policy, many insureds just use their personal liability limits as the limit for uninsured motorist's protection (*without* the property damage component).

Coverage D (Physical Damage or Loss Coverage)

Physical damage protection for your car is available through two separate types of coverage under the PAP:

1. *Collision* coverage applies whenever your car hits another car, a fence, a telephone pole, a tree, or a building (essentially, *any* inanimate object). Collision coverage will also pay for damages to your car regardless of who was at fault in an accident.
2. *Other-than-collision,* or comprehensive, coverage is for property damage to your car that results from something other than collision, such as a broken windshield, damage from fire or hail, theft, or damage from collision with animals.

Depending on the company issuing the policy, physical damage coverage may or may not apply for rental cars. Typically, for short-term rentals (less than thirty days), coverage is afforded; however, the issue is much less clear for longer-term rentals. You should check with your insurance company before renting a car for longer than a month as you are likely *not* covered. As a substitute (unless you are renting a car in a foreign country), you may be able to get coverage if you rent the car with a major credit card such as MasterCard, Visa, or American Express.

As mentioned, you can reduce your car insurance premium substantially if you choose the highest deductible available with respect to collision and comprehensive coverage. Better yet, if you can afford the loss of a car damaged beyond repair ("totaled"), purchasing physical damage coverage of any form is probably not wise. If your car is financed and pledged as collateral for a loan, the lender will probably require physical damage coverage, regardless of its estimated salvage value.

No-Fault Insurance

The traditional method of settling claims resulting from an automobile accident is through the *tort system*. A *tort* is a civil wrong wherein one driver is generally found to be at fault in an accident. Negligence is the most common example of a tortuous act. Under the tort system of liability, the at-fault driver's insurance carrier is required to pay for damages suffered by the other parties to the accident. This means that if *you* are the driver at fault in an accident, your insurance company will likely either raise your premiums or, worse, cancel any further coverage.

An alternative method of settling claims is the *no-fault insurance system*. In this system, the insured's insurance company pays the insured for his or her damages, then seeks reimbursement from the at-fault driver and his or her insurer. Most states that have a no-fault system have adopted a *modified* form of the system that permits a lawsuit by the injured party only when his or her policy limits are exceeded. A *pure* form of the system does not allow *any* lawsuits, regardless of the amount of damages or physical injuries. However, no state (at least to date) has adopted the pure form. To combat the rising costs of premiums, many states are abandoning the no-fault system altogether and returning to tort liability.

Umbrella Liability Insurance

Umbrella liability policies are *extended personal liability insurance*—that is, they *supplement* or *add to* your existing, or underlying, personal liability coverage under your homeowner's or automobile policies. For example, if you are sued for negligence in an automobile accident and the plaintiff wins a verdict of $1 million in damages, an umbrella policy will cover you for this amount, even though the underlying maximum limit on your personal automobile policy for injuries to all individuals is only $300,000.

An umbrella liability policy may not only increase liability coverage amounts, but will oftentimes *broaden* such coverage. Most automobile and homeowner's policies exclude the risks of libel or slander from liability protection; in contrast, an umbrella policy typically includes them. Other additional risks may be covered by an umbrella policy, although, since most policies are customized to the needs of the insured, the covered risks may vary.

The premiums charged for umbrella coverage are relatively inexpensive. This is primarily because an umbrella policy is written on an *excess basis*—the policy only pays when the underlying coverage limits (from your automobile or homeowner's policy or both) have been used up. The nature of an umbrella policy limits the number of claims that the insurance company will experience and potentially have to pay. When the umbrella policy is the only coverage for a claim (for example, if slander is alleged), the policy typically has its own deductible or self-insured retention amount, which may be as high or low as the insured chooses. Alternatively, if the liability claim is covered by one of the underlying policies (for example, negligence), the deductible for the underlying policy is also effectively the deductible for the umbrella.

You should think of an umbrella policy exactly as the name implies. The excess coverage provided by the "umbrella" protects you against sizable damage amounts that may be awarded as a result of litigation. Purchasing umbrella coverage is particularly important for individuals who are often the subject of lawsuits, including professionals (lawyers, doctors, accountants, engineers, etc.) and any person of higher net worth. Be aware that any claim arising out of a business activity in which you (or any other insured) are engaged is *not* covered under an umbrella policy; rather, to be protected against these types of claims, a professional liability policy (typically, a malpractice or *errors and omissions* policy) is necessary.

Business Property Insurance

There are two types of *business property* insurance: a *commercial package policy* (CPP) and a *business owner's policy* (BOP). The type of policy you purchase will depend on the size and organizational form of your business. For example, the CPP is usually required by *larger* businesses, typically corporations, whereas the BOP is designed for *small to medium* businesses, usually operating in an unincorporated form as a sole proprietorship or partnership.

The CPP combines commercial property, liability, and business automobile coverage into a single policy. As a result, each part of the CPP specifies covered business property, an applicable deductible, valuation provisions, and a requisite cause of loss. In practical effect, these types of property coverage are very similar to a homeowner's policy, but are much broader and comprehensive in scope. Hence, the advantage of listing and insuring business property in this manner is that there are fewer gaps in coverage and administrative savings may be achieved that can lead to lower premiums.

The general liability portion of the CPP protects the business against legal liability arising from business activities, excepting injuries incurred by employees while on the job, for which separate worker's compensation insurance is needed. Typically, the CPP will have additional coverage for business automobile liability, but all claims arising out of employee injury must be handled as part of the worker's compensation policy that most businesses are required to maintain by law. It is also possible to write a separate policy for commercial general liability, although this may result in additional cost.

The BOP is specifically designed for the needs of small- to medium-sized businesses and covers all business-related real and personal property without a separate listing. There are two forms of this policy: basic and special. The basic form covers the possibility of loss from all listed perils and the special form covers loss from all perils not excluded. All forms of the BOP cover liability for bodily injury and property damage caused by employees while engaged in an activity on behalf of the business.

119

If you are business owner, you should be aware that there is another type of policy that protects business property while that property is *in transit* to another location. This is known as an *inland marine policy* and covers domestic goods while they are being moved from one location to another, mobile equipment and property, and certain types of property that are still in the dealer's store (such as inventory). The term *inland marine* has nothing to do with water or oceanic activities, as the name seems to imply.

We have now concluded our look at personal and property risk exposures and how to insure them. However, if you are employed, additional forms of insurance benefits may be available to you in *group form*. Such forms, along with other benefits commonly offered by an employer, is the subject of our next chapter.

CHAPTER 8

OPTIMIZING YOUR EMPLOYMENT BENEFITS

Our look at how to *protect* your wealth concludes with this chapter on how best to take advantage of benefits offered by your employer. Unlike the humorous television commercial, benefits offered by your employer do not come from France ("French benefits"), but rather are commonly referred to as fringe benefits. The nature and amount of fringe benefits at the workplace depends on your employer, its current and future cash flow, and its attitude toward providing (usually) tax-free benefits to its employees. Typically, employers not only offer fringe benefits for competitive reasons, but also because they receive an income tax deduction for providing them, thereby assisting with managing future cash flow. Perhaps the most popular benefit for employees that has evolved through the years is employer-provided group medical and dental insurance. Other common benefits offered to employees are group term life insurance coverage, accidental death insurance coverage, group long-term disability coverage, dependent care assistance (usually through some form of flexible spending account), educational assistance, and group long-term care insurance. Recently, employers have implemented retirement savings options such as the Section 401(k) (after the Internal Revenue code section of the same number) retirement plan. Executives of companies may have special or discriminatory benefits established to encourage performance goals.

This chapter will consider how you, as a valued employee, can best take advantage of these benefits to help meet your financial goals.

Group Medical and Dental Insurance

In a chapter 5 we discussed what an informed purchaser of health care services should take into account before selecting a health insurance policy. However, most wage earners only have the option of whatever group medical and dental plans are offered by their employer. Historically, the most popular type of group medical plan provided by employers has been comprehensive major medical coverage, sometimes known as fee-for-service programs. Recently, however, managed care plans such as HMOs and PPOs have come onto the scene, and more recently still, a close cousin of the health savings account (HSA) has begun to be offered by employers: the health reimbursement arrangement (HRA).

An HRA is an employer-sponsored health spending account that permits employees to accumulate funds for health expenses. Employers offering HRAs typically pair them with a high-deductible group health insurance plan in order to cover any sizable medical expenses incurred by the employee. Once the employer funds set aside in the HRA are used up in a given year, the employee's health expenses are then covered by the high-deductible plan after the deductible and co-insurance requirements are met. If any funds remain in the HRA at the end of the year, these funds may be carried over to the following year, which allows the employee to "save" for his or her future medical expenses.

A major advantage of an HRA from the point of view of the employee is that preventative care, such as routine physicals and child immunizations, are *not* charged against the fund. In addition, because of the savings element associated with the arrangement, HRA participants have an incentive to use their health care dollars wisely.

Employers like HRAs because they allow them to minimize health-care insurance costs since the underlying policy providing coverage has a high deductible and the policy may never be used by relatively healthy employees.

Unfortunately, most group dental insurance coverage plans have not yet adopted the HRA approach to payment of expenses. Most dental insurance uses managed care as a model, operating either as an HMO or PPO. If you have a dental HMO, the premium payments on your group coverage will be sent directly to your dentist or specialist. If your plan is structured as a PPO, a network of participating dentists has agreed to provide services for a reduced fee to group insureds. You may go out of the network to an unaffiliated provider, but you will pay a higher deductible and co-payment to do so.

In summary, unless you participate in an HRA at work, your group medical plan probably provides you with little incentive to save your health care dollars. Further, the high cost of paying for your own medical care will likely dissuade you from purchasing an individual policy. You have to seek ways of paying for your share of the group medical costs (deductibles and co-payments) in as tax-efficient a way as possible, such as by participating in a flexible spending account. You should also turn your attention to other employment-provided benefits that may need to be supplemented with individual coverage, such as life insurance and disability income insurance.

GROUP LIFE INSURANCE

The most common form of life insurance offered by employers is *group term* insurance. By its nature, this form of insurance is temporary and covers you only for a specific period, normally only as long as you work for the employer providing coverage. As such, you need to keep in mind that you will likely *lose* coverage when you leave the job. However, at that point, you typically have an opportunity to convert the group term coverage into some form of permanent insurance (either whole life or universal life) offered by the same insurance company. Generally, this conversion privilege is only available for thirty to sixty days following the date the employee is no longer employed, but, if taken advantage of, the privilege of converting is usually a *guaranteed benefit* (you cannot be denied coverage regardless of your health status at the time).

Group term insurance is generally offered to employees as a multiple of salary. For example, the death benefit provided by the policy is one or two times the current salary of the employee. Often, however, the employer portion of this benefit is capped at a specified amount, usually $50,000. This is because the employee is limited to a $50,000 cost-of-coverage exclusion before he or she must be attributed some cost of the protection as a taxable employee benefit. Stated another way, if the employer pays for more than $50,000 of group term life insurance on your life, you must report the economic benefit of the extra insurance as income. (It is typically reported on the IRS Form W-2 at the end of the year.) Fortunately, this attributed amount of income is relatively small and the cost that the employer pays for the insurance is still likely much less than you would have to pay if you tried to obtain the insurance coverage on your own. Plus, as mentioned above, you probably have the right to convert the group term insurance once you have left that employer.

Nevertheless, even with your group term insurance coverage, you should analyze whether you have *enough* life insurance protection. Don't assume you have enough coverage simply with what the insurance provides, and remember, unless you convert, you will lose the insurance when you leave the job. Rather, look at the group term coverage only as a starting point to be supplemented with individual life insurance, either with an individual term or a permanent policy or perhaps both.

Another commonly provided group insurance is **accidental death benefit** (ADB) insurance, sometimes simply referred to as double indemnity insurance. Historically, this insurance has been purchased as a rider to a group life policy and *doubles* the death benefit payable to an employee's beneficiary if death results from an accident while the employee is conducting employer business. Like group term insurance coverage, the accidental death benefit is typically limited in amount. However, this is to minimize employer cost and not to minimize the income tax consequences to the employee. If you have ADB insurance protection, consider yourself one of the lucky few, as i However, increasing numbers of employers are dropping such coverage. Moreover, it is difficult to envision a situation in which your need for life insurance protection is greater in the case of accidental death than it is under normal circumstances of death. Therefore, the doubling of the benefit is essentially free money for your heirs, which you would not have otherwise provided.

More and more employers are offering group *permanent* types of life insurance policies—notably, group universal life. A group universal life insurance policy is very similar in structure and provisions to an individual universal life policy, except that the group coverage is provided (up to a limit) *without* any evidence of insurability. Therefore, an employee in poor health who may not be able to qualify for individual coverage may obtain insurance through group underwriting. Unlike group term policies, group universal life policies are *portable*, meaning that you can take the coverage with you when you leave the job (although a higher premium may then be charged).

GROUP DISABILITY INSURANCE

If individuals have disability insurance, they have it through their employer in the form of group *long-term* coverage. (As has been discussed, the purchase of an individual disability income insurance policy is likely one of the best moves you can make to protect your future wealth.) A group long-term disability policy normally has an elimination period of thirty to one hundred and eighty days before you can draw benefits, but this period may be even longer if the policy is coupled with short-term disability coverage. Therefore, you need to find some way to cover your expenses while you wait for the long-term benefits to begin. This underscores the importance of maintaining an adequate emergency or contingency fund.

If you are fortunate, your employer will also offer *short-term* disability coverage. This coverage may have an elimination period as short as seven days for illness and one day for injury. If written to cover illness, short-term policies generally function as a kind of sick leave from your job. The policy pays you a specified dollar amount not tied to a percentage of monthly compensation—as is the norm with long-term coverage. If written to cover injury or disability, the short-term definition of disability used is usually that of *total disability*, which will preclude payment if you are only partially disabled or temporarily experience a loss of income.

Group disability coverage is often less expensive than individual coverage. However, it is important to realize that you cannot customize coverage in a group policy nearly as effectively as with an individual policy. For example, in an individual disability policy, you can purchase coverage that will pay when you are unable to perform your own occupation; this is generally *not* possible with a group long-term policy that uses a combination of *any occupation* and *modified any occupation* definitions of disability. Additionally, the group policy may not provide you with a cost-of-living increase in benefits (as is possible with the purchase of a rider to an individual policy). You will pay taxes on any disability benefits received from the policy if the employer pays the cost of the policy premiums during your employment years.

Group Long-Term Care Insurance

The offering of group long-term care insurance by employers is a relatively new phenomenon. As a result of the rising cost of long-term care (and the relative paucity of government-provided benefits to assist in the payment of this cost), more employers are encouraging their employees to plan for this need and are helping them do so through group insurance plans.

There are essentially three types of group long-term care plans. The one that is right for you depends on the status of your current health. For example, the most liberal and favorable type of group long-term care policy (but also the most expensive) is a *true group* policy. This type of policy is underwritten as *guaranteed issue*, meaning that no employee can be denied coverage, even if he or she *already* has a debilitating health condition that would preclude him or her from otherwise obtaining coverage. The price for this coverage is a high premium, in part designed to discourage what is known in the insurance industry as adverse selection—meaning that the sickest and most disabled employees will be the most likely to enroll.

A modified form of a true group long-term care policy uses no medical underwriting but asks one or more disqualifying questions intended to eliminate the sickest and most disabled employees. This is known as a modified guaranteed issue policy. The premiums are lower on this type of policy and if you are relatively healthy (and could otherwise qualify for individual coverage), this is preferable to a true group policy.

Third, individual long-term care plans are offered to employers for group coverage to their employees on a discounted basis (typically, anywhere from 5 to 15 percent below the individual plan premium). While these types of plans are medically underwritten (in other words, they are neither guaranteed issue nor modified guaranteed issue), they permit *more* benefit options for employees. Employers like to "carve out" these policies for a select group of employees (usually executives) since the benefits are significant but cost much less than true group policies. If you are an executive in a company, a discounted individual long-term care plan is likely for you.

If you currently do *not* have a group long-term care policy available to you as an employee, ask your human resources department to investigate the possibility of offering such a benefit. It is possible to offer a group policy on a ten-year paid-up basis—something that is generally not available with an individually obtained policy.

One last thing: The frequency of claims made on individual long-term care policies is relatively high—so high that many insurance companies are choosing not to enter the long-term care market or are getting out of the business of underwriting individual long-term care policies entirely. Accordingly, that is all the more reason you should be investigating whether your employer will offer a group policy for the benefit of all employees.

DEPENDENT CARE ASSISTANCE

Your employer can provide you with a substantial amount of dependent care assistance as a nontaxable fringe benefit. Currently, up to $5,000 per year of such assistance per family (or the total amount of the lower paid spouse's salary, if less than $5,000) is not includible in your taxable income.

You may also wish to reduce your salary and contribute this amount to a *flexible spending account* (FSA) on your own behalf. Two primary reasons for doing so are

1. You can pay dependent care costs, such as full-time child care, after-school day care, or the cost of a nanny, out of this account and receive reimbursement on a tax-free basis.
2. You never pay any income or Social Security tax on the amount you contribute to the account; as such, you are contributing to the account from your paycheck on a pretax basis.

You also need to be aware of two related income tax consequences as you consider whether to fund an FSA in payment of child care expenses:

1. You may *not* claim the **dependent care** and **child tax credit** for any child-care cost that is reimbursed out of the account (in other words, it is an either/or proposition).
2. You *lose* any amount contributed to the account that is not spent on employment-related child-care costs during the year. (Unlike an HSA, where you can use the account as a savings vehicle for the next and subsequent years, an FSA is contributed to on a use-it-or-lose it basis.)

As a general rule, the *higher* your taxable income, the *more advantageous* it is for you to utilize the FSA salary reduction in the payment of child-care expenses. Conversely, the *lower* your taxable income, the *less advantageous* the salary reduction and the *more valuable* the child tax credit will be.

Do not overlook the possibility of dependent care assistance for more than your young child or children. Under current law, the tax exclusion is available not only for expenses incurred on behalf of a dependent child under the age of thirteen, but also for any individual who is physically or mentally incapable of caring for themselves and who resides with the taxpayer in their principal place of residence for more than six months out of the year. Therefore, the $5,000 exclusion from income is also potentially available for dependent elderly parents or a dependent spouse for whom you are the primary caregiver.

EMPLOYER EDUCATIONAL ASSISTANCE

Some employers, particularly those who need highly skilled employees, offer educational assistance benefits. In most instances, under employer rules to achieve reimbursement, this education must be job-related. However, under current tax law, an exclusion from employee income of up to $5,250 per year is permitted even for non-job-related education courses. Further, the exclusion is (in most cases) not limited only to degree programs, and the employer payment may be in reimbursement of either undergraduate or graduate degree courses. As a result, you may be able to obtain and be reimbursed for that doctoral degree in underwater basket weaving you have always wanted.

There is a second related educational benefit in tax law that you may be able to take advantage of *without* getting your employer involved. This is an itemized tax deduction for un-reimbursed educational expenses that you pursue in advancement of your career. As you might suspect, this education must be related to your career. For example, if you are an accountant, pursuing a master's degree in accounting will qualify as job-related education. The major issue here for many young fast-track employees is whether educational costs expended for a master's degree in business administration will qualify for the tax break. Generally, the answer is yes; however, if your current job is so unrelated to traditional business activities (say, you are a professional musician), you may find it difficult to make a strong argument that the deduction should be permitted. Regardless, if you *do* qualify, and itemize your tax deductions, you may be able to offset some of the cost of advancing your career.

SAVING FOR RETIREMENT THROUGH EMPLOYER-SPONSORED PLANS

In recent years, employer-provided plans designed to provide for retirement have undergone major changes. Historically, employers promised their employees a pension (guaranteed retirement income) at a certain age (usually sixty-five) as long as the employee completed a specified number of years of service. As such, the employer assumed the risk of investment performance on the retirement monies set aside to make good on its pension promise.

Beginning in the 1990s, the methodology of providing for an employee's retirement changed from a guaranteed employer-provided pension to one where the employee was made responsible for his or her own financial future. *Defined contribution retirement plans*—in which the amount of retirement benefit is *not* guaranteed but rather depends on the employee's own investment expertise to accumulate the needed savings—became predominant. According to Boston College's Center for Investment Research, among workers with retirement plans, 83 percent had traditional employer-provided pensions in 1980. By the year 2004, that number was down to 39 percent, a rather significant reduction.

However, there was a major problem in the shift away from pensions to defined-contribution plans: most employees did not possess the investment expertise to optimally plan for their own retirement. This is still the case today. While recent legislation (notably, the Pension Protection Act of 2006) has been passed to make it easier for employers to assist employees with their retirement investment decisions, employees are generally not yet well educated enough to take on the responsibility of making retirement plan investment choices. Hopefully, after finishing this book, you will feel more comfortable in making such choices. If not, I strongly urge you to seek the assistance of a CFP professional.

Section 401(k) Retirement Plans

Many employees today are participating in one or more types of defined-contribution retirement plans at work, but the Section 401(k) plan has become the savings plan of choice. While many employees believe that employers match a percentage of their 401(k) plan contributions primarily for altruistic reasons, this is not usually the employer's motivation. Rather, there are special **nondiscrimination tests** that must be met before the employer can offer and maintain a 401(k) plan on behalf of any employee, including **highly compensated employees**, whose job satisfaction and performance is the employer's *primary* concern. In addition, highly compensated employees are the kind of employees most likely to already contribute to a Section 401(k) plan; therefore, the employer needs to motivate the *non*-highly compensated employee to contribute to the plan as well in order to satisfy nondiscrimination tests. Employers typically encourage the non-highly compensated employee to contribute via a matching-of-employee-contributions program.

According to Fidelity Investments and their excellent publication *Building Futures*, the average 401(k) plan contribution (or salary deferral percentage) in the year 2005 was 6.9 percent. However, only approximately 65 percent of employees actually participated in 401(k) plans. This means the aggregate plan savings rate was only 4.5 percent. Even with a 3 percent employer match of employee contributions (the most common matching-of-employee contributions in the United States is 50 percent of the first 6 percent of salary deferrals), the aggregate savings rate is only 6.5 percent (6.9 percent plus 3 percent times 65 percent). This is not nearly enough for most 401(k) plan participants to live adequately during their retirement years.

If you are lucky enough to have an employer that sponsors a Section 401(k) plan (many companies, particularly smaller ones, do not), the first thing you must do is *participate*. You should then elect to defer on a pretax basis as much of your salary as possible into the 401(k) plan. (Note: While there are annual dollar limits on how much you can defer, these limits are usually important only for highly compensated employees such as corporate executives.) Certainly, you should be deferring at least 3 percent of your salary (or whatever percentage your particular employer will match), since that is a *guaranteed* 100 percent investment return on your money. But beyond that, at least a 10 percent total annual contribution (15 percent is better) should be your goal. If you are closer to retirement and have let the prime saving years of your thirties and forties pass, you will need to save an *even greater* percentage to fund retirement—either that or you will need to consider one of two unpleasant alternatives: (1) work longer and extend your planned retirement date, or (2) reduce your postretirement standard of living. There is also a third choice: continue working after your planned retirement date and hope that your good health continues.

As a result of the Pension Protection Act (PPA) of 2006, many 401(k) plans are adopting automatic enrollment plans. This alternative, also known as a negative election, allows an employer to enroll employees in its Section 401(k) plan *without* the employee's consent, so long as the employee has the right to opt out of contributing. Some employers are also supplementing the automatic enrollment with a progressive savings feature, meaning that they will automatically *increase* an employee's savings deferral percentage by a set amount (for example, 1 percent) each year that the employee participates in the plan. These two features, when used together, may go a long way in helping employees—and particularly those who have opted out in the past—save for their own retirement.

As an incentive to offer automatic enrollment, the PPA of 2006 included relief from employer liability if the employer provides investment advice to 401(k) plan participants. To be eligible for this relief, however, the employer's investment advice arrangement must include an unbiased computer model certified by an independent expert to create a recommended portfolio for a participant's consideration. As a result, *life cycle investment funds* or *target retirement funds* are now being adopted as an employer's default investment option for employees who are automatically enrolled. Overall, this is not a bad thing, particularly if you are an employee who would not save otherwise, but if you are at all serious about saving for your own retirement (you're reading this book, aren't you?), it does seem that you can invest your retirement plan contributions more wisely than the default option. At least, you—or your financial planner—should definitely try!

Section 403(b) Retirement Plans

The Section 403(b) plan, also referred to as a tax-sheltered annuity, is the equivalent of the Section 401(k) plan for employees who work for specified *not-for-profit employers*, such as public or private schools, churches, and some hospitals. The maximum annual salary reduction contributions for the 403(b) plan are generally the same as those allowable for the Section 401(k) plan, as are the nondiscrimination rules that must be met by the employer. Today, more and more not-for-profit employers are *matching* the salary reduction contributions made by their employees (historically, many 403(b) plans were funded solely by employee salary reductions with no employer matching).

However, there are a few differences between the 403(b) and 401(k) retirement plans. Only certain not-for-profit employers (called "501(c)(3) organizations" after the Internal Revenue code section of the same number) may implement a 403(b) plan. As mentioned, these employers include schools and churches, so if you are a public school elementary or secondary school teacher, you likely have a 403(b) plan and not a 401(k) plan. I use the word "likely" here since increasing numbers of not-for-profit employers have been implementing a Section 401(k) plan and adding it to or substituting it for a Section 403(b) plan. A Section 401(k) plan generally has more investment choices than the Section 403(b) offering. For example, a Section 403(b) plan has to be invested in either an **annuity**, fixed or variable, or mutual funds. It cannot be invested in individual stocks or bonds. Therefore, if you are an investor who likes to play the market, a Section 403(b) plan may not be for you.

Another advantage of the Section 401(k) plan, as compared to the Section 403(b) plan, is the ability to elect a special income tax treatment if the participant chooses to take a lump-sum distribution. This special election, known as ten-year averaging tax treatment, is not available for Section 403(b) plan participants. Specifically, ten-year averaging allows 401(k) plan participants born before 1936 to pay income taxes on a lump-sum distribution in one year as if they were paying it over ten years, thereby significantly lowering their tax bill.

With the exception of these two advantages for the 401(k) plan, the 403(b) is probably the more favorable of the two. While not discussing the other technical reasons why this is so, the 403(b) plan generally beats the 401(k) for one big reason: you can put *more* money into the 403(b) plan the *closer* you are to your planned retirement date. For example, if, as a not-for-profit employee, you have worked for the same or another qualifying employer for at least fifteen years, you may be able to contribute as much as $15,000 per year *in addition to* the normal contribution limits. As such, you can attempt to make up for those years in your thirties and forties when you did not or were not able to adequately save for your own retirement. You cannot do this with the 401(k) plan since the special catch-up annual contribution exception doesn't apply.

Other Retirement Plans

Other employer-sponsored retirement plans (and IRAs) will be discussed later in the book when we address distributing your wealth at the time of retirement, but some employers offer plans in addition to the Section 401(k) and Section 403(b) plans. If they do, they may permit you to make contributions to these plans on an after-tax basis. While this may not seem like something you want to do, particularly if you have already maxed out your before-tax contributions to the 401(k) or 403(b) plan, consider this: if you contribute after-tax money to any employer-sponsored plan, once that plan makes a distribution of those same funds to you, you do *not* have to pay income taxes on that portion of the distribution. That is not quite as good a deal as the **Roth IRA** or **Roth 401(k)**, where the *earnings* from those after-tax contributions are also generally income tax-free, but it is close. All in all, if you have the opportunity to make after-tax contributions to an employer-sponsored plan and can afford to do so, you should. Making after-tax contributions is an attractive way to add to your retirement savings.

COMPANY STOCK PURCHASE PLANS

There are two basic types of company stock purchase plans: employee stock ownership plans (ESOPs) and employee stock purchase plans (ESPPs). Both plans permit the employee to purchase and own employer stock, although, as the name implies, only the ESOP permits controlling ownership to be transferred to the employees.

If you work for a corporation or incorporated business, the employer may have established an employee stock ownership plan. An unincorporated business, such as a sole proprietorship or partnership, cannot have an ESOP since it has no stock. An ESOP is a retirement plan designed to invest primarily in employer stock. Some closely held (non-publicly-traded) corporations also establish ESOPs to provide a market for employer stock that would otherwise not be very marketable. (Would you want to buy into a business where you did not know the owners or, worse, if you did, found them to be overbearing and inflexible?) Thus, if establishing an ESOP, the employees become the market and ultimately the owners of the closely held business.

There is another major advantage to the employee of an ESOP: you now have a tax-favored retirement plan in which to save for your own retirement. Further, once the employer stock is distributed to you at the time of retirement, you do *not* have to pay any capital gains tax on the appreciation of the stock (technically known as **net unrealized appreciation** or NUA) until you sell the shares. This amount of appreciation is then taxed at favorable long-term capital gains rates (15 percent or 5 percent, depending on your regular income tax bracket) if you have owned the stock for at least a year, which is extremely likely since you have accumulated the stock for long-term, retirement planning purposes anyway. Through the end of 2012, the 5 percent capital gains rate is temporarily *zero* for those who qualify for the tax break.

In contrast to the ESOP, an ESPP is simply a means for you to own stock in your employer under very favorable terms. It is typically not structured as a retirement plan, but rather as an employee investment option. The ESPP permits the employee the right to buy company stock on a future date for an amount that is no higher than its current, publicly traded value. If the stock price *increases* between the time this right is granted and the time that the employee purchases the stock, the employee may choose to buy the stock at the *lower* or discounted price. The tax advantages are generally the same as the ESOP.

As the employees of Enron found out, there is a fundamental disadvantage to owning too much employer stock, either as part of an ESOP or an ESPP. That disadvantage is the inherent lack of portfolio diversification, such that if the company's financial prospects decline (or, as was case with Enron, bankruptcy results), you are left with an asset of little value. To avoid this problem, you should return to the basic asset allocation principles discussed in chapter 3 and make sure you have diversified into other assets *beyond* your employer's stock. Lack of diversification is a major problem for many corporate executives, who commonly end up owning too much of their employer's stock either through stock option arrangements or other forms of incentive-based compensation. If you suspect you are not as diversified as you should be and hold too much of your employer's stock as a total percentage of your portfolio (say, over half of your net worth), I would advise you to see your tax or investment advisor as soon as possible.

Stock Options and Other Forms of Incentive Compensation

This last section about optimizing your employment benefits probably best pertains to corporate executives, since they are the kinds of employees most likely to be offered stock options and other forms of incentive compensation.

There are two main types of stock option plans used for compensating executives: incentive stock options (ISOs) and nonstatutory or regular stock options (also known as nonqualified stock options or NQSOs).

ISOs are primarily used only by larger, publicly traded corporations to compensate their executives. They are not generally used by closely held corporations (including family businesses operated as corporations). The few owners of a closely held corporation do not typically want or need unrelated outsiders or even executives as additional owners. This same dichotomy also holds for NQSOs except, for the reasons about to be stated, NQSOs are much more prevalent than ISOs. If you are a corporate executive, your options are more than likely to be NQSOs instead of ISOs. If you are unsure, ask your human resources department.

An ISO plan is a tax-favored, written arrangement for compensating executives by awarding them options to buy employer stock. Unlike regular stock options, ISOs generally do *not* result in regular taxable income to the executive either at the time of the grant or at the time that the executive exercises the option (purchases the employer stock for which the option was granted). In other words, there is no regular taxable consequence to the executive until he or she *sells* the employer stock, the timing of which is completely at the executive's discretion.

However, the exceedingly favorable income tax consequence associated with ISOs is *not* available with NQSOs. At the time that the executive exercises a regular stock option (purchases the employer stock), he or she has taxable *compensation income* to the extent of the difference between the fair market value of the shares at the date of purchase and the greatly discounted option price (or the price that the executive actually paid for the option). Further, the employer must withhold and pay Social Security tax and Medicare tax with respect to this compensation income.

Why, if the tax consequences are much more favorable for the executive with an ISO than a regular stock option, is the regular stock option much more prevalent? There are two reasons:

1. At the time of exercising the ISO, the executive incurs an *alternative minimum tax* consequence—an exceedingly disadvantageous tax where the taxpayer must pay a greater amount than the already high regular tax liability.
2. Unless extraordinary circumstances occur, the employer or company who grants the ISO to an executive does not ever receive a corporate income tax *deduction* for the compensation, thereby potentially disrupting the cash flow of the company (and the net earnings reported to the shareholders or owners).

If you are an executive holding a regular stock option (usually numerous options), you can anticipate that, at the date of exercising these options, there will be income tax due. So what do you do if you do not have the cash or other liquid assets necessary to pay this tax? A viable planning strategy is to undertake what is known as a cashless exercise of options

A cashless exercise arrangement takes place in three steps:

1. Exercise the regular option or options at the specified date.
2. After the exercise, sell just enough of the employer stock to pay the exercise price of the stock plus any income taxes due.
3. Ask your employer to pay you the net amount remaining after the sale of the stock *in cash*, and then retain the additional shares for a subsequent sale date of your own choosing.

Another planning alternative is to further defer the taxation of these options by combining the options with a subsequent agreement entered into with your employer that restricts your access to the shares purchased until a later time, such as your planned retirement date.

Restricted Stock

Recently, more executives have been receiving incentive compensation in the form of restricted stock instead of stock options. This trend is partially taking place because of the corporate abuses that have occurred with options, including the backdating of the exercise date of these options to a more favorable time for the recipient. There is also a more technical reason for this trend: under general accounting rules, corporations must now account for the value of these options (known as expensing the options) on their income statements. In turn, this *reduces* corporate earnings and ultimately perhaps the value of the company's publicly traded stock to its shareholders.

Therefore, if you are an executive, do not be surprised if you are now offered a restricted stock incentive-based compensation arrangement instead of stock options. Employers may also adopt a restricted stock plan to keep you from going to work for a competitor, specifically providing that if you leave the company for a rival business, your right to receive the stock at little or no cost is lost.

The taxation of restricted stock to an executive is substantially similar to that of the exercise of a regular stock option. That is, when the restriction expires (known in tax law as becoming substantially vested in the stock), the difference between the fair market value of the stock when substantially vested and what was paid for it, if anything, is taxable compensation income. But, unlike a regular stock option, there is something you can do immediately to limit the amount of tax you might end up owing. If you make a special tax election (commonly referred to as a Section 83(b) election after the Internal Revenue code section of the same number) to recognize income as of the date that you *receive* the restricted stock rather than when the restriction *expires*, any subsequent appreciation in value of the stock is now treated as *capital gain income* and potentially taxable at a much lower rate.

For example, assume that you received restricted stock in the year 2011 when its publicly traded value was $35 per share. You paid nothing for this stock. Further assume that you anticipate that, with your efforts, the value of this stock will be $85 per share five years from now (in 2016), which is also the date when the restriction of the stock expires. Thus, if you make the Section 83(b) election, you will have $35 of compensation income in the year 2011, but $50 of capital gains income ($85 less $35) in 2016, taxable at a much lower rate (currently, no more than 15 percent). Compare this to $85 of compensation income in 2016, currently taxable at a rate as high as 35 percent, and you can see why making a Section 83(b) election may be a prudent planning technique.

Be careful! What happens if you leave the company and forfeit the stock before 2016 and previously made the Section 83(b) election in 2011? In that case, you are *not* permitted to go back and amend your 2011 tax return to claim a $35 per share loss. That's right: you are gambling that the stock will increase in value from the date you make the election and that you will not leave the company prior to the restriction expiring.

Nonqualified Deferred Compensation

We end this chapter with an employee benefit that is only available to a very select few—the very top echelon of many corporations and businesses. This is a nonqualified deferred compensation agreement, commonly funded with life insurance or securities made payable only to the executive or his or her family.

Nonqualified deferred compensation is not that far removed from the employer-sponsored retirement plans in which many participate. Both are really forms of setting aside current compensation to be paid out later, typically at the retirement date of the employee. But employer-sponsored retirement plans generally have to be available to *all* employees, regardless of compensation level and employment status (an exempt or nonexempt employee for purposes of labor law). In contrast, nonqualified arrangements may *discriminate* in favor of whomever the employer decides. Usually, these favored employees are the CEO and senior management of the company.

If you are lucky enough to be offered any of the several forms of nonqualified deferred compensation (an example is a special trust arrangement known as a **rabbi trust**), be sure that you do not sacrifice your future benefit security for a current tax advantage. For example, while a mere promise from an employer that it will pay your deferred compensation at some point in the future achieves tax deferral (the current tax advantage), if the employer goes out of business in the future, you have sacrificed payment of your current compensation needlessly (the future benefit security). Fortunately, there are ways to accomplish both objectives.

Most deferred compensation arrangements require the drafting of skilled legal counsel. Therefore, the risk that you, as a valued executive, will not be adequately protected by your corporate legal office or an outside law firm is relatively small. Nevertheless, it is always important to remember that the corporate legal office primarily represents the business and you as an employee only secondarily. As such, you may wish to secure your own attorney and financial planner to advise how best to proceed if presented with this opportunity.

SECTION III

ACCUMULATING WEALTH

CHAPTER 9

INVESTING IN FINANCIAL ASSETS

There are two basic categories of investment assets: financial and real assets. It is possible to diversify *across* both categories, although most investors choose to diversify *within* each one—that is, they choose to invest in either financial or real assets, but usually not both. A possible exception to this rule is the purchase of a personal residence, which some individuals intend as an investment in real assets, although, more properly, this purchase is really a *use* asset.

This chapter discusses what most people think of when the term *investment* is mentioned: financial assets such as stocks and bonds denominated and traded in U.S. dollars. However, to be properly diversified, many financial planners also recommend some exposure to foreign markets or financial assets denominated and traded in local (non-U.S. dollar) currencies. Unless the investor invests in an American Depository Receipt (ADR) of foreign stock, he or she needs to understand that there is a currency or exchange risk when converting the proceeds from the foreign stock into U.S. dollars. This is in addition to other systematic risks that are assumed when accumulating wealth via financial assets.

Why, with all the inherent risks we discuss in this chapter, should you invest in financial assets? The reason is very simple: because to generate an investment *return*, you have to assume some form of investment *risk*. For example, some investors believe that if they hoard cash and stuff it in a mattress in their basement, they are immune to investment risk, but this isn't true. Because of inflation (also known as purchasing power risk), when the investor is ready to spend the cash some years later, he or she will not have as much money (purchasing power) as when the cash was first stuffed in the mattress.

The key to investing in financial assets and to accumulating wealth generally is to assume as *little investment risk* as possible in order to generate as *great an investment return* as possible. The methods required to do this are the subject of another book—probably several books—but any serious investor understands the risk/return relationship and structures his or her portfolio accordingly.

CASH INVESTMENTS AND WHEN TO USE THEM

You may think you know what is meant by the term *cash*—namely, that it is green and tangible (you can see and touch it). However, in the investment and financial planning world, cash has a very specific meaning. It refers to investments that possess a high degree of liquidity with little or no risk to principal (the sum of money that you originally invest). Many planners use the term *cash equivalents* to differentiate a cash *investment* from the more general "green and tangible" definition.

In general, cash investments are short-term (not more than twelve months in maturity) interest-bearing securities and deposit accounts. This includes not only bank deposits such as savings accounts, certificates of deposit (CDs), and money market deposit accounts, but also investments that are made in the money market, including money market mutual funds, corporate commercial paper, and U.S. Treasury Bills. Sometimes, patriotic investments, such as the purchase of U.S. government Series EE bonds, are also included among cash equivalents. None of these investments will generate a great deal of investment return, but they are very liquid, which is a fundamental attribute of cash equivalents.

Bank Deposits

Many conservative investors do not venture away from bank deposits as an investment strategy. This is likely because they prefer the assurance of knowing that these deposits (up to a certain limit) are insured by the Federal Deposit and Insurance Corporation (FDIC). As a result of relatively recent legislation, all non-IRA bank deposits are now insured up to an amount of $250,000 per account (up from $100,000 previously). IRAs are also insured up to an amount of $250,000 per depositor per bank.

Certificates of deposits (CDs) are probably the most popular form of bank deposit. Also known as time deposits, CDs are monies deposited with a bank for a specified period of time, usually anywhere from three to twelve months. The bank typically pays a fixed rate of interest for the term of the certificate, with rates increasing with the length of the term. If you redeem the CD and convert it to cash prior to its stated expiration or maturity date, a penalty is imposed by the bank in the form of a one-time fee or a lower overall interest rate.

If you have a substantial amount of money to invest (for example, a lump-sum distribution from a retirement plan), you may wish to purchase *multiple* CDs rather than investing in only *one* certificate. In order to obtain as much FDIC insurance as possible, you may wish to purchase each of these multiple CDs at a different bank. A viable investment strategy is to sequence or *ladder* the maturity dates of the multiple certificates to take advantage of interest rate fluctuations (hopefully up rather than down). For example, if interest rates increase, dividing an investment into two six-month certificates (rather than one twelve-month certificate) may be prudent. As each six-month certificate matures, you can then reinvest it at a higher interest rate without penalty.

Many people are unaware that banks also offer money market deposit accounts (MMDAs) in addition to the standard savings account. An MMDA generally pays a higher rate of interest than a savings account, but it also requires a minimum deposit and account balance to avoid bank fees. Typically, six pre-authorized transfers are permitted from the account each month, up to three of which may be by personal check. Unlike the money market mutual fund, an MMDA is federally insured, and for that reason may offer a slightly *lower* interest rate accrual than the money market fund.

Although many investors purchase Series EE bonds through payroll-deduction plans at their places of employment, you can also obtain these bonds at banking institutions. Also known as savings bonds, Series EE bonds are cash investments that must be purchased at 50 percent of their face amount and they range in denomination from $50 to $10,000. The value of the bond is *guaranteed* to double after twenty years, after which time it may be extended for another ten years at a fixed rate of interest. An advantage of the bond is that the interest earned is not taxable until maturity (or when the investor redeems the bond), unless the investor elects to accrue the interest annually. As we shall discuss later when we look at funding your child's college education, there is a special type of EE bond for which the interest is entirely income-tax free if the bond proceeds are used to pay qualified education expenses, provided that the parents' income does not exceed a certain annual amount.

Money Market Deposits

The term *money market* is used in the investment world to refer to the market in which short-term securities (technically defined as securities with a maturity date of twelve months or less) are borrowed and re-loaned by financial institutions. The money market is contrasted to the capital market, which generally involves the trading of securities with longer-term maturities or no maturity date at all (like a stock). While banks and bank deposits are part of the money market, the term is used here to refer to cash investments obtained through brokerage firms and mutual fund companies.

There is no doubt that most investors are familiar with money market mutual funds, if for no other reason than because they use such funds as emergency assets and as a conduit to park money before it is invested somewhere else. An investor who works with an investment advisor or financial planner to establish a separate, fee-based account of securities uses a money market mutual fund to "sweep" money from one investment to another.

A money market mutual fund is offered by a mutual fund company that invests in high-quality, short-term investments such as U.S. Treasury Bills, corporate commercial paper, bank repurchase agreements, and large CDs. The typical minimum investment in the fund is $1,000 and funds may be withdrawn at any time by telephone or if the investor has check-writing privileges on the account (you should request this as a convenience to easily access your money). Most funds also offer owners the ability to wire-transfer money from the fund to a bank account.

While money market mutual funds lack FDIC insurance protection, they are very safe, primarily due to the quality of the assets in which they are invested. You can also invest in a *tax-exempt* money market fund that invests only in short-term municipal securities that are backed by *full faith and credit* and the taxing power of the municipality. This not only increases the potential safety of the fund, but may also increase your after-tax return from since interest from municipal securities is typically exempt from federal taxes (and may be from state taxes as well if you are a resident of the state that has issued the security).

Like any serious investor, you want to invest in securities *beyond* what is included in a money market mutual fund. However, in the wealth accumulation process, you want to make sure you always maintain some money (known in the investment world as "a position") in a money market fund. As mentioned earlier, this is primarily to protect yourself in the event of a financial emergency, but also because you may be waiting on the sidelines until broader capital market conditions improve. Regardless, remember that the *money market* is for *short-term cash investments* whereas the *capital market* is for *longer term security investments*.

Another type of money market deposit that you may wish to consider as a separate cash investment is a U.S. Treasury Bill (T-Bill). T-Bills are sold on a discount-from-face-value basis, and the interest portion (the difference between the issue value and the face value) is exempt from state and local taxes. T-Bills are offered by the U.S. Treasury in denominations of $1,000 and have maturity dates of four, thirteen, and twenty-six weeks. Most investors find it easier to purchase T-Bills through their local bank, but they can be purchased at the Federal Reserve Bank in your area. The primary T-Bill market is an auction by mail.

T-Bills are very important as a reference for the benchmark short-term interest rate from which all other short-term rates are established, including bank CDs. Since the U.S. Government stands behind the issuing of all Treasury securities, including the short-term Treasury bill, T-Bills are often said to be default-risk free. As such, the investor assumes no credit risk when purchasing the obligation. This is not the case with other debt obligations such as corporate bonds (or even bank CDs in excess of the FDIC limit). Thus, if you want to determine what short-term interest rate you will receive on your cash investment, start with the thirteen-week T-Bill rate and add a half-percentage point or so for a credit risk premium.

BONDS AND WHEN TO USE THEM

Unlike stocks, in which you own an *equity* interest in the company issuing the stock, bonds are *debt* obligations. That is, when you purchase a bond from an issuer—usually a corporation or government—you are making a *loan* to the issuer in exchange for the right to receive semiannual or annual interest payments. In this way, we have the first key to timing the purchase of a bond: when you are interested in regular income payments to assist with your ongoing cash flow. Concomitant to this stream of income, there is the expectation that you do not need back your original investment (the *principal* of the bond) or loan to the issuer until some known date in the future, otherwise referred to as the *maturity date* of the bond.

Generally speaking, the *longer* the maturity date of the bond, the *higher* the interest or coupon rate of payment. The coupon rate is the stated percentage rate of interest on the bond. This is because you are loaning your money to the issuer for a longer period of time and thus want a higher interest rate for doing so (like a bank CD). But be careful: the amount of interest you will get depends on the interest rate payable by the bond, which is determined by a number of market-related factors, a measure of which is represented by something known as the *yield curve*. This curve is published regularly in financial newspapers like the *Wall Street Journal* and tells you roughly how much more interest you are likely to receive, the longer you commit your money to the issuer of the debt or bond. If this curve is relatively flat, this indicates that you are not receiving any investment reward (increase in the rate of return) for promising the issuer the use of your money for a longer period of time. If the trend is a flat yield curve, do not invest in bond obligations with a maturity date of more than several years. That way, you can reinvest your money much sooner in another bond issue when longer term interest rates have increased—in other words, when the yield curve has turned *normal* or positive.

Corporate Bonds

Bonds are usually issued by a corporation or government. Corporations issue bonds in the form of a secured obligation, known as a mortgage bond, or an unsecured promise, known as a debenture. As an investor who may be concerned about not getting all of your original investment back at the bond's maturity date (referred to as the bond's *default risk)*, you may want to limit your purchases only to mortgage bonds, since the corporation pledges property as collateral that may be sold in the event of the issuer's default. However, commensurate with the investment risk/investment return tradeoff, the *yield* on the bond (essentially, its rate of return) will be less on a mortgage bond than on a debenture since you are assuming less risk of possible default.

Corporations can issue bonds that are callable and convertible into stock. If the corporation issues a *callable* bond, it means that it can pay off or *call* the obligation before its maturity date. Thus,

151

you will get your money back sooner rather than later. However, this result is not as attractive as it appears. The corporation has likely called the bond because market interest rates declined, meaning it is less expensive for the corporation to pay off the existing bond and issue another one at a lower interest or coupon rate of payment. As an investor, you are now confronted with reinvesting the bond proceeds at the current, lower interest rate. To protect investors who are relying on the security of a fixed payment from the bond, corporations usually issue bonds with a provision that they may not be called until a certain number of years have passed. Nevertheless, if you have to choose between a callable bond and one that is not, choose the noncallable bond.

A *convertible* bond gives an investor both the certainty of semiannual income payments and the opportunity for significant capital gains if the bond is converted into the underlying stock of the issuer. Actually, a convertible bond provides the investor with *two* opportunities for capital gains—not only is there the opportunity for the underlying stock price appreciation, but as the stock increases in value, so does the price of the bond.

For example, assume that a bond convertible into thirty shares of ABC common stock is issued at $1,000 and at the time of issuance, ABC common stock is trading for $25 per share. If the price of ABC stock increases to $35 per share, the convertible bond will now sell for at least $1,300 (or $1,000 plus the $300 of appreciation in the value of the stock shares).

How do you minimize the default risk associated with noncallable and nonconvertible corporate bonds? The primary way is to invest only in investment-grade bonds. An investment-grade bond is a bond of the highest quality, or next-to-highest quality, as rated by one of several bond-rating organizations—notably, Standard & Poor's Corporation or Moody Investors Service. While these rating services are not infallible, they can give you guidance in differentiating an investment-grade bond from a non-investment-grade or high-yield bond. A high-yield bond is not, by definition, a bad investment, although it does involve greater default risk than an investment-grade bond.

This table can be used to help determine what is and is not an investment-grade bond, according to Standard & Poor's Corporation and Moody's. Generally, you will want to purchase only investment grade bonds since they have the lowest amount of default risk as determined by the rating agencies.

	Standard & Poor's	Moody's
Investment Grade:		
Highest Quality	AAA-AA	Aaa-Aa
Next-to-Highest Quality	A-BBB	A- Baa
Non-Investment Grade		
Speculative	BB-B	Ba-B
Default	CCC-D	Caa-C
Overall Range	AAA-D	Aaa-C

Government Bonds

Like U.S. Treasury Bills, if the U.S. Government issues a note or bond, you do not need to be concerned about default risk.

U.S. Treasury notes and bonds are debt obligations of the federal government that are primarily distinguished by their maturity dates. A *Treasury note* is a medium-term debt security issued with a maturity date of two, three, five, or ten years. The minimum denomination is $1,000, but notes may be issued up to a maximum of $1 million. The yield on the ten-year note has taken on added importance in recent years as the most widely quoted benchmark in establishing current mortgage rates. A *Treasury bond* is a longer term debt security with a fixed maturity date of more than ten years. The Treasury discontinued issuance of the *long bond* (thirty-year maturity date) in October 2001, but recently (effective February 2006) resumed the auctioning of this bond as an additional method to finance the ever-expanding federal deficit. Interest from U.S. Treasury notes and bonds is paid semiannually to the owner and is exempt from state and local taxes.

There are several other forms of government securities popular with conservative investors. The first is a form of *zero-coupon bond* known as a Treasury STRIP (Separate Trading of Registered Interest and Principal of Securities). A zero-coupon bond is a bond for which the semiannual interest coupons are not attached but instead are omitted or "stripped" off. There is still an interest payment made on this bond, but it is accrued as part of the bond principal and payable only at the maturity date. As a potential investor, you would have an obligation to pay federal taxes on the accrued interest, but you would not have any cash from the bond with which to pay them. So where is a Treasury STRIP (or any other form of zero-coupon bond, since corporations can also issue them) best positioned? In one of two places, and for one of two purposes:

1. If it is a *taxable* STRIP, position the bond in a tax-deferred account such as a retirement plan.
2. If it is a *tax-exempt* STRIP, include the bond as a part of a college education savings program for a child under the age of nineteen.

In both cases, you know with absolute certainty when the STRIP will mature, which is the primary attraction of any zero-coupon bond. Further, you also know with certainty how much the principal and accrued interest will amount to at maturity. As such, you can match the bond's maturity to the date you need the funds to meet your financial goal. This is the beauty of any zero-coupon bond, but particularly of the Treasury STRIP, since, as an obligation of the U.S. government, it also has no default risk.

The second—and an increasingly popular—form of government security (actually, a series of securities) is the Treasury Inflation Protected Security (TIPS). TIPS were first issued in 1997 and are now auctioned by the Treasury four times each year. They are sold in five-, ten-, and twenty-year maturities and in minimum $1,000 denominations. As the name indicates, they are designed to offer protection against the effects of inflation.

The principal is adjusted semiannually to keep pace with inflation as measured by the Consumer Price Index (CPI) over the previous six-month period, but the interest rate remains fixed. At the maturity date, you receive the *greater* of the inflation-adjusted principal value of the security or its face value at the time of issue.

Simply stated, if you invest in TIPS, you will be taxed annually on the interest payment plus the appreciation in the face value of the security once adjusted for inflation. However, you do not receive the inflation-adjusted principal until the security is sold or matures (more than likely the latter, since you should look at TIPS as a longer term investment). To avoid the potentially adverse tax consequences, it is best to hold TIPS in a tax-deferred account such as a retirement plan or a Roth IRA. If you are the treasurer of a tax-exempt (not-for-profit) organization, consider TIPS as a possible investment for the nontaxable entity.

Municipal Bonds

State and local governments issue bonds typically to finance long-term projects such as road improvement or other infrastructure needs. Such bonds primarily come in two types: general obligation bonds and revenue bonds, although a third type of hybrid bond—a private purpose bond—is increasingly being used to finance football stadiums and the like. General obligation and revenue bonds are issued by public municipalities, whereas private purpose bonds may be shared with a private developer or sports promoter. General obligation bonds are backed by the taxing authority of the municipality and as such are safer than revenue bonds, which must depend on the revenue from a specific project to pay the bondholders. As a result, general obligation bonds feature a lower interest rate.

Historically, municipal bonds have been most attractive to high-income taxpayers because their semiannual interest payments are generally free from federal income tax, and may also be free from state and local taxes, in some circumstances. You can easily compute what your after-tax return from a municipal bond will be if you know your **marginal income tax bracket** and the coupon rate of the municipal bond. Once you have computed the after-tax return, you should then compare this return to the return you would receive on a taxable obligation, such as a corporate bond, to determine the higher paying investment.

For example, assume you are trying to decide whether to purchase a municipal bond (only federal-income-tax free) featuring a tax-exempt yield of 5 percent or a corporate bond yielding 7 percent. Also assume you are currently paying taxes in the highest marginal federal income tax bracket of 35 percent. To compute your after-tax return on the municipal bond, use the following formula:

$$\text{After-tax return (or tax-equivalent yield)} = \frac{\text{Tax-exempt yield}}{(1 - \text{marginal tax rate})}$$

Your after-tax return on the municipal bond is 7.69 percent (0.05 divided by (1 - 0.35)). This compares to the corporate bond yield of 7 percent, so you should likely invest in the municipal bond. It also means you should probably not purchase the corporate bond until its yield-to-maturity exceeds 7.69 percent.

It is also possible to invest in a municipal bond or tax-exempt mutual fund, usually as part of a money market mutual fund. However, if you do so, you lose control over the time at which you have to recognize capital gains from the sale of bonds. This is a distinct disadvantage of investing in bonds via a bond mutual fund.

Bonds as a Part of Your Portfolio

It is a common misconception that as people age, they become more financially conservative, meaning that safety of principal and reliable income from that principal is paramount. Savvy investors—even retirees—know that protection of purchasing power and achieving an after-tax return in excess of inflation is just as important as safety of principal and preserving the value of the original investment. As mentioned when we discussed asset allocation, there is an argument to be made for the inclusion of stocks and stock mutual funds in any retiree's portfolio. Bonds also play an important diversification role.

Certainly, a primary relationship that must be understood before investing in an individual bond is that *bond prices move in the opposite direction of market interest rates.* Hence, if you believe that interest rates are likely to decline in the future, you should have a position in bonds, since sizable capital gains are likely. This was proven in the bear market of 2007–2009, when bond returns significantly exceeded that of stocks, and interest rates declined at the same time. If interest rates are likely to decline, you should also buy *long-term bonds*, since they will appreciate more in price than shorter term issues.

Beyond that, as the stock market exhibits volatility—seemingly random price moves up and down—bonds *compete* with stocks for investors' money. If the stock market moves down (called *bearish* movement), investors will seek a positive return and, more important, *safety*. Next to cash, there is no safer investment than a U.S. Treasury security bill, note, or bond. Conversely, if the stock market goes up consistently over time (a bull market), investors will prefer the higher returns of stocks, even though there is more investment risk. No matter your age, you should probably include some bonds or bond funds in your portfolio since no one, including esteemed security analysts with many years of experience, can predict with absolute certainty whether the stock market is going to be up or down on any given day.

You will likely need to decide between an investment in individual bonds and bond mutual funds, but be aware they exhibit different characteristics. With an individual bond, if you hold the bond to maturity, you will almost always get back your original amount invested plus interest. However, with a bond mutual fund, your total rate of return is uncertain since the value of that fund constantly fluctuates. Nevertheless, a bond mutual fund provides additional diversification of your portfolio that is not available with individual bonds.

STOCKS AND WHEN TO USE THEM

More investors are probably familiar with individual stocks and stock mutual funds than are familiar with bonds.

Stocks represent an ownership or *equity* interest in a corporation. As a shareholder, you will realize a return from the corporation's earnings after they have paid all their creditors, including their bondholders. This return can come from a declaration of *dividends* each year by the corporation's board of directors or from *capital appreciation* of the shares once the earnings are reinvested back into the corporation or from both. Dividends are taxable to you, the shareholder, if they are declared for any given year and you receive them. However, capital appreciation is not taxable until you sell shares and then perhaps at very favorable rates if you have owned the shares for a certain period of time (currently, more than one year from the date you bought the shares).

There are two forms of stock: common and preferred. The most widely held is *common stock*, which may or may not provide dividends, depending on whether a dividend is declared for that year by the corporation's board. Most individuals, particularly younger investors, do not purchase common stock for its income potential, but rather for its possibility of significant capital appreciation. In contrast, investors purchase *preferred stock* for much the same reason that they purchase individual bonds: to generate income. The term *preferred* in preferred stock means that if a dividend is declared by the corporation's board of directors, those shareholders are first in line before any payment is made to the common shareholders. The preferred shareholder also receives payment before the common shareholder in the event of the corporation's liquidation.

Common stocks are highly *marketable* since they can generally be easily bought and sold on publicly traded exchanges such as the New York Stock Exchange. However, they are not very *liquid*, because the investor may or may not receive back his original investment. Rather, the value of common stocks may change significantly during the course of a trading day. The risk that an investor takes in purchasing common shares is referred to as *market risk*—risk that can be minimized but not entirely eliminated by proper asset allocation and portfolio diversification.

Publicly traded stocks may be thought of in a number of ways, but most frequently they are categorized in terms of the market behavior of the stocks, the sector or industry in which the stocks are situated, and the size of the company issuing the stocks.

Examples of categorizing stocks on the basis of their *market behavior* include

- Income stocks: These types of stocks consistently pay high dividends to the investor.
- Growth stocks: These stocks exhibit considerable capital appreciation.
- Value stocks: Value stocks are currently undervalued in terms of price compared to their marketplace peers.
- Defensive stocks: These stocks do not decline as much in a bear market as other stocks.
- Cyclical stocks: Cyclical stocks are very sensitive to current economic and market conditions.
- Blue chip stocks: These are stocks of the largest and oldest companies, including many of those on the Dow Jones Industrial Average—the most frequently quoted index of market activity.

The Standard & Poor's rating service divides stocks into ten market *sectors* and into many more industries within those sectors. In general, however, technology, health care, and financials tend to be the fastest-growing market sectors, whereas consumer staples and utilities tend to be more stable. The other sectors, such as industrials and materials, tend to be cyclical in nature.

The *size* of the company issuing the stocks is referred to as its market capitalization. Market capitalization is computed as the price per share of a company multiplied by the number of common shares outstanding. The *higher* the price per share and the *more* the number of outstanding shares, the *greater* the market capitalization of the company issuing the stock. With reference to this measurement, stocks are classified as follows:

- large capitalization (large-cap): the stocks of companies with market capitalizations of more than $5 billion
- medium capitalization (mid-cap): the stocks of companies with market capitalizations of between $1 billion and $5 billion
- small capitalization (small-cap): the stocks of companies with market capitalizations of less than $1 billion

Growth stocks usually are found in the small capitalization category of stocks.

A major advantage of owning stocks rather than bonds is the right to vote with respect to significant company matters, including election of the company's board of directors. However, shareholders who do not own enough shares to be in a controlling position (51 percent or more of the total outstanding shares) must band together as a block to influence the course of future action by the corporation. Even then, if the majority or the controlling shareholders think differently, it is unlikely that the minority shareholders' views will be considered.

There are many ways to value whether you should buy an individual stock, but the most common is a relative valuation technique known as a price-to-earnings (P/E) ratio. This estimation of value relies on the premise that the stock's value bears some relationship to the earnings per share generated by the issuing company or corporation. This premise is supported by remembering that the rate of return to the investor, whether in the form of dividends or capital appreciation, derives from the corporation's residual earnings after all other creditors have been paid.

For example, assume that ABC stock is trading on the stock exchange for $40 per share. It is a value stock. ABC's earnings over the next twelve-month period are estimated to be $2.50 per share and you have determined that the relevant P/E ratio for the stock is twenty. Therefore, using the P/E ratio approach, ABC stock should be trading for $50 per share ($2.50 times twenty). Since it is currently selling for only $40 per share, ABC is *undervalued* and you should *buy* the stock at your earliest opportunity.

Stocks as a Part of Your Portfolio

Since 1926, the average large stock has generated a compounded annual rate of return of slightly more than 10 percent. Inflation has averaged 3 percent, so that is a 7 percent real, before-tax rate of return. A pretty good track record, notwithstanding the gloomy results of the stock market in recent years!

However, if you were to look at a risk pyramid, you would find individual common stocks near the top. That means there is a great deal of volatility associated with the investment; certainly, more so than with investment-grade bonds. If you are going to include individual stock in your portfolio, you need to research the stock carefully before you purchase it (either that or let your financial planner do it). Fortunately, there are various print services, such as *Value Line*, and online reference sources that you can use before making a potential purchase.

If you decide you want individual stocks as a part of your portfolio, the types of stocks you will select likely depends on your style of or orientation to investing. For example, if you are primarily a *growth investor*, you will likely select stocks with above-average earnings potential. If you are primarily a *value investor*, you will prize stock that is undervalued in relation to its industry or sector peers. To be properly diversified, a portfolio should consist of approximately fifteen to eighteen stocks spread across five or six different market sectors. Particularly with stocks, you should be a long-term or *buy-and-hold* investor. While you may be able to make a killing in a short period of time from purchasing a hot stock (typically a newly issued stock), usually stocks increase in price only over *long* periods of time. Buy-and-hold should not be a problematic investment strategy for you if you did sufficient research before you bought the stock and you believe in the financial prospects of the company issuing it.

MUTUAL FUNDS AND WHEN TO USE THEM

The proper name for a mutual fund is an *open-end investment company*, meaning that the fund or company does not have a fixed number of shares to issue. Instead, the number of outstanding shares varies as investors purchase and redeem their shares. The value of a share in a mutual fund is determined by its net asset value (NAV), which is computed by dividing the value of the fund's total net assets by the number of shares outstanding. The NAV is computed at the end of each market trading day and is the price at which you must buy and sell shares.

A mutual fund is a type of *professionally managed asset*. Practically, this means that you deposit a sum of money with the fund along with thousands (or millions) of other investors and the fund's professional money manager buys stocks, bonds, or other securities with that money. In recent years, other types of professionally managed asset pools, such as exchange traded funds (ETFs), hedge funds, and private equity funds, have become popular. Hedge funds and private equity funds will not be discussed here since they are not for the average investor, but you should be aware that *all* of these other types of professionally managed assets are growing in importance, primarily because of increased access to skilled money managers that would not otherwise be possible for an individual investor.

Mutual funds are for the *small* investor. They allow the "little guy" to purchase a percentage ownership in securities that they may not otherwise be able to afford. Thus, the investor achieves instant portfolio diversification since he or she now owns a small piece of many stocks or bonds across many different market sectors or industries. The investor does not have to keep track of all of his or her holdings in the fund or the cost basis of purchasing the shares since the fund company usually assumes these responsibilities. Combining the dollar-cost averaging strategy discussed earlier with contributions to a number of good, low-expense funds has been a very effective wealth accumulation technique for a great number of small investors.

There are thousands of different mutual funds, including money market funds, but practically, they can be broken into stock funds and bond funds or a combination of both stocks and bonds known as a balanced fund. You can also purchase funds that invest only in foreign stocks or those that invest in foreign and U.S. stocks, called global funds.

There are three basic types of *stock* mutual funds:

1. Growth fund: This is a fund that invests primarily in stocks that offer potentially significant capital appreciation. A subcategory of this type of fund is an *aggressive* growth fund, which invests in stocks of considerable risk and also offers the possibility for maximum capital appreciation.
2. Income fund: An income fund invests primarily in stocks that pay higher-than-average dividends, such as utility stocks. The name can also be used to describe a fund that invests a high percentage of assets in bonds.
3. Growth-and-income fund: There are many names for this type of fund, including *equity income* and *total return* fund. Operationally, a growth-and-income fund invests in stocks that aim to achieve *both* long-term capital appreciation and current income. It is here that you will find a concentration of value stocks that will be of primary interest to the value style of investor.

There are also three basic types of *bond* mutual funds:

1. Corporate bond fund: This is a fund that invests in either short-term bonds (generally not more than a five-year maturity date) or longer term bonds or both, as issued by corporations. Usually, these bonds are investment-grade, but not always. A clue that the bond fund is investing in non-investment grade bonds is if the name of the fund

includes the phrase "high-yield." Historically, that type of fund has been referred to as a junk bond fund, although the term "junk" is likely a bit extreme, as you can find very good investments among the fund's holdings.

2. U.S. Government bond fund: This is a fund that invests in U.S. Treasury securities, typically Treasury notes or bonds. As mentioned, the securities within the fund are free of default risk, which is a major safety advantage but also an attribute that results in a lower yield than that of corporate funds.

3. Municipal bond fund: This is also known as a *tax-exempt* fund since it invests primarily in bonds issued by cities and states. Dividends paid by municipal funds are free from federal taxes and, if the purchaser is a resident of the state or city that issues the bond, the dividends are typically free of state and local taxes.

Index Funds

An index fund is a mutual fund that attempts to replicate the performance of a particular market index, such as the Standard & Poor's index of five hundred stocks. As such, the fund implements what is known as a passive management investment style; that is, there is no actual intent by the fund manager to attempt to exceed the return of a specified market index. Additionally, index funds are fairly income-tax efficient, given that very little selling of securities occurs within the fund, the tax consequences of which are passed along to the investor in the form of capital gain distributions.

In contrast to an index fund, most stock and bond mutual funds are actively managed. This is an effort on the part of the mutual fund's money manager to outperform the market or some appropriate market index on a risk-adjusted basis. However, academic studies have shown that, on average, approximately 95 percent of all mutual fund money managers *fail* to outperform the Standard and Poor's index of five hundred stocks on a long-term basis. This means that as a potential investor you should seek out mutual funds with relatively low expenses (in comparison to funds that have the same investment objective) that have achieved above-average market performance over at least five years. Fortunately, this is not too difficult, given the thousands of funds available in the marketplace.

Exchange Traded Funds (ETF)

In recent years, a variation of the mutual fund investment called the *exchange traded fund* (ETF) has been introduced. While these funds still occupy a relatively small part of the investment marketplace, they are growing in popularity, particularly among tax-savvy investors.

An ETF is essentially an index fund that trades like a stock. Instead of being priced at net asset value at the end of the day like the traditional mutual fund, an ETF trades throughout the day based on market supply and demand. Most ETFs are designed to match the performances of various market benchmarks, such as the Standard & Poor's index of five hundred stocks. Other ETFs try to match the performance of a market sector, such as technology, energy, or finance. Still others are engaged in the trading of international securities.

There are two primary reasons you should be interested in an ETF as a possible wealth accumulation vehicle:

1. Since it acts like an index mutual fund, an ETF is passively managed and therefore the expenses of operating the fund are very low—sometimes even lower than an index mutual fund.
2. An ETF trades equivalent securities or what are known as in-kind trades. According to the IRS, this exchange of essentially similar securities does *not* constitute a taxable event, and thus no capital gains or losses are incurred. ETFs are very income-tax efficient. Alternatively, a traditional mutual fund must trade its securities in the open market, with the investor paying taxes on those gains.

Mutual Funds as a Part of Your Portfolio

Many small investors begin and end their portfolio construction with mutual funds. They also work with an investment advisor or financial planner to position these funds in an advisory services account.

If you are not inclined to work with an investment advisor or financial planner but wish to invest in mutual funds (or *have* to invest in such funds as part of a self-directed retirement account such as a 401(k) plan), consider the following:

- Try to invest in no-load or low-load funds. These are funds that do not assess a sales charge for purchase. Note, however, that most advisory accounts will waive the sales charge if the fund is held within the account.
- Try to invest in funds with low maintenance expenses in relation to their peers. There is no rule of thumb here except that the *lower* the annual expenses to operate the fund, the *better*. An alternative is to invest in all index funds, but you will lose the potential for excess market performance that an excellent mutual fund money manager may generate.
- Try to invest in funds with a relatively low turnover of assets. Investing in a fund that does not constantly sell and buy securities is an effective tax management technique, which, as we will see later, is a key component to defending the wealth you accumulate.
- Make sure the fund is investing in securities consistent with its investment objective. For example, if the fund states that it is a growth stock fund, it should not be investing in short-term bonds.
- Understand how much investment risk you are willing to assume and match up your risk profile with the investment objective of the fund. This is critical in mutual fund investing. If you are most covetous of income (generally, a conservative risk profile), many stock funds are not for

you. Alternatively, an aggressive growth risk profile usually means that investing in a U.S. Government bond fund is *not* the most appropriate use of your money.

In summary, you may wish to invest in a combination of actively managed mutual funds and passively managed index funds. Many investors that have adopted this strategy are the wealthier for it.

INTERNATIONAL INVESTING

It has frequently been said in recent years that we are becoming a globalized economy. As such, what happens financially in one country—particularly in emerging growth economies such as China and India—almost instantaneously impacts the economy of the United States. A globalized economy presents investment opportunities beyond purchasing only domestic stocks, bonds, or mutual funds.

There is additional risk in international investing. *Currency* or *exchange rate risk* originates in the uncertainty associated with the value of foreign currencies in relation to the U.S. dollar. For example, let's say that you have invested in a stock of a UK company and you pay for it in the currency of the UK pound. Even if the share value of this stock appreciates, you may still lose money if the pound depreciates relative to the U.S. dollar. Conversely, you may reap a double benefit (including the appreciation of the UK stock) if the pound appreciates with respect to the U.S. dollar.

How is currency or exchange rate risk effectively minimized? This question leads us to the investment strategy of purchasing foreign stocks using a financial instrument known as an *American Depository Receipt* (ADR). An ADR is a receipt issued by a U.S. bank on foreign securities purchased by the bank through a foreign representative and held in trust for the benefit of the ADR owner. These receipts are listed on most U.S. stock exchanges, including the New York Stock Exchange, and represent an alternative to direct foreign investment. The ADR is denominated in U.S. dollars, meaning that you never have to worry about the relationship of the foreign currency to its American counterpart.

Another way of investing internationally is to purchase shares of an international or global mutual fund. An *international* mutual fund invests in securities (either stocks or bonds or both) of companies that are located and do business *outside* the United States. Alternatively, a *global* mutual fund (also known as a world fund) invests in securities of international companies *and* those of U.S. companies. There are also region-specific funds, notably in the Pacific Rim.

You should consider international investing as another way to diversify your portfolio. In recent years, international and global investing has generated returns considerably in excess of those in the U.S. market and, depending on future political events in foreign countries, global investments are likely to continue to outperform domestic funds. This is particularly the case if the relevant country's currency *strengthens* in relation to the U.S. dollar.

Here are the major currencies of the global economy:

1. United States: U.S. dollar
2. European Union: euro
3. United Kingdom: UK pound
4. China: yuan or renminbi
5. Japan: yen
6. Australia: Australian dollar
7. India: rupee
8. Canada: Canadian dollar
9. Brazil: real
10. Russia: ruble

Now let's move on to the other major category of investments and wealth accumulation: investing your money in *real assets* or in real property.

CHAPTER 10

INVESTING IN REAL ASSETS

Most individuals own real estate; approximately 70 percent of Americans own their own homes. Indeed, owning your own home is an integral part of the American Dream and of accumulating wealth. According to the U.S. Census Bureau, in the year 2000, 32.3 percent of the typical American's net worth consisted of the equity in his or her home. This decreased considerably with the real estate bust that began in the summer of 2007 in most areas of this country.

For most people, owning a home is not an investment in the sense of stocks and bonds or rental real estate. On the statement of personal financial position, your home or primary residence should be listed as a *use asset*. This is to be contrasted with *direct investments* in real estate, such as the ownership of a rental home, vacation home, or even raw land, and *indirect* investments, such as a share of a real estate limited partnership (RELP) or a real estate investment trust (REIT).

DIRECT INVESTMENTS IN REAL ESTATE

Vacation Homes

According to *American Demographics* magazine, approximately 70 percent of Americans view the purchase of a vacation home as the number one indication that an individual has accumulated wealth. Further, partly as a reflection of this fact, some 60 percent of Americans anecdotally say they would like to own a vacation home. Although this is a common financial goal, it is not of tantamount importance for many people, since buying a vacation home is beyond their financial means. (With any luck, this book will show you how to change that situation!)

If you are interested in purchasing a vacation home, you should take three major factors into consideration: (1) the location of the home; (2) the financing costs associated with buying and maintaining the property; and (3) how long you plan to own the home, including how you may wish to ultimately divest yourself of ownership.

As is a standard rule in any purchase of real estate, when buying a vacation home, the most important factor is location, location, location. As of 2005, according to an EscapeHomes.com survey, with the exception of Las Vegas, Nevada, *all* of the top ten preferred locations for buying a second home were near the ocean or in the mountains. They were also close to or part of a major city (San Diego, California, was number seven in the survey). You can bet that those locations demand premium prices and are likely suffering from a paucity of attractive vacation properties.

As such, you may wish to take a different approach. Look for areas that more than one print publication or website describe as up-and-coming. For example, in recent years, properties along both coasts of Mexico have become more attractive to retiring and vacationing Americans. If you concentrate on areas that are not yet well known to the wealthy and aspiring wealthy, you are less likely to buy at the top of the market and can thus anticipate that your second home will enjoy future appreciation that may not be possible in more established locations.

Financing a second home, particularly if you do not have much equity in your first home or primary residence, is always an issue. Most lenders expect you to put down at least 20 percent of the second home's fair market value before closing. Renting out the home is a good way to recover some of this down payment, but if you do so, charge a rent that is approximately 10 to 20 percent higher than your mortgage payment to take care of maintenance expenses. You will also very likely need to hire a property manager, particularly if the second home is some distance from your primary residence or in another country. If you can avoid it, try *not* to tap into the equity of your first home to make the down payment on the second. If the property value of your first home declines, it will make it all the more difficult to recover the lost equity, not to mention present a cash flow challenge if an interest-only adjustable rate mortgage (ARM) has been used to finance the first home.

Do not expect your vacation home to pay for itself immediately. Over the long term, a vacation home can be self-sustaining (particularly if you are renting it out when you are not there), but careful financial planning is required. Like most real assets, the *longer* you own the vacation home, the *greater* the chances of its significant capital appreciation. Ultimately, you will have to determine whether you wish to pass it on to family members now or at your death, or whether you wish to sell it and realize a (hopefully) sizable percentage return on it. As we shall see, the value of highly appreciated vacation homes may be a significant estate planning issue, although a competent estate or financial planner can assist you in removing or reducing the value of the home from your taxable estate.

Rental Homes

Most individuals become landlords in one of two ways: as a result of a conscious decision to buy homes and renting them out to others, or because their primary residence does not sell in the time frame they anticipate and they convert the residence to a rental property.

The obvious practical disadvantage of becoming a landlord is that, unless you hire a property manager, you have to deal with tenants, but there *are* tax advantages associated with rental homes. Notably, as a landlord, you can depreciate the home and, at least to a limited extent, you can take an annual operating loss if your adjusted gross income is not deemed to be too high.

Under current tax law, a rental activity is treated as a passive activity. A passive activity is one that involves the conduct of any trade or business in which the taxpayer does not *materially participate*. However, there is a lesser standard of participation—*active participation*—that most individuals can easily meet with respect to their rental real estate activities. An individual meets the active participation standard if he or she participates in making management decisions with respect to the rental property or arranges for others (for example, a property manager) to provide rental property services. If this lesser standard is met, as the owner of the rental property, you can deduct up to $25,000 of losses annually from your rental real estate activities *provided* your adjusted gross income (AGI) for that year does not exceed $100,000. The $25,000 maximum is then reduced by 50 percent of the amount by which your AGI exceeds $100,000, meaning that if your AGI (and your spouse's income, if you file jointly) reaches $150,000, no loss deduction is permitted.

For example, assume that you own an apartment building that is managed by an on-site property manager. You meet frequently with the property manager and make all decisions with respect to improving the property. As such, you actively participate for purposes of the rental real estate loss deduction. Further, assume that your AGI for the year 2011 is $110,000 and the building generates $26,000 in losses during that year. You are allowed to deduct only $20,000 of these losses on your 2011 income tax return since the maximum deduction is $25,000, and the maximum deduction is reduced by $5,000 (the portion of $110,000 in excess of $100,000—or $10,000—times 0.50 equals $5,000).

As we will learn when we discuss the primary residence as a use asset, generally, you are *never* allowed to take an income tax loss when selling that residence (your home). But there is a favorable exclusion of gain provision that applies to the sale of a personal residence previously converted into rental property. While the sale of a rental home is taxed in accordance with the normal capital gain and loss rules (remember, you have turned your home into an investment), there is the additional tax benefit of the up-to-$25,000 annual loss provision, if you qualify. This may even be enough reward to compensate you for the daily hassles of putting up with tenants.

Commercial Real Estate

Typically, given the investment risk, only experienced investors (usually high-net-worth individuals or institutions) purchase commercial real estate. Accordingly, you may wish to avoid this investment opportunity entirely.

However, if you do wish to invest in commercial properties, you will likely do so for one of two reasons: to receive annual income or to hold such properties for capital appreciation before eventual sale. Most investors who participate in the commercial real estate market do so to generate income since a primary reason of investing in raw land is capital appreciation. If you are after income from the commercial property, you first need to determine how much to pay for it. For that, fortunately, there is a relatively easy computation known as the *net operating income* (NOI) formula.

The formula for NOI is as follows, although if you hire an appraiser to help you with the investment decision, the appraiser will likely compute the NOI for you.

Gross rental receipts from the property
+ Nonrental or other additional income from the property
= Potential gross income
- Vacancy and collection of receipts losses
= Effective gross income
- Operating Expenses (excluding interest and depreciation)
= Net operating income (NOI)

Since NOI is a cash flow computation from the commercial property, any charges you have incurred to finance the purchase of the property, such as interest on a loan, and tax-related charges, such as depreciation, do *not* enter into the computation.

Once you or your appraiser have computed NOI, then in order to determine how much you should pay for the property, you need to divide the property's NOI by a prevailing **capitalization rate** (cap rate) to arrive at a final value. This cap rate is not easy to determine, but think of it as the rate of annual compounded return you would like to receive from the property. It is also the reciprocal of the number of years it will take for the property to pay for itself. For example, a standard cap rate is 12 percent, meaning that you will want your original investment back in a period of slightly more than eight years (100 divided by 12 = 8.33 years). Similarly, if you want a 20 percent return, you will want your original purchase price back in five years (100 divided by 20 = 5). You are more aggressive and factor in more risk of the initial investment with a 20 percent cap rate than with a 12 percent cap rate.

Appraisers use the income approach, comparable property, and cost replacement methods to determine the value of commercial and residential rental real estate. The income approach relies on the establishment of a realistic cap rate to determine whether a property is currently under- or overpriced.

Raw or Unimproved Land

Mark Twain is famous for saying, "Buy land, they're not making it anymore." This is true, but it does not provide a great deal of guidance if you are an investor trying to decide *where* to buy land.

The most valuable land or unimproved real estate is probably land that is adjacent to already developed (or soon to be developed) residential or commercial property. It is likely that, before long, the adjacent property will also be developed, given that its highest and best use is no longer as farmland, grassland, or other land lying fallow. As an investor, you are likely to enjoy significant capital appreciation from this land when you subsequently sell it.

However, there are certain significant investment risks associated with any undeveloped land. Among these risks are

- The land may be adversely rezoned. For example, property bought for residential development purposes may be rezoned by the city or county for commercial purposes.
- You may not be able to obtain permits from the county, city, or township to build on the land in the manner that you (or the developer) intend.
- Access to your land may be restricted by an adjacent landowner's property or property rights.
- The population growth that you anticipate in the area may not occur.

As a result, many investments in undeveloped land are extremely risky. If you have borrowed money to buy the land (known as leveraging your investment), you must find a way to service the debt from income or assets other than your original purchase or be forced into a position to sell the land well before you would have otherwise intended.

INDIRECT INVESTMENTS IN REAL ESTATE

There are two basic ways to invest indirectly in real estate: as a limited partner owning an interest in a real estate limited partnership (RELP) or as a shareholder in a real estate investment trust (REIT). Let's look at the REIT first, since it is generally the more marketable of the two investments.

Real Estate Investment Trusts (REITs)

A REIT is like a mutual fund except that its shares are not always valued at net asset value (NAV) but are traded at a premium or discount to NAV on a publicly traded exchange. In most cases, the REIT will invest in income-producing real estate properties such as apartment buildings, shopping centers, office parks, hotels, and, increasingly, retirement communities. Some REITs, known as mortgage REITs, also invest in the financing of real estate properties.

The REIT entity is not subject to federal income tax as long as it distributes at least 90 percent of its annual income to shareholders each year. As a result, many REITs distribute 100 percent of income to shareholders. Taxes are paid by the shareholders on dividends received (like stocks or stock mutual funds) and any passed-through capital gains. But be careful: Unless the REIT tells you that the dividend is a qualifying dividend for federal income tax purposes, you will *not* be able to claim the favorable 5 to 15 percent rate that otherwise applies to stock or mutual fund dividends. Further, unlike the RELP, REITs cannot pass through any losses experienced in the sale of their underlying properties.

There is a relatively *low* **correlation** between the price movement of REIT shares and that of a typical stock or stock mutual fund. A primary advantage to you, as a potential investor, is the opportunity to further diversify your portfolio with the purchase of a REIT. Other advantages of REITs include

- relatively stable dividend income
- high dividend yields
- the possibility of significant capital appreciation
- liquidity
- access to professional management of the property

The long-term total return (defined as dividend income plus capital appreciation of the underlying real estate investment) of a REIT is likely *less than* a high-performing, higher risk growth stock, but *more than* the return of a lower risk investment-grade bond.

Before you invest in a REIT versus, for example, a mutual fund, you must first decide that you want to invest in real estate properties. Then you must decide in what manner you wish to invest in those properties—directly or indirectly. If you decide that you want to invest indirectly, you must decide what type of REIT to invest in. There are three types:

1. an *equity* REIT, which generally acquires income-producing real properties
2. a *mortgage* REIT, which makes construction loans and otherwise invests in the financing of real estate ventures
3. a *hybrid* REIT, which both owns properties and makes financing loans

As a general rule, a mortgage REIT is a bit riskier than an equity REIT, since the mortgage REIT does not have established properties from which to generate an income stream to the investor. However, your ultimate rate of return from a mortgage REIT may be greater than from an equity REIT.

Real Estate Limited Partnerships (RELPs)

If you want a high-risk real estate investment and the possibility of a high return, purchasing an interest in a RELP may be for you.

A RELP is most commonly structured as a real estate syndication with one or more general partners or real estate developers and many investors as limited partners. The limited partners have no say in the management or control of the real property investments or in when the underlying properties may be sold. Unlike a REIT, however, a RELP *is permitted* to pass on losses to its limited partner investors, although because of a series of income tax rules known as the passive activity rules, it is doubtful that you, as a limited partner investor, may be able to claim this loss on your annual income tax return. Typically, you cannot claim this loss until the general partner or syndicator sells the partnership property that has generated the loss. Remember, as a limited partner, you cannot legally force him to do so.

A RELP is usually *not* a publicly traded entity, so cashing in your interest at something close to what you paid for the interest is difficult, if not impossible. Some RELPs are organized and publicly traded in the form of **master limited partnerships**

(MLPs), but the trading is very thin and tax rules generally restrict the claiming of any losses on your income tax return. Thus, an interest held in a RELP is generally both illiquid and relatively unmarketable.

So why invest in a RELP? You would do so almost always because you believe in the ability of the syndicator to develop and sell the underlying real properties for a significant profit. In addition, you are able to invest in commercial and residential real estate properties for a relatively small amount and are limited in your potential liability as a creditor only to the extent of your investment.

THE USE OF LEVERAGE IN REAL ESTATE INVESTING

The financial concept of leveraging is the use of borrowed money (typically that of a bank or other lender) to increase your profit on a real estate investment. The concept may also be used with financial assets, most notably through the use of margin (borrowing money from your broker to purchase stock), but one of the oft-cited advantages of real assets is the ability to employ leverage effectively.

For example, assume that you have directly invested $100,000 in a residential real estate property. Further assume that this real estate is in a good location and appreciates at a rate of 10 percent annually. At the end of year one, your investment has grown to $110,000, and the end of year two, the property is worth $121,000. You have earned a $21,000 profit in the property.

Now, let's assume that you have put down $100,000 on a $500,000 tract of residential real property (you have borrowed the remaining $400,000 from a bank at a low interest rate). Again, the property appreciates at the rate of 10 percent annually. Now, however, at the end of year one, your investment has grown to $550,000, and at the end of year two, the property is worth $605,000. Thus, you have increased your dollar profit from $21,000 to $84,000 ($105,000 less $21,000). That is *four times* your original profit or a total percentage return of *400 percent* (before figuring in the dollars and percentage rate you have to pay to the bank for borrowing the money).

How do you put the concept of leveraging into practice as a real estate investor? By putting the minimum down on real property that has a strong likelihood of *appreciating* in future years. Generally, on other than primary home purchases, the bank will ask you to put down at least 20 percent on the initial investment. If you can find a bank that will let you put down less, and you are relatively sure that the property you are interested in will go up in value, you can see the benefits of using someone else's money.

Be aware that leveraging also compounds your dollar *loss* if the property goes *down* in value. Using our two examples above, if leverage is not used, you end up with a $19,000 loss after two years. Since this is residential rental property, you may or may not be able to take all of that loss depending on the amount of your adjusted gross income at the end of year two. If you used leverage, your loss is now $95,000, a difference of $76,000 ($95,000 less $19,000). Regardless of your adjusted gross income, you definitely cannot take all of that loss for income tax purposes, as you are limited to $25,000 in any year. In addition, you still have to pay the bank for any interest incurred on the loan during the two years.

In summary, if you are going to employ leverage, stay away from purchasing questionable properties in less than desirable areas. As mentioned in the first chapter, there is both *good* debt and *bad* debt. Bad debt is any debt incurred on property that is likely to *depreciate* in value over the anticipated time frame of the investor. The misuse of leveraging proves the truth of that statement many times over.

CORRELATION

In the financial world, correlation measures the direction and extent of a relationship between two investment assets, but you can also use this concept to diversify your portfolio and *accumulate* wealth.

A correlation of +1.0 means that two assets move exactly *together* in direction, whereas a correlation of -1.0 means that the two assets move exactly *opposite* of each other—that is, when one goes up, the other goes down. A correlation of 0.0 means that there is *no* relationship whatsoever between the two assets—that is, they move independently of each other.

Since 1970 (and through 2004), there have been correlations of various financial asset classes and real estate to the most often used stock market index—the Standard & Poor's index of five hundred stocks:

- large-cap stocks: 0.96
- mid-cap stocks: 0.86
- small-cap stocks: 0.79
- international stocks: 0.55
- intermediate-term bonds: 0.23
- cash: 0.02
- real estate: 0.52

As you can see, with the exception of cash and medium-term bonds, real estate and international stocks have the *lowest* positive relationship to the broad domestic stock market. Thus, if possible, given your budget and appropriate risk tolerance, you should add real estate and international stocks to your portfolio as diversification tools.

FINANCIAL OR REAL ASSETS: WHICH IS BETTER?

A lot of wealth has been created (the *accumulation* part of the PADD process) by individuals investing in financial and real assets. Nevertheless, this process is *not* a zero-sum game. The wealth accumulation techniques involved with each type of asset are not mutually exclusive.

Many investors prefer either financial or real assets but not both, because such investors are investing in assets that they understand (or someone has convinced them that they understand), or they are comfortable with either general category of assets but not both. Therein lies a fundamental rule of investing: *if you do not understand the potential investment, you should not be investing your hard-earned money in it.* Note that prior to the most recent recession that began in December 2007, investors *ignored* this basic rule and piled money into exotic derivative investments such as credit-default swaps, in which they neither appreciated the underlying risk nor understood the investment to begin with.

There are now real estate investments that look more like financial investments (for example, a REIT is a mutual fund that invests in real estate and real estate properties). Alternatively, you can invest in securities issued by real estate development companies and home builders. Once you understand your ability to assume differing amounts of risk, you may wish to invest in *both* financial and real assets. History has shown that adding real assets to a primarily financial portfolio will improve diversification and reduce overall risk and vice versa. Remember: the goal of wealth accumulation is to achieve not only as great an annual percentage return as possible, but to do so with as little amount of risk as possible.

Let's move on to a topic of great interest to investors and non-investors alike: how to buy a home and take best advantage of *use* assets in accumulating wealth.

CHAPTER 11

USE ASSETS

If you think back in the financial planning process to when you prepared your personal financial statement, you will notice that your home and automobile were properly listed as use assets and not as investments. While a profit motive for an investment may attach to some use assets (particularly luxury automobiles or antique collectibles), generally such assets are purchased to make efficient and enjoyable *use* of them.

YOUR HOME AS AN INVESTMENT

Your home likely means a lot of things to you, not the least of which is adequate and enjoyable shelter. Further, owning your own home is an integral part of the American dream.

One of the things your primary residence should *not* be is an investment, or, as many baby boomers are relying on, a retirement planning vehicle. As noted earlier, studies have shown that the average annual real rate of return on residential real estate is only 1.62 percent after considering all costs of maintenance and improvement. It is generally not good financial planning to have too much of your net worth tied up in any one asset. We have just discussed the importance of diversification when investing in financial and real assets, yet millions of individuals now (and when they retire) will hold approximately 70 percent of their net worth in just one asset: the equity in their home.

According to the *Wall Street Journal* (the *Journal*), as a homeowner, you can easily spend up to *three times* the purchase price of your home in additional costs, such as mortgage interest, property taxes, and major home improvements. For example, today's buyer of a $300,000 single-family dwelling who finances with a thirty-year fixed rate mortgage will end up paying the price of the dwelling all over again just in mortgage interest. Then add thirty years of property taxes, ongoing maintenance of the home, and several major home repairs or improvements, and the total cost of buying the home could approach $1 million.

Does this mean you should not buy a home and should instead rent? No, not at all! But it does argue for a new method of analyzing why you bought the home in the first place.

A house is one of the few assets (perhaps the only one) that does not violate the basic rule of debt management: *only go into debt for an asset that is likely to appreciate in value.* Notwithstanding the current housing crises in many cities, over the long term, depending on their location, houses tend to go up in value. As mentioned, you have already spent your initial purchase perhaps several times over, so as the *Journal* suggests, think of the sales proceeds as a *rebate* of your money. In other words, some of the thousands of dollars you spent on the upkeep and improvements to the house will be returned to you (in future value dollars, meaning that they are worth *less* in terms of purchasing power than when you first expended them).

Let's look at the average cost of home ownership over the thirty-year period from 1977 to 2007 according to an Office of Federal Housing Enterprise Oversight (OFHEO) study. The OFHEO assumes a purchase price of $50,000 for a single-family home in 1977 (not much above the national median home price of $48,800 at that time) and then compares the total cost of owning the home by financing its purchase with a thirty-year fixed-rate mortgage and with an all-cash purchase. According to the OFHEO, the house would have appreciated to a value of $290,500 by the year 2007 at a nominal annual compounded rate of return of approximately 6.04 percent. The average mortgage interest rate for a thirty-year fixed-rate mortgage in 1977 was 8.72 percent and the homeowner is assumed to be in a 33 percent marginal income tax bracket.

Here are the actual results in table form:

Average Cost of Home Ownership Over Thirty Years (1977–2007)

	Mortgage Financing	All Cash
Down Payment/Cash Price	$10,000 (20% down)	$50,000
Principal on Loan	$40,000	-0-
Interest at 8.72%: $112,796 total less $40,000 principal= $72,976 interest amount	$50,000 ($72,976 times (1-0.33 or 0.67)) (rounded up)	-0-
Taxes and insurance ($3,000 per year)	$90,000	$90,000
Ongoing maintenance ($150 per month)	$54,000	$54,000
Major Repairs and Home Improvements	$150,000	$150,000
Total Costs	**$394,000**	**$344,000**
Sale Value	$290,500	$290,500
Net Profit/(Loss)	**($103,500)**	**($53,500)**

There are several striking facts to acknowledge when analyzing this table. The first is that even an all-cash purchaser suffered a dollar loss over the thirty-year period (although not as much as the borrower, after itemizing his or her mortgage interest deduction). The second is that the net loss in both instances could have been turned into a net profit *if* not nearly as much money was expended on major repairs and home improvements. This speaks to the next major point that needs to be made with respect to home ownership: *exercise as much financial discipline as possible over aspects of the home purchase and ongoing ownership that you can control.*

Specifically, as a prospective home purchaser and owner, you have control over two significant home-owning costs:

(1) the amount of interest you pay, and (2) the extent of home improvements you make. With respect to the interest payments, even though some of this cost is offset by an income tax deduction, you are doing nothing to pay down the principal on which the total interest amount is computed. Thus, accelerating your principal payments (paying off the note as quickly as you can) will result in considerable savings. Another option, if you can afford it, is to finance the purchase of the home with a fifteen-year fixed rate mortgage rather than the standard thirty-year note.

Limiting the amount of home improvements you make is even more difficult. However, very few improvements will pay off for you at the time of sale. Studies have shown that a new kitchen or bathroom will return the greatest rebate at the time of sale, but even those improvements do not often return *all* of the money you expended. Watch the addition of a backyard swimming pool or dog run. The next buyer of your house may not have kids or a dog and these additions will be a disadvantage at the time of sale, not an advantage. A swimming pool can be an attractive nuisance to neighborhood kids and if one of them falls in the pool and is injured, you will likely be sued (thereby potentially adding significantly to your total cost of home ownership).

In addition to accelerating your mortgage payments and limiting the extent of your home improvements, there are several other planning strategies you can adopt with respect to managing your home as a use asset:

1. Adopt a different attitude. Treat your home as any other consumer purchase and buy it at as low a price as possible. Monitor price trends in your local housing market closely, and, when there is dip in the market, consider houses to be on sale. Buy then if you can.

2. Stay put as long as possible. Be a buy-and-hold home purchaser as long as possible. The average homeowner lives in his or her home only seven years before moving on, usually to a more expensive residence. Depending on your area and market conditions, this is likely *not* long enough to ensure a net profit at the time that you eventually sell.

3. Pay as much cash as possible. If you can afford an all-cash purchase, it is preferable, but absent that, make as much of a down payment as possible. A large down payment limits the amount of principal you have to borrow and interest you have to pay.
4. Be careful about refinancing. Yes, if you refinance, you will lower your monthly payment, but you have now extended the time of your loan (and thus added to your total interest payments). If you are going to refinance, consider going from a thirty-year fixed-rate mortgage to a fifteen-year fixed-rate mortgage (especially as you grow closer to your planned retirement date).
5. Stay away from interest-only mortgages. This is not so much a cash management tool as it is straightforward, practical advice. Many individuals who financed their home purchases with interest-only mortgages bought more house than they could afford and thus probably paid too much. Interest-only mortgages contradict the first strategy of paying as little for the house as you can.
6. Diversify, diversify, diversify. After accelerating your payments, take whatever money you have left and make sure you are contributing as much as possible to your employer's 401(k) retirement plan and any personal retirement savings vehicles, such as traditional or Roth IRAs. But don't go overboard: if you can pay off your house (or as much of it as possible) before you retire, you will *increase* your cash flow considerably and enjoy your retirement years that much more.

Buying versus Renting a Home

It can be argued that buying a home with a mortgage is just another form of renting. Instead of paying the rent to a landlord, as a homeowner paying interest, you are just paying the mortgage lender. You get a tax deduction for paying mortgage interest if you itemize your deductions, but until about the twenty-year point in the standard thirty-year mortgage, the interest payments are not doing much to reduce your principal. This result is only made worse by the homeowner moving soon after purchasing the home. As just discussed, that is also why it is so important to accelerate the payment of your mortgage as quickly as possible.

A sample home buy-versus-rent analysis worksheet is provided below:

Home Buy or Rent Analysis
A. Cost of Buying
1. Annual mortgage payments (twelve times monthly mortgage payment)
2. Property taxes
3. Homeowner's insurance
4. Maintenance
5. After-tax cost of interest on down payment and closing costs ($ times % after-tax rate of return)
6. Total costs (sum of items 1 to 5)

Less:
7. Principal reduction in mortgage loan balance (from amortization schedule)
8. Tax savings due to itemized mortgage interest deduction (interest portion of mortgage payments times marginal income tax rate)
9. Tax savings due to itemized property tax deduction (item A 2 above times marginal income tax rate)
10. Total reduction and deductions (sum of items 7 to 9)

Equals:
11. Annual after-tax cost of home ownership (Line A 6 less line A 10)

Plus:
12. Anticipated annual appreciation in fair market value of home, if any (percentage of price of home)

Equals Total Cost of Buying (Line A 11 less Line A 12)

B. Cost of Renting
   1. Annual rental costs (twelve times monthly rental rate)
   2. Renter's insurance
Equals Total Cost of Renting (Line B 1 plus Line B 2)

There is one important positive component of buying a home that is not an issue for renters: the estimated annual *appreciation* in the value of the home. This underscores what was just discussed: it is critical that as a prospective homeowner, you research the local market carefully and do *not* overpay for the property. If you do overpay, you limit the amount of potential appreciation in home value. If you buy in the wrong area or at the wrong time, you may be better off renting.

An oft-overlooked *protection* strategy of the wealth accumulation and management process for the renter is the need for a tenant's property insurance policy. In almost every lease, exculpatory language is included whereby the landlord bears no liability for damage to or theft of the tenant's personal property. A tenant's policy provides for this protection plus liability coverage for guests who may be injured while on the property. The policy protects the tenant from the consequences of his own injurious acts, wherever they may occur.

In addition to securing a property insurance policy, a tenant should be sure to check on the status of any security deposit required by the landlord. Some landlords, in an attempt to attract tenants, invest this deposit for the tenant and pay them the interest at the end of a long-term lease. However, more commonly, this deposit is simply maintained in escrow by the landlord and refunded to the tenant at the expiration of the lease, provided that the rental unit is left in good physical condition. Regardless, as a prospective tenant, you want as low a security deposit as possible and a return on your money in the form of protected premises and timely landlord maintenance.

SELLING YOUR HOME

Most of the issues involving the sale of your home are income-tax related, but you should not overlook practical questions such as whether to sell the home yourself or use a real estate broker.

With today's internet-savvy society, increasing numbers of individuals are opting to list and sell their homes themselves. However, as attractive as it might seem to avoid the cost of using a real estate broker, consider the following if you choose to sell your home on your own:

- You must establish a reasonable price for your home. While this may appear easy given the widespread availability of comparable market data these days, you need to be as realistic as you can about what your home may be worth. As such, you must separate emotion and the natural tendency to ask for more rather than less. Be as objective as possible.
- You need to market your home. This is much more than sticking a For Sale By Owner sign in the front yard. You need your house listed in your area's multiple-listing service (MLS). According to the National Association of Realtors, over 60 percent of home sales occur with the assistance of a buyer's agent (real estate agents or brokers typically work only for the *seller*). As such, try to list your house with such an agent, who typically works as part of a network and represents any number of qualified buyers.
- You need to separate the serious prospects from the merely curious. Neighbors are notorious for taking sales brochures or flyers simply because they want to see what you are asking for your house. Instead, ask them to refer to your attention any friends or family who may be looking for a new home. You should then prequalify the serious buyers so as not to waste your time negotiating a price with someone the mortgage lender will not approve.

- You have to close the deal. This is where many for-sale-by-owner sellers stumble. Many buyers are skilled in the art of negotiating for the absolute lowest price (sometimes even a below-market price). Hence, as a seller, you have to know what price you will accept while recognizing that it is the most the market will bear at that particular time.

Assuming that you or your real estate agent have been successful in getting a fair price for your home, you now have report the tax on any gain from that sale. Fortunately, the gain from the sale of any primary residence is considered a gain on the sale of a *capital asset*. Depending on your income tax bracket (and if you have owned the house for at least one year), the gain is generally taxed at either a 5 percent or a 15 percent rate. More importantly, if you meet certain conditions, any gain on the sale of a home is only taxable to the extent that it exceeds $250,000 (or $500,000, if you file a joint return). This $250,000 or $500,000 exclusion may be used as often as once every two years.

To determine your taxable gain, you must subtract your *basis* in the home from its sales price minus all costs and commissions. This underscores the importance of keeping good records since your basis in a home is generally equal to what you paid for it plus any improvements made while you owned it.

For example, assume that you paid $150,000 for your home ten years ago. While you owned it, you finished the basement at a cost of $30,000. Thus, your adjusted basis in the home is now $180,000 ($150,000 plus the $30,000 in improvements). Also assume that you have recently sold the home for $270,000 with the assistance of a real estate broker. You must pay your broker a commission of 6 percent of the sales price. Your sales price for determining capital gains tax is $253,800 ($270,000 less the $16,200 broker's commission). Accordingly, your total, potentially taxable gain is $73,800 ($253,800 net sales price less $180,000 basis); however, if you qualify for the $250,000 exclusion, you have *no* recognized gain for tax purposes.

To qualify for the $250,000 or $500,000 exclusion, you must meet both an *ownership test* and a *use test*. Specifically, you must have

- *owned* the residence for at least two out of the five years prior to when you sold it
- *used* the home as your primary residence for this same period of time

If you are married and file jointly at the time of sale, either you or your spouse can meet the ownership requirement, but you *both* must meet the use requirement (a particularly difficult requirement for divorced or divorcing couples).

If you fail to meet these tests because of a change in employment (for example, if your employer transfers you to a new location) or other unforeseen circumstances, you can exclude the fraction of the $250,000 or $500,000 exclusion that is equal to the fraction of the two-year period in which these tests were met.

For example, assume that you purchased a home on January 1, 2010, and on January 2, 2011, your employer transferred you to another city. You have owned your home for at least twelve months and, as a single taxpayer, are entitled to exclude up to $125,000 ($250,000 times 0.50 or (12 divided by 24)) of any gain you make on the sale of it.

As mentioned previously, like any other personal asset, losses on the sale of a home used as a personal residence are *not* allowed for income tax purposes.

Automobiles—Do You Really Need That New Lamborghini?

Unlike a home that has historically appreciated in value, there is no other use asset that depreciates in value more quickly than an automobile. From a debt management perspective, you should think twice before borrowing to purchase a new luxury (or any other type of) automobile. Remember, *it does not make financial sense to borrow to buy a depreciating asset.*

Nevertheless, in most places in America, an automobile is not a discretionary purchase, but a necessity for getting around. Accordingly, what are some tips for taking the most advantage of this necessary tool of daily living?

- If you can suffer what is, for some, an indignity, purchase only a quality *used* automobile. An automobile broker can assist you in finding one. Then, as with a house, do not overpay for it.
- Do some research before you buy. For example, if you have decided on a pre-owned car, consult the *Kelley Blue Book* to determine what you should be paying as the retail price. If it is a new car, there are online services that you can consult to find out the dealer's invoice cost. Start your negotiation with the dealer about 2 percent above that cost and try to work down from there.
- Try to determine before you buy if the car you are interested in is likely to become a classic model. For example, individuals who were fortunate enough to buy a 1957 Chevrolet or a 1965 Ford Mustang transformed a depreciating asset (a car) into a collector's item (a classic automobile).
- Buy only one quality automobile at a time and keep it for at least ten years or 100,000 miles (longer if possible). Fortunately, automobiles are improving in quality all the time, so this should not be too difficult.
- Keep your car in good repair and maintenance. It has been proven that well-tuned cars conserve gasoline and thus, in the longer term, save you money.

Another decision that you may need to make with respect to an automobile is whether to buy or lease the car. Generally, when a high percentage of the car's use is for business purposes, it may be more advantageous to lease instead of buy. This is because not only can the business portion of the lease payments be deducted for income-tax purposes, but the business portion of the interest on the loan may be deducted. Depreciation of the vehicle (within certain limits) is also possible as a tax deduction.

However, if the vehicle is to be used for primarily *personal* purposes, buying and owning the car for a significant period of time is preferable. This is particularly the case if the lease agreement does not provide for an option to purchase the car at its depreciated value at the lease's expiration date (a closed-end automobile lease agreement).

TANGIBLE PERSONAL PROPERTY AND COLLECTIBLES

Tangible personal property, such as art, stamps, and coins, may be transformed from a use asset to an investment based on the rarity and quality of the property. Likewise, a hobby, such as stamp collecting, may turn into a business depending on whether there is intent on the part of the collector to earn a profit from the activity (as determined by the IRS and the courts).

Examples of popular investment-quality collectibles include artwork, gemstones, rare coins, antique dolls and furniture, and even baseball cards. All share certain attributes—notably, rarity and popularity within a sizeable market. But collectibles generally do not provide any current income to the owner and are best held for capital appreciation. Once disposed of, the items are taxed at a special long-term capital gain rate of 28 percent. (That's right, they do *not* qualify for the typical maximum 15 percent rate.)

While there is a market for collectibles, in most cases it is not an *organized* market. Both buyers and sellers are at a disadvantage, since unless they are very skilled, neither is likely to have an idea as to what constitutes a fair price for the item. As with so many other consumer purchases, the Internet and a multiplicity of websites (particularly eBay) have improved access to reliable information about collectibles. Still, by and large, the market for collectibles is generally inefficient.

Another problem with tangible personal property that may become collectible is that the market may only be temporary. For example, several years back, Cabbage Patch Kids dolls were a heavily sought-after item that demanded high retail prices (and even higher tempers of potential purchasers). Today, however, the craze has passed and the price has returned to a more normal level. This is bad news if you bought at the top of the market, intended to make a subsequent profit, and now have no practical use for the dolls.

It is possible to obtain insurance coverage for valuable tangible personal property. If it is standard use property, as mentioned in chapter 7 you will need to schedule or endorse the property for an agreed-upon value with the insurance company. If it is truly a collectible with a recognized and sustainable market, you will have to enter into insurance negotiations with a specialized underwriter, such as those found at the Lloyds of London market.

The next section and relevant chapters take up the "defense" of accumulated wealth, most notably from the harmful effect of income taxes.

SECTION IV

DEFENDING WEALTH

CHAPTER 12

INCOME TAX PLANNING AND MANAGEMENT

This chapter begins the section of the book on how to *defend* your wealth, the first *D* in the PADD process of wealth accumulation and management. Chapter 12 focuses on income tax planning and management, with subsequent chapters addressing transfer tax (gift and estate tax) planning and life events that threaten wealth, such as divorce or loss of a job.

Now that we have discussed the *protection* and *accumulation* of wealth steps in the PADD process, we now move to the *defense* or preservation of that wealth. There are two primary threats that you must manage effectively in order to maximize wealth: *inflation* and *taxes*. While the rate of inflation is largely out of your individual control, you can be proactive when it comes to effective tax management. The step in effective tax management is to become familiar with the basic provisions of the income tax system.

BASICS OF INCOME TAX RATES, WITHHOLDING, AND ESTIMATED TAXES

A basic rule of wealth accumulation and management is to determine not only how much income you have to spend or save, but also how much of this income you *get to keep*. To maximize the *keeping* part, you need to know your federal income tax rate. (Note: You should also know what your *state* income tax rate is if you work in a state that imposes an income tax. However, because of the wide variation in state laws with respect to income tax, only the basics of the *federal* system are discussed here.)

There are actually two types of income tax rates: marginal and effective. Normally, when someone asks what your tax rate or bracket is, they are referring to your *marginal* income tax rate, which is the percentage of tax applying to your *next* dollar of taxable income. Your *effective* tax rate is the total tax payable divided by your taxable income as reported on your federal income tax return.

Through the end of 2012, there are six federal marginal income tax rates that apply to salaries and wages (and most other income other than capital gains income). These are 10, 15, 25, 28, 33, and 35 percent.

This is more than the two income tax rates (15 percent and 28 percent) implemented by the Tax Reform Act of 1986, but, historically, six is still a relatively small number of rates. Income is taxed in each of these rates according to a range of income known as an income tax *bracket*. Your bracket depends on the amount of taxable income you make in a year and the filing status you use to report this income (for example, single or jointly filed with your spouse). As a tax management technique, you want to do everything legally possible to not progress into the next higher marginal tax rate, where all remaining income is then taxed at a greater percentage.

There are preferential capital gains tax rates if you hold appreciated investment or business property for a required time (currently, more than one year) before selling. This is known as *long-term capital gain property* and the tax rate that is assessed depends on your marginal income tax rate. For example, if you are in the 10 or 15 percent marginal tax bracket, long-term capital gains are generally taxed at a rate of 5 percent. However, beginning in 2008 (and continuing through 2012), there is a one-time reduction in the capital gains rate for those in the 10 percent and 15 percent marginal tax brackets to *zero*. If you are in the 25 percent or above marginal rates, long-term capital gains are currently taxed at a rate of 15 percent. (Note: This will continue to be the case through 2012 since the one-time reduction to zero does *not* apply for higher bracket taxpayers.) *Losses* from investment or business property in both sets of marginal tax brackets are first offset against any capital gains and, if there is any remaining loss, are taken against salary or wages (or any other non-investment or business property income) up to a maximum of $3,000 in any given year. Any excess loss is then carried forward indefinitely until used up.

For example, assume that you or your tax preparer have reported that you have a long-term capital gain of $4,000 and a $5,000 long-term capital loss in the current year (2011). You are in the 15 percent marginal income tax bracket. As such, you have no long-term capital gain (it is completely offset by the long-term capital loss), but a remaining $1,000 long-term capital loss. As a result, you can use the total of this loss ($1,000) to reduce your salary or wages (or other non-investment or business property income), since it is less than $3,000 in the current year.

Once you know what your marginal income tax rate is (you can determine this by referring to past tax returns and checking the amount of taxable income against the bracket range), the next step is to figure out how much to withhold from your paycheck for future taxes. You do this by obtaining and filling out an IRS Form W-4. Your goal in completing this form is to withhold enough taxes to be equal to 90 percent of what you think you will owe to the federal government at the end of the year. The IRS Form W-4 lets you claim *allowances* or *exemptions* based on your projected income in estimating what these taxes will be at year-end. An exemption *reduces* the amount of taxes withheld and *increases* the amount of your take-home pay. Therefore, the *greater* the number of exemptions claimed, the *higher* your take-home pay, and the *lower* the number of exemptions, the *lower* your take-home pay.

Before January 31 of the subsequent year, your employer must report your amount of earnings for the previous year and the taxes withheld, as based on the number of exemptions you claimed on the IRS Form W-4. The form your employer uses to report these earnings is IRS Form W-2, which you are then required to attach to your income tax return before April 15 of that year.

Some individuals, notably self-employed taxpayers, are also required to pay *estimated taxes*. If, as a salaried individual, you have a great deal of additional income such as rental real estate income, you may also have to pay these taxes. Retirees with a large lump-sum distribution from their retirement plan are the third candidates for estimated taxes. If subject to estimating your taxes, your first payment is to be made by filing IRS Form 1040-ES on April 15 of the current year and then June 15, September 15, and January 15 (of the next year).

SOCIAL SECURITY AND MEDICARE TAXES (FICA)

Sometimes known as payroll taxes, under the Federal Insurance Contributions Act (FICA), all salaried employees have to pay (or have withheld from their paycheck) 7.65 percent of their salary to fund the Social Security and Medicare social insurance systems. Specifically, 6.2 percent of the total portion of 7.65 percent is the employee's contribution to fund his or her own Social Security retirement benefit, and the remaining 1.45 percent is Medicare funding. Note that there was a temporary 2 percent reduction in the employee portion of the Social Security tax in the year 2011, making the total tax only 4.2 percent of applicable income. The Social Security portion is assessed only up to a certain amount of the employee's salary (referred to as the taxable wage base—for example, $106,800 in 2011) in any calendar year, whereas the Medicare portion is assessed on an *unlimited* amount of employee salary.

Unlike state and local income taxes, which many taxpayers can separately deduct against their federal income taxes, Social Security and Medicare taxes are *not* deductible. Effectively, this *increases* the overall marginal income tax rate that an individual pays. For example, if you are in the highest marginal income tax bracket of 35 percent, you effectively pay 10.33 percent *more* in taxes (7.65 percent plus 2.68 percent or (0.35 times .0765)) because you cannot deduct these amounts.

REGULAR INCOME TAX VERSUS INDIVIDUAL ALTERNATIVE
MINIMUM TAX (AMT)

We just discussed the most important provisions of the
regular income tax system—the one that most taxpayers must
protect against as an ongoing threat to their accumulated wealth.
However, there is *another* tax system that certain high-income
(and increasing numbers of middle-income) taxpayers must plan
for each year. This system is referred to as the individual *alternative
minimum tax* (AMT).

The AMT is a parallel tax system originally designed to
prevent a small number of high-income taxpayers from avoiding
paying regular tax. Under the AMT system, taxpayers pay the
greater of the regular tax or alternative minimum tax due in any
given year. But because the AMT system has not been indexed
for the effect of inflation, more middle-income taxpayers are
now being impacted by it. While the AMT top rate is only 28
percent (compared to the regular system's top rate of 35 percent),
certain deductions and other tax breaks that are provided in the
regular system *do not count* in the AMT computation. Even
though it appears at first glance that if you are in the top three
regular income tax brackets (28, 33, and 35 percent), you do not
have to worry about the AMT, unfortunately, this is not the
case.

The deductions and other regular income tax breaks not
allowed to you under the AMT system are generally referred to
as *tax preference items*. These items are added back to your regular
taxable income to compute your alternative minimum taxable
income (AMTI)—upon which an AMT tax rate of 26 percent
or 28 percent is imposed. Among such preference items is the
income portion of an incentive stock option occurring on the date
of exercise of that option, the disallowance of the regular standard
income tax deduction, and the disallowance of any personal
or dependency exemptions. As a result, according to the *Ernst
&Young 2011 Tax Guide*, if your regular taxable income is at least
$100,000 in the year 2011, you file as a joint taxpayer, and you

have more than $32,223 in tax preference items, you are likely to be subject to the AMT for that year.

How do you avoid the application of this onerous tax? First, understand what constitutes a tax preference item (they are in the separate instructions to the AMT tax form), then try to limit them. For example, if you hold incentive stock options (ISOs) as an employee benefit from your employer, postpone exercising them for as long as possible (to when your total income is relatively low in a given year). Next, as curious as it seems, you may wish to consider *accelerating income* into the current year in the hope of increasing your regular tax liability to *above* that of the AMT. Finally, *postpone deductions* that you cannot take for AMT purposes into the next taxable year. The deductions at risk here include certain itemized deductions, including the deduction for state income taxes and property taxes. If you currently live in a high income tax state such as New York, you should ask your accountant or financial planner to separately compute your possible AMT liability.

Also note that the last two of AMT planning techniques—accelerating income and postponing deductions—is the exact *opposite* of what you would do in regular income tax planning. As a result, AMT planning essentially requires that you think *backward* with respect to how you would otherwise try to minimize taxes. This requires that you accelerate income for regular tax purposes, thereby trying to avoid the imposition of the AMT, and defer deductions to a later year if those deductions are not allowed for AMT purposes.

One further planning technique with respect to the AMT: write your congressperson and ask them to do something about it. Since the exemption amounts under the tax have not been indexed for inflation, the imposition of the AMT is an accident waiting to happen for many middle-income taxpayers.

BASIC TAX PLANNING TECHNIQUE #1: TAX AVOIDANCE

The term *tax avoidance* may be used narrowly, as when a higher bracket taxpayer gives property to a lower bracket taxpayer and the lower-bracket taxpayer then pays the income tax at a reduced rate, or broadly, meaning that the higher bracket taxpayer does not incur income taxes on the income. In the context that the term is used here, you should think of tax avoidance as broadly as possible. The most common example of tax avoidance is to take full advantage of all income tax deductions to which you are entitled under the tax law. Another example is to attempt to qualify for any income tax credits provided under law.

A tax *deduction* is a percentage reduction of your taxable income based on your marginal income tax rate. For example, if you are in the 33 percent marginal bracket, you are only paying tax on 67 percent (1 less 0.33) of your income. Alternatively, a tax *credit* is a dollar-for-dollar reduction against an individual's income tax liability and is therefore not affected by the marginal income tax rate of the taxpayer. For example, if you have computed your income tax liability before credits to be $10,000 this year and you qualify for a credit of $1,000, you only owe the government $9,000 ($10,000 less $1,000). In practical effect, and as a tax avoidance technique, a *credit* is worth more to a *lower bracket taxpayer* (15 percent rate and below) and a *deduction* is worth more to a *higher bracket taxpayer* (25 percent and above).

As a regular taxpayer, you are entitled to choose one of two general deductions: a specified *standard deduction* under law, based on your filing status, or a series of deductions known as *itemized deductions*. The one you want to choose is the *higher* of the two deductions, since that will afford you the greatest tax benefit. As a practical matter, if you own a home that you have financed with a mortgage and are paying a sizable amount of interest on that mortgage, you are likely able to itemize your deductions. If you rent, have not financed your home, or have paid off your mortgage early, more than likely you are limited to choosing only the standard deduction.

You may potentially be able to take advantage of the following deductions, if you itemize your deductions:

- unreimbursed (by health insurance) medical expenses
- state and local income and property taxes
- sales taxes
- home equity loan or line-of-credit interest payments
- charitable contributions
- casualty and theft losses

There are also a number of miscellaneous itemized deductions, such as unreimbursed employee expenses, home office expenses, and tax return preparation fees, that may only be deducted in limited circumstances. Generally, you will be unable to deduct *any* miscellaneous itemized deduction unless the *total* of those deductions exceeds 2 percent of your adjusted gross income (AGI) as reported on your federal income tax return.

As mentioned, if you qualify, regardless of whether you take the standard deduction or itemize, certain tax credits are allowable. There are two general types of credits: refundable and nonrefundable. A *refundable* credit is one where money is paid to you even though you have no income tax liability. An example is the earned income tax credit. Conversely, a *nonrefundable* credit is one where, at best, your tax liability can be reduced to zero (in other words, you are not separately paid if you do not owe any taxes). Of the two, as a tax avoidance technique, you want the refundable credit. Unfortunately, however, most credits are nonrefundable.

Among the most popular nonrefundable credits are

- the child and dependent care credit
- the child tax credit
- the adoption credit
- the credit for the elderly or disabled
- certain higher education expense credits, such as the HOPE scholarship credit and the Lifetime Learning credit

The Hope Scholarship and Lifetime Learning credits will be discussed later in the book in the education planning section of *distributing* your wealth during lifetime.

As a general tax management strategy to avoid as much regular income tax as possible, you should *accelerate deductions* and credits into the current tax year and *postpone income* into the next or subsequent tax years. Salaried taxpayers typically find it difficult to postpone income since they are not in control of when they actually receive it. However, self-employed taxpayers have much more latitude with respect to this tax planning technique. For example, a self-employed taxpayer can choose to bill a client early in January of the following year rather than in late December of this year, thereby deferring taxes due on the income.

A valuable tax-avoidance technique is to invest in tax-exempt mutual funds such as a municipal bond fund. As discussed earlier, generally, the *higher* the marginal income tax bracket you are in, the *more* you will benefit from tax-exempt investments. This is because the after-tax return on a taxable investment has to be relatively high to match your nominal tax-free return on a tax-exempt investment.

TAX AVOIDANCE VERSUS TAX EVASION

You should distinguish between income tax avoidance planning techniques and tax evasion. *Avoidance* techniques are perfectly legal and take advantage of tax benefits such as deductions and credits afforded to you under the tax law. Conversely, tax *evasion* is illegal; it means that you *intended* to not comply with the tax law. The most common form of tax evasion is the failure to report all of your taxable income for the calendar year.

If, in filing your tax return for any given year, you intend to break the law, the IRS must prove this fact (typically in a court of law). If it does so, you are guilty of a felony offense punishable by severe monetary fines or imprisonment in a federal penitentiary. Fortunately, imprisonment is rarely the punishment. Restitution (paying what you should have owed) and fines are the preferred recourse of the government. Nevertheless, if you are involved in a tax evasion case, either as the subject of the investigation or as someone who knows something about it, you should immediately contact a tax attorney to speak with the IRS Criminal Investigation Division (CID). Do not speak voluntarily to the CID as anything you may say may be used against you later.

BASIC TAX PLANNING TECHNIQUE #2: TAX DEFERRAL

The most common tax deferral technique is to contribute to a retirement plan at work or to a personal retirement savings plan such as a **traditional** or **Roth IRA**. We have already talked about the importance of contributing to your employer's 401(k) or 403(b) retirement plans to take advantage of the matching contribution. However, from a tax planning perspective, you are also deferring the tax on any contributions made to the 401(k) or 403(b) plans *and* deferring the tax on any earnings generated from those contributions. Since 401(k) or 403(b) plans are tax-advantaged retirement plans under law, you must later pay tax on your contributions and earnings beginning in the year after you reach the age of seventy and six months. In the meantime, you have enjoyed the financial advantage of the tax-free compounding of your money. Let's try to understand the importance of this advantage.

If you are asked, "Would you rather have $1,000 today or $1,000 ten years from now?" you would likely intuitively answer "$1,000 today." Why? The logic is that is if you receive the $1,000 today, you can invest the lump sum and make even more money with it. How much more depends on your investment rate of return. Assume that you invest your $1,000 in a U.S. Treasury bill that returns 5 percent annually. At the end of ten years, you will have $1,628.89. Alternatively, if you were to take the $1,000 ten years from now, this same amount would only be worth $613.91 in today's dollars. In financial language, this

$613.91 is known as the present value of that $1,000 if you were to receive it ten years from now.

Instead, think of the 5 percent annual rate of return as a tax percentage. If you have an income tax liability this year of $1,000 but you can somehow defer that liability for ten years, the present value of that liability is now only $613.91 (a savings of more than $386). And, using time-value-of-money principles, the *longer* you postpone that liability, the *lower* your present value and the *greater* your savings. Moreover, you should be aware that by year forty, your $1,000 liability is only worth $142.05 in present value dollars—approximately 14 cents on the dollar. You have generated the other 86 cents on the dollar completely income-tax free, which is the beauty of income-tax deferral with respect to retirement plan accumulations of wealth.

There are also other tax-deferral techniques involving financial products. Notably, if you purchase either a tax-deferred fixed or variable annuity product, the taxes on the earnings from the after-tax contributions to that product are deferred (in some cases, until age one hundred). You can also purchase a tax-deferred annuity with a lump-sum distribution that you make from an employer's retirement plan (such as a 401(k)), but, since those contributions are really made with before-tax money (you never paid taxes on it), distributions will have to be made in the year after you reach the age of seventy and six months.

Another financial product that provides for tax deferral is a cash value life insurance policy. If you do *not* access the cash surrender amount in this policy during your lifetime, the death proceeds from the policy to your named beneficiary are completely *income-tax free*. Alternatively, the earnings on the cash value accumulated within a whole life, universal, variable, or variable/universal life insurance policy are tax-deferred until you surrender the policy, assuming that the cash value you receive is in *excess of* the premiums paid on the policy at the time of surrender.

For example, assume that you have owned a whole life insurance policy for some time and have accumulated $70,000 of cash surrender value. During the course of the year, you surrender this policy for cash, but have only paid $50,000 in premiums on the policy to date. Thus, the portion of the lump-sum payment of $70,000 in excess of the premiums paid of $50,000 ($20,000) is taxable immediately, payable at your current marginal income tax rate.

BASIC TAX PLANNING TECHNIQUE #3: THE CONVERSION OF INCOME

Ultimately, every item of income is classifiable as either *ordinary income* (such as salary and wages) or *capital gains* (generally, income deriving from the sale or disposition of an investment product such as a stock or business property).

As noted, there are significantly different tax rates that potentially apply to each of these types of income. For example, ordinary income is taxed at a maximum rate of 35 percent, whereas long-term capital gains income (a sale of a stock owned for at least one year) is taxed at a maximum rate of only 15 percent. This rate spread of 20 percent suggests a tax planning strategy of converting as much income as possible from ordinary income to capital gains income. It also underscores the importance of saving and investing as much as possible, since the appreciation on investment assets is taxable at a rate no higher than 15 percent.

For example, assume that you have earned $1,000 in salary and are currently (in the year 2011) in the maximum ordinary income tax bracket of 35 percent. Your after-tax, disposable dollars are $650 ($1,000 less $350). If you take this same $1,000 and invest it in ABC stock, and you sell it for $2,000 at least one year after your bought it, your after-tax, disposable dollars are now $850 ($1,000 less $150). Note that you incur a 15 percent capital gains tax, since you are in a 25-percent-or-higher ordinary income tax bracket. If you were in the 15-percent-or-lower ordinary income tax bracket, you would not pay any capital gains tax on this sale.

Since 2003, you can take advantage of capital gain income rates on most investment income generated from stocks or mutual funds (5 percent or 15 percent, depending on your ordinary income tax bracket). However, dividends payable from indirect real estate investments such as a **real estate investment trust** or REIT do not typically qualify for this same advantage. As such, a conversion of income is not possible with these types of investments.

There is a common *reverse conversion* of income that many taxpayers unwittingly commit without realizing it. This occurs when a taxpayer invests in mutual funds (or individual stocks and bonds) within a retirement plan—either an employer-sponsored plan such a 401(k) plan or a traditional deductible IRA. In such case, what the taxpayer has really done is invest in a capital asset, which could potentially be taxed at lower capital gains rates on sale, and instead converted it to an asset that requires the payment of ordinary income taxes on distribution. This happens because, for income tax purposes, a distribution from a retirement plan or IRA is in lieu of salary, which would otherwise be taxable as ordinary income. Nonetheless, this disadvantageous conversion of income is likely *outweighed* by the extremely favorable, long-term tax deferral of earnings and contributions associated with an employer-sponsored retirement plan or IRA.

Tax-Smart Investing

Now that we have discussed both investing—the *accumulation* of wealth in the PADD process—and income taxes—*defending* your wealth—we need to combine the two. In other words, which type of account—tax-deferred or taxable—is most efficient to position a given type of financial asset?

Tax-deferred accounts such as retirement plans allow for the growth of assets over many years without paying taxes on the earnings. Therefore, it makes sense to position those investments that are *not* income-tax-efficient in retirement plans. An example of such an investment is a zero-coupon bond where taxable phantom income is generated each year, but no corresponding cash is received. Among other investments you may wish to position within retirement plans are individual corporate, investment-grade bonds and bond mutual funds, as well as Treasury STRIPs and Treasury Inflation Protected Securities (TIPS). Conversely, one type of financial asset you should *not* position within a tax-deferred account is a municipal bond or municipal bond fund. Interest from a municipal bond is tax-exempt, so if you position it within a tax-deferred account, you are converting income from tax-free status to taxable status once withdrawn from the retirement plan.

As a general rule, individual stocks and stock mutual funds belong in a *taxable* account. This is because they are more tax-efficient than bonds and bond mutual funds. Index funds or exchange-traded funds (ETFs) are also good choices for taxable accounts since they are passively managed and generally very income tax-efficient. However, with respect to stocks and stock mutual funds, an argument may be made that, given their growth potential and the total compounded dollars at time of withdrawal, they may also optimally fit as part of a tax-deferred portfolio. If you are working with a financial planner or investment advisor, ask him or her to give you perspective with regard to this argument.

WHAT YOU CAN LEARN FROM YOUR OWN TAX RETURN

Although most taxpayers do not prepare their own tax returns, they should understand the entries so as to plan more effectively for coming years. The following points provide a brief explanation of some of the basics of filing a tax return.

1. What is your filing status? If you are married and living together throughout the year, you should file your return jointly with your spouse, since generally you will be taxed more favorably. Alternatively, if you are a single parent with a dependent child or children, you should investigate filing your return by using the advantageous head of household status.

2. How many personal exemptions can you claim? This depends on whether your personal circumstances meet a number of qualifying conditions, but you can always claim yourself and spouse as an exemption.

3. Should your investment interest be taxable or tax-exempt? As discussed, the *higher* your marginal income tax rate, the *greater* the advantage to you of investing in tax-exempt assets such as municipal bonds or municipal bond funds.

4. Do you have any self-employment income? If you do (to be reported on IRS Form 1040, Schedule C), you may be entitled to a number of business deductions that you would not otherwise be able to claim.

5. Do you have capital losses (losses from the sale of any investment or business property)? As a tax planning technique, should you recognize capital losses in years when you have capital gains? These losses can offset capital gains and further offset ordinary income to the extent of $3,000 per year.

6. Are you required to make required minimum distributions from your IRA this year? Just as with distributions from employer-sponsored retirement plans, you have to begin taking distributions from a traditional deductible IRA (not a Roth IRA) no later than April 1 of the year after you reach the age of seventy and six months.

7. Can you contribute to and deduct contributions to your IRA this year? The answer is somewhat complicated and depends on your filing status, but if your income is low enough, you can both contribute to and deduct a specified amount annually from your IRA.

8. Do you have enough deductions to itemize? If you own a house and have financed it with a mortgage, chances are that your amount of itemized deductions will exceed the standard deduction afforded to you under law for a given year.

9. What is your taxable income? Depending on your filing status, this amount determines what marginal income tax bracket you are in and your applicable marginal income tax rate.

10. Do you qualify for any additional tax credits this year? All allowable credits have qualifying conditions or limitations. However, if you qualify, a credit affords you a dollar-for-dollar tax reduction.

11. Do you owe household employment taxes? Generally, you are responsible for paying Social Security and Medicare taxes if you employ a household domestic worker such as a nanny. This is one of the most overlooked sections of income tax law and has resulted in the imposition of tax penalties for many salaried and self-employed workers.

12. Did you pay tax or receive a tax refund? A goal of many taxpayers is to receive as big a refund as possible when they file their tax return, but think about it: if you receive a refund, you have just given the federal government an interest-free loan for the entirety of the previous tax year. Alternatively, you do not want to withhold so little tax that penalties are imposed for the previous year. Your goal here should be a small tax *payment* with the filing of your individual income tax return (for example, a payment of no more than $100).

We now move on the other major tax that can reduce your accumulated wealth very quickly: the transfer tax imposed under federal tax law.

CHAPTER 13

TRANSFER TAX PLANNING AND MANAGEMENT

Many individuals think that transfer tax (gift and estate tax) planning is only for very high-net-worth taxpayers. This is not really true. For example, did you know that you can give away $13,000 per year, regardless of the amount of your net worth, to donees without having to file a federal gift tax return? Just as important, did you know that once you exceed this $13,000 limit, you are *required* by law to file a federal gift tax return? Yes, that includes Christmas gifts if you have given away the $13,000 amount earlier in the same year.

This chapter explains gifts and the advantages of making gifts in transfer tax planning and management and subsequently considers how to minimize your taxable estate at death. While there has been a great deal of discussion in Congress about the repeal of the estate tax (sometimes referred to as the death tax), it is still with us—and likely will be with us in some form for years to come.

THE ADVANTAGES OF LIFETIME GIFTING

Once an individual has *accumulated* wealth, his or her motivations not only turn to how to protect or defend this wealth but also how to *distribute* it. We will talk more about the distribution of wealth in the next section of the book, but the beauty of lifetime gifting is that it accomplishes two steps of the PADD process at once: the *defense* of one's wealth against transfer taxes as well as the *distribution* of that wealth for the benefit of others (typically, your spouse and children).

You may have many reasons for making gifts. Among these are personal reasons, such as assisting a family member or close friend in immediate financial need. There also may be tax reasons. Whereas lifetime gifting (other than to charity) does *not* generate an income tax deduction, it does shift the income generated from the gifted property to someone else. There are numerous tax rules that restrict the outright assignment of income to others, but if you gift them an income-producing asset such as a stock, bond, or real estate, the donee—and not you—will pay the future income tax on the income.

Under the gift tax rules, there are three ways to make gifts to others without worrying about the payment of any gift tax (or the filing of a gift tax return, IRS Form 709). The first has been mentioned: as of 2011, you can give up to $13,000 per year to as many donees as you like. Technically, this $13,000 allowance per donee is known as the gift tax annual exclusion amount. For example, if you have ten children, you can give up to $130,000 per year ($13,000 times 10) without concerning yourself about reporting these gifts to the federal government. But be careful: some taxpayers, believe it or not, are so concerned about reducing their income and estate tax liability that they forget to ask the first basic question before making the gift—can I afford to make this gift without sacrificing my own future financial security?

The second method of making a lifetime gift is to transfer assets or property to your spouse or a **qualified charity**. Unlike gifts to others, you can make a gift to your spouse or a qualified charity in an *unlimited amount*. Particularly as it relates to estate tax planning, it may be beneficial to make gifts since the gifted property is now completely removed from your taxable estate at death. However, as we shall see later, if your spouse is the donee, you may be causing a further estate tax problem for him or her if he or she is already of high net worth in his or her own right (or expects to be shortly).

The third method of prudent lifetime gifting is to pay the educational or medical expenses of a loved one. However, the payment needs to be made *directly* to the educational institution or medical provider and not to the donee, who would then pay the institution or provider. If the donee is the intermediary, the $13,000 or other indexed-for-inflation limit applies rather than the unlimited amount that is possible if the institution or provider is the payee.

If you give more than $13,000 annually to any donee, under law, you must file a gift tax return and have the excess applied against an overall lifetime exemption limit of $5 million through the end of calendar year 2012. There are two consequences to making a gift of more than the annually permitted limit:

1. You begin to use up the overall lifetime limit of $5 million such that once you exceed $5 million in lifetime taxable gifts, you pay federal gift tax out of pocket.
2. The gift tax value of the gift that you make (the property's fair market value at the time that you gift it) is included in the estate tax computation as an adjusted taxable gift, meaning it *adds* to your potential taxable estate at death.

For example, assume that you make a gift of appreciated stock to your adult son in 2011. The fair market value of this stock at the time you give it is $100,000. Thus, you have made a taxable gift of $87,000 ($100,000 less $13,000) for which you must file a federal gift tax return. As a result, you now have only $4,913,000 ($5 million less $87,000) of your lifetime limit left. This taxable gift of $87,000 is also added to your taxable estate at your date of death. Note that while you think the amount of $4,913,000 is a lot of money (and it is!), the $5 million lifetime exemption is only for gifts made before the end of 2012, when the exemption amount is likely to be substantially reduced.

So why, given these tax consequences, do you want to make a taxable gift? Because you have removed any *future appreciation* of the gifted property from your taxable estate. In the example above, let's say that the $100,000 in stock that you gave your son appreciates to $600,000 at your death twenty years later. The appreciation amount of $500,000 ($600,000 less $100,000) is now forever removed from possible future transfer taxation in your estate.

Let's go back to taking maximum advantage of the $13,000 annual gift tax exclusion. In the example given previously with the ten children as donees, the person who gave the gift immediately removed $130,000 from his or her taxable estate and did not have to file a gift tax return or worry about reducing the overall $5 million exemption limit. This strategy is known in estate planning as a systematic annual gifting program and takes advantage of as many gift tax annual exclusion amounts as possible, to as many donees as possible, to reduce the donor's taxable estate. Therefore, as a transfer tax planning technique, you should look first to adopting a systematic gifting program by making as many annual exclusion gifts as you can afford at the *beginning* of each calendar year. In this manner, you will not only reduce your taxable estate, but you will also remove an additional year of income from the gift from your current year's taxable income.

GIFTS TO MINORS

If you are going to make gifts to a minor (someone who is under the state-specified age of legal majority, usually eighteen), you have to be concerned not only about gift tax laws, but also about state property laws. Minors cannot take title to property in the same way that individuals of legal majority—adults—can. Instead, minors have to take title through custodial arrangements as specified by each state.

There are two basic types of custodial arrangements: arrangements provided by the Uniform Gifts to Minors Act (UGMA) or by the Uniform Transfers to Minors Act (UTMA). In many states, UTMA has superseded the previously enacted UGMA and is now the approved form of making property transfers to minors. Under both uniform laws, the minor is given title to property, but as managed by a custodian, usually the parent or grandparent of the minor. This custodian invests and manages the gifted property on behalf of the minor and does not own the property in any respect. As such, the custodial arrangement is similar to a trust on behalf of the minor but without the complexity and cost of implementing the trust document.

All states have simple forms to title property gifted to a minor in custodial arrangement, but be aware that custodial gifts to minors are completed gifts for federal gift tax purposes—in other words, the gift becomes the *minor's property* and not yours, if you are the donor. At the state-specified legal age of majority, the child can do whatever he or she wants with the gifted property, including *not* going to college or pursuing higher education. Income used for your minor child's maintenance and support is taxable to *you* if you are the child's parent, even though you may *not* be the named custodian. This is because, under all state property laws, as the child's parent, you have the legal obligation of support to raise that child until he or she attains the legal age of majority.

Fortunately, as we will see in chapter 15, in recent years, a much better technique than a custodial arrangement for saving for college has been legislated by Congress. Private savings plans are made possible under Section 529 of the Internal Revenue Code (commonly referred to as Section 529 savings plans).

A Basic Primer on the Use of Trusts

A trust is an arrangement to which there are three parties:

1. the individual who establishes the trust (known as the creator or grantor)
2. the trustee of the trust
3. the individual or individuals for whose benefit the trust is established (known as the trust beneficiary or trust beneficiaries)

In any trust arrangement, the trustee must act solely and exclusively on behalf of the trust beneficiaries. As such, the trustee has the legal title to the trust assets, but the beneficiaries have what is known in the law as equitable title to the assets.

Trusts have many uses in transfer tax planning and management, as well as in estate planning generally. Among these are

- the ability to benefit one or more specified beneficiaries
- being able to afford the expertise of professional or other skilled management in the investment of trust assets
- asset protection
- probate avoidance
- being able to achieve income and transfer tax savings

There are many types of trusts, including those established on behalf of minors, but all may be categorized as either revocable or irrevocable trusts.

Revocable Trusts

A *revocable* trust is a trust that is created during your lifetime over which you retain the power to revoke or take back the trust assets. Accordingly, you do *not* make a completed gift, nor do you lose the right to the income from the trust assets. However, if you make someone else the beneficiary of the trust, a gift *does* occur at that time. Once you die, if you have not revoked the trust, the trust becomes irrevocable and can operate in lieu of a will to distribute your assets.

There are two major advantages of a revocable trust, neither of which involves transfer tax savings. These advantages are

1. If you transfer assets to the trust during your lifetime and re-title them in the name of the trustee (which is typically you), the trust assets avoid the probate process in the state where you die.

2. If you become mentally incompetent (for example, if you contract Alzheimer's disease), the successor trustee of the trust can assume the management of your financial and personal affairs.

Additionally, you can reduce the beneficiary's estate tax using a revocable trust—once it becomes irrevocable at your death—if the trust is drafted properly.

Generally, these advantages far outweigh the lack of transfer tax savings from the revocable trust at your death. Since you keep complete control over the trust and its assets, the assets are included in your taxable estate. But if you are below the estate tax allowable exemption amount ($5 million in 2011), you should not be concerned about this disadvantage.

Revocable trusts, which are also known as living trusts, are heavily promoted by trust sponsors and marketing firms as the panacea to all estate tax problems. While this is decidedly *not* the case, living trusts can be a very effective estate-planning tool, particularly for individuals who own a vacation home or other real estate in a state other than their primary residence. For owners of out-of-state vacation homes, a second or *ancillary* probate proceeding is required in the state where the vacation home is located. By transferring the title of the vacation home to the trustee of the revocable trust, your estate can avoid multiple probate proceedings.

Irrevocable Trusts

An *irrevocable* trust, which may be created during your lifetime or at death, can result in estate tax savings at your—the creator's—death. The term "irrevocable" means just what it implies: *you cannot change, revoke, or amend this trust in any way after you create it.* This disadvantage alone is incentive enough for many creators to shy away from even considering the implementation of an irrevocable trust—with one or two notable exceptions.

The first reason you may wish to create an irrevocable trust has to do with the usual motivations of individuals who purchase a life insurance policy. Most individuals purchase a life insurance policy for death-motivated reasons; that is, to protect their survivors from the loss of income resulting from their death. While there are lifetime reasons for the purchase of a cash-value type policy, they are usually not predominant. Given the at-death motivation and the fact that there is a very low gift tax value associated with most policies, the life insurance policy is usually an *excellent* asset to transfer to an irrevocable trust. Funding a trust with only a life insurance policy known as an **irrevocable life insurance trust** (ILIT) is a commonly used estate-planning technique.

The second reason you may wish to create an irrevocable trust is for asset protection from creditors. This type of trust, particularly popular among doctors and lawyers and other professionals who are frequently the target of lawsuits, is known as a foreign situs or offshore trust. Be careful: the offshore trust is very controversial and the IRS monitors its operation very carefully. In part, this is because the income from property transferred to the trust is still taxable to its creator or **grantor**. Unless the trust is drafted very skillfully, and for appropriate estate planning reasons, the trust may be rendered void on its face in violation of the creator's state fraudulent conveyance laws.

COMPONENTS AND VALUATION OF THE GROSS ESTATE

In transfer tax planning and management, more individuals are concerned or upset about the imposition of a possible estate tax at their death than they are about lifetime gift taxes.

The estate tax is ultimately assessed on an amount known as the tentative tax base, which is your taxable estate plus any adjusted taxable gifts made during your lifetime, but the computation begins with assets that make up the taxpayer's *gross estate*. The gross estate is similar to gross income under income tax law, but with one major difference: in income tax law, the tax is assessed on your *annual income*, whereas in estate tax law, the tax is assessed on the fair market value of your *lifetime assets* as of the date of your death. Operationally, the income tax is a government levy on the inflow items you show on your *personal cash flow statement*; conversely, the estate tax is a government levy on the asset items you show on your *statement of personal financial position.*

The gross estate consists not only of assets you die owning, but also certain lifetime transfers (gifts) over which you retain control or enjoy the benefit from at your death. For example, if you make a gift to an irrevocable lifetime trust, but at your death are an income beneficiary of that trust, the *total* fair market value of the trust assets at your date of death is taxed. Similarly, if you have previously gifted an out-of-state vacation home to your favorite child but you retain by agreement with that child the right to use the home whenever you want, the fair market value of that home at your date of death is taxed.

Assume that you live in North Dakota but own a winter home in Florida. In 2011, you transfer the title to the Florida home to your oldest son, but, per an agreement with him, are allowed to use the home whenever you want. If you die still holding this power, the fair market value of the Florida home will be included in your gross estate, as if you had never transferred the title to your son in the first place.

Property is included in your estate at its fair market value at of the date of your death (contrast this with gifted property that is valued at its fair market value as of the date of the gift). Most of the time, the date-of-death fair market value may be easily established. For example, publicly traded stock may be valued based on the average of the highest and lowest trading price on the date of death. Real estate may also be relatively easily valued by referencing comparable sales in the neighborhood or area. If a decedent (the individual who dies) is the owner of a small, family, or closely held business, the value of his or her business interest may not be so easily determined. There are many factors that must be considered when establishing this value, not the least of which is whether the owner owns a controlling or minority interest in the business at death. If you are an owner of a closely held business, it is best to contact a qualified appraiser to help you value it properly for estate or gift tax purposes.

One final comment with respect to the assets included in the gross estate and their respective value. If you die owning or having incidents of ownership with respect to a life insurance policy, you have to include the *death proceeds* or *face value* of that policy in your gross estate. This is a much *greater* amount than the fair market value of the policy, which, depending on the type of policy, is usually relatively small. For example, if you own a cash-value type policy, its fair market value is very close to its accumulated cash value; if you own a term policy that has no cash value, its fair market value is very close to zero. This is all the more reason to consider making a lifetime gift of a life insurance policy to another: if you gift it, the policy has a very *small* value, whereas if you die owning it, the policy has a very *large* value.

Assume that you die owning a whole life insurance policy with a face value of $500,000. The accumulated cash value in this policy at your date of death is $80,000. For estate tax purposes, the policy is included in your gross estate at a value of $500,000. If you had previously gifted it, the policy value for gift tax purposes would be no more than $80,000 (and probably less, since the policy would not have accumulated the same amount of cash value at your death years later).

DEDUCTIONS AND CREDITS AVAILABLE TO THE ESTATE

As with the income tax system, there are deductions and credits available to the estate for transfer tax purposes. But, unlike income tax, these deductions and credits are not usually limited in amount.

The two most useful—and probably the most frequently claimed—estate tax deductions are those for property transfers at death to either your spouse or a qualified charity. Respectively, these are known as the estate tax *marital deduction* and the estate tax *charitable deduction*. They are unlimited in amount, as is also the case for transfers to a spouse or qualified charity during an individual's lifetime for gift tax purposes. However, both types of property transfers need to be left in a qualifying form before the deduction is permitted. For example, property transfers to a spouse at death must be left without restriction and property transfers to a qualified charity must be left in a charitable trust form.

Assume that you leave all your property outright (with no restrictions) to your spouse at your date of death under your will or by beneficiary designation. This is acceptable and will qualify for the unlimited estate tax marital deduction. However, if you left your property to your spouse only for his or her lifetime use (in other words, with restrictions), the transfer will typically *not* qualify for the unlimited marital deduction.

Then assume that you leave property in remainder interest to a qualified charity, but keep the right to the income from the property during your lifetime. This is a **charitable remainder trust** (CRT) and the remainder interest left to charity will qualify for the unlimited estate tax charitable deduction. However, if you had tried to accomplish this same transfer without establishing a trust, the unlimited charitable deduction would likely *not* be allowed.

There are also several credits available in estate tax planning, the most useful of which (indeed, its use is mandatory) is the *unified credit.*

The unified credit is equal to a certain amount of property that may be transferred estate-tax-free at death. However, as with income tax, this credit is applied only *after* computing the total tax liability. For example, in 2011, the amount of estate tax on $5 million of taxable estate property is $1,730,800. To that amount, you must apply the allowable unified credit of $1,730,800, so your net estate tax liability is zero. When you hear that you may transfer up to $5 million in property free of estate tax (actually more, if your only beneficiary is your spouse or a qualified charity), you know it to be true, since you have an allowable unified credit of $1,730,800 to offset the tax due on that amount.

You need to be aware of one circumstance that will *reduce* the $1,730,800 unified credit at death. Since the gift and estate tax systems are linked (which is where the term *unified* comes from), any taxable gifts that you make during lifetime in excess of the gift tax annual exclusion impact the amount of unified credit that is available to your estate at your death. As such, if you make any taxable gifts during lifetime, the credit amount that you use to offset that gift tax liability *reduces* your allowable unified credit at death.

For example, assume that you die with a taxable estate of $5 million in 2011 and you leave it all equally to your two children. During your lifetime, however, you made taxable gifts of $100,000 to each of those children. In operational effect, this means that you have a taxable estate of $5.2 million, leaving you with an estate tax due of $70,000 ($200,000 times the applicable marginal estate tax rate of 35 percent). Looked at another way, you have *reduced* your allowable unified credit by $70,000 and thus only have available at your death an allowable unified credit of $1,660,800 ($1,730,800 less $70,000).

Tax Rates and the Possible Repeal of the Death Tax

In recent years, one of the transfer taxes—the estate tax—has become somewhat of a political football. Specifically, some legislators have urged the repeal of what they believe to be an unnecessary and even punitive tax, while others are worried about the revenue effects of eliminating the estate tax. Hence, we find ourselves on uncertain ground with the continuation of the tax through 2012 but no knowledge of whether the estate tax will continue thereafter. This makes estate tax planning very difficult—if not impossible—for most estate planners.

In 2011, the top marginal estate tax rate is 35 percent. This will remain the case through 2012, when the amount of property that may be left estate- or gift-tax-free to anyone other than your spouse or a qualified charity will be reduced to a total of $1 million. At that time, the top marginal estate tax rate is scheduled to increase to 55 percent.

As you might recognize, the 55 percent scheduled *transfer* tax rate in 2013 is much higher than the current maximum marginal *income* tax rate of 35 percent. Thus, if you (or you and your spouse combined) currently have a gross estate of at least $5 million, the need for transfer tax planning is particularly acute—otherwise, the government, rather than your family, may be the chief beneficiary. Even if you are currently below $5 million in total net worth but think you may exceed that amount at your death (perhaps through the wealth accumulation and management techniques explained in this book), you need to plan. Moreover, I would engage in transfer tax planning *today* even if your current or anticipated net worth is only $1 million.

Do I Really Want to Leave It All to My Spouse or Charity?

As we have discussed, the deduction available for transfers made at death to a spouse or charity is *unlimited in amount*. But as a planning technique, do you really want to take full advantage of either deduction?

Although the tax law allows you and your spouse to leave each other all property free from estate tax, you may end up increasing or overfunding your spouse's estate if you leave everything to him or her. This is particularly the case if your net worth is already at or near the estate tax exemption equivalent of tax-free property ($5 million in 2011 and 2012). If your spouse is much younger than you (and thus there is considerable time for your bequeathed assets to grow in value), it may *not* be the best idea to leave it all to him or her. This possibility is one of the major problems with titling all your property in **joint tenancy with right of survivorship** (JTWROS) with your spouse: from a planning perspective, JTWROS titling limits your flexibility, since all property passes directly to your spouse.

Moreover, in so far as federal transfer tax law is concerned, there is *no* debate about who constitutes a spouse for purposes of taking advantage of the unlimited marital deduction allowance; that is, the spouse must be a member of the opposite gender. This is the case even if your state of residence recognizes same-sex couples as being legally married. When it comes to transfer tax law advantages, *federal* law and not *state* property law is in control. This means that gay and lesbian couples of fairly sizable net worth cannot plan their individual estates to pass to the other partner free of estate or gift tax as traditional married couples can. If you are part of this population, you not only need to consult an estate planning attorney, but an estate planning attorney that specializes in planning for gay and lesbian couples.

If your estate, or the combined estate of you and your spouse, is currently equal to or more than the allowable exemption equivalent, you may wish to consider seeking the counsel of an estate planning attorney relatively soon. This is also the case if you anticipate your estate exceeding that level in the near future. However, when and if you do seek assistance, ask the attorney about including in your estate plan a **disclaimer trust** to allow your spouse or estate executor to do some after-death planning and legally refuse the amount of your property that may **overfund** his or her estate. It will save your ultimate estate beneficiaries a great deal of money in the long run.

In contrast to property left to your spouse, you do not need to be concerned about possibly overfunding a charity. If the charity is tax-qualified, it is a tax-exempt entity and will not pay any income or transfer taxes. You do need to take into account how best to take care of family members who have otherwise been disinherited because their portion of your estate went to a charity. In most states, your surviving spouse may elect against your will to take the portion of your estate that he or she normally would have been entitled to—usually half of all your property at death—but your children, siblings, and close friends are not permitted this election.

There are several ways to benefit or "re-inherit" your children or other disadvantaged heirs. The most popular is to buy a life insurance policy and name your children as the beneficiaries. If you buy this policy in the name of an irrevocable life insurance trust (ILIT), the death proceeds from the policy are removed from your gross estate for transfer tax purposes. Since the proceeds are paid from a life insurance policy, they are *not* taxable to your children or other beneficiary for income tax purposes. In estate planning terminology, setting up an ILIT in this manner, and for the reason of making up an inheritance otherwise lost to charity, is known as a **wealth replacement trust.**

For example, assume that, as an unmarried individual with two adult children, you wish to benefit the American Cancer Society (ACS) with the majority of your $5 million estate. You make a bequest in your will of $4 million to the ACS. At the time you write your will, you establish an ILIT and name your two adult children as the trust beneficiaries. You then have the ILIT purchase a $4 million life insurance policy on your life. Accordingly, you get the benefit of both the estate tax charitable deduction and accomplishing your philanthropic goals. Plus, you meet these objectives *without* disadvantaging your children, who would otherwise expect to be the beneficiaries of your estate.

THE UNINTENDED DANGER OF GENERATION-SKIPPING TRANSFERS

A number of high-net-worth individuals are unaware that there is actually a *third* transfer tax: a transfer tax on transfers that skip a generation and are instead gifted to a subsequent generation. A common example is a gift made by a grandparent to a grandchild. The additional transfer tax that is assessed on this transfer is known as the generation-skipping transfer tax (GSTT).

The rules with respect to skip transfers are very complex, but here is what you need to know to avoid the GSTT:

- The tax is designed to impose the equivalent of the gift or estate tax that the intervening generation (or the parent's generation) would have paid for the transfer.

- The tax is imposed *in addition to* either the estate or gift tax; thus, the tax can only add to an otherwise sizable transfer tax burden.
- The tax is assessed at the *maximum* estate tax rate in a flat rate at the time of a generation-skipping transfer (for example, in 2011 and 2012, a flat 35 percent rate applies to any generation-skipping transfer). There is no progressivity leading up to this maximum rate as there is with other lifetime or testamentary transfers.
- The tax potentially applies either to a gift made directly from grandparent to grandchild during lifetime (known as a direct skip) or at death via a trust, where the grandchild is benefited to the exclusion of the parent (otherwise referred to as a taxable termination or indirect skip).
- The tax potentially applies to a gift made from one unrelated individual (transferor) to another (transferee), where the transferee is at least thirty-seven and a half years younger than the transferor.
- The liability for paying the tax falls upon different individuals, depending on the type of generation-skipping transfer made.

Fortunately, most individuals can escape the payment of the tax—even if they do make a generation-skipping transfer—rather easily. This is because the transferor has a $5 million exemption (in 2011) that he or she can allocate to the transfer to avoid the imposition of the tax. This allowable exemption, to be used on an elective basis by the transferor or his or her estate, tracks the estate tax exemption equivalent previously discussed. Direct gifts to grandchildren that qualify for the gift tax annual exclusion ($13,000 in 2011) during the grandparent's lifetime are also not subject to the tax.

For example, in 2011, a grandfather makes a direct gift of $5,013,000 in appreciated stock to his adult granddaughter. If he *elects* to allocate his full $5 million generation-skipping exemption to the transfer (the $13,000 gift tax annual exclusion is automatic and does *not* need to be elected), there is no generation-skipping transfer tax imposed. However, be aware that the generation-skipping tax exemption amount, since it tracks the estate tax exemption equivalent, may only be $1 million, effective for generation-skipping transfers made in 2013 and thereafter. Also, not only may the generation-skipping-transfer tax apply to the direct gift, but so will the federal gift tax on any transfers made from a donor to a donee in excess of $13,000 annually.

In summary, the generation-skipping transfer tax may be easily avoided with a little planning. If your will or trust was drafted before 1987, when this tax came into effect, you should ask your estate planning attorney or financial planner to review it to see if the tax applies. If the tax does potentially apply, amend your will so as to *defend* your hard-earned wealth. If you are fortunate enough to avoid the imposition of the tax in your estate planning, just be aware that the generation-skipping transfer tax constitutes an unintended danger to the *accumulation* and *distribution* of wealth from one generation to the next.

CHAPTER 14

LIFE EVENTS THAT ENDANGER WEALTH

As we go through life, we sometimes experience events that endanger or threaten the amount of wealth that we have accumulated. Among these are divorce, the loss of a job for an extended period of time, unemployment while retraining to pursue a new career, the death of a spouse or life partner, a parent incurring a debilitating condition, caring for a developmentally disabled child, and physical or mental incapacity.

We have already discussed the importance of obtaining an individual disability income policy in the event of physical disability and will subsequently discuss how to plan for your own possible mental disability. In this chapter, we identify important planning considerations with respect to each of these six, potentially financially devastating life events.

Divorce

Statistics indicate that one of out of every two marriages ends in divorce or separation. Divorce is the legal ending of a marriage; separation does not end a marriage, but does involve the establishment of a separate and independent lifestyle. How do you financially make the best of (and hopefully recover) from divorce or separation?

Likely the first financial task that you, your attorney, or your financial planner should undertake—either before the divorce is finalized or immediately after property settlement—is to separate the assets and liabilities of you and your spouse. In other words, you will need to prepare new statements of personal financial position. Unlike before, when assets and liabilities could be listed as joint or individually owned on one statement, you will now potentially need to prepare *three* personal financial statements: his, hers, and ours. If you are in a community property state such as California or Texas, the division of assets and liabilities will be easier, since all marital property must be divided equally between spouses, but preparation of separate financial statements is still prudent divorce planning.

Once you have identified and reduced to writing your total assets and liabilities, you will need to prepare separate income or cash flow statements. This will assist you in determining whether temporary alimony or child support is possible before the divorce is finalized, as well as in establishing any future amounts that may need to be paid. As a general rule, many divorcing spouses (particularly women) do not fully understand how their living expenses will change after divorce. As a result, ex-spouses typically *underestimate* how much money they will need to sustain their pre-divorce standard of living. The notable exception to this rule is a celebrity divorce, where they typically *overestimate* their needs.

There are three basic provisions of most divorce or separation agreements that should be carefully considered by separating spouses:

1. the amount and necessity of alimony payments from one spouse to the other
2. the amount of child support payments, if there are minor children from the marriage
3. the division of property accumulated during the marriage (otherwise known as the property settlement agreement)

If the spouses own a home at the time of the divorce, attention should be given to how to divide equity in that important asset.

Alimony

Alimony, if it is to be paid, is often the most contentious aspect of any divorce. This is complicated by the fact that the payer of the alimony receives an income tax deduction for payments made, thereby encouraging him to allocate *as much* of the total payments to alimony as possible. To prevent this abuse, some years ago Congress added a provision to the Internal Revenue Code known as excess front-loading alimony rules, commonly referred to as alimony recapture. If violated, these rules make the payer go back and include in his or her income statement some portion of the alimony paid and deducted.

For example, assume that a husband made an alimony payment of $50,000 in the first year subsequent to a divorce and nothing thereafter. Under the alimony recapture rules, at the end of the third year after the divorce, the husband is required to file an amended income tax return and include a portion of the $50,000 first-year payment in his income. This excess payment is referred to as disguised alimony since, inevitably, the real intent of the payment was as part of a property settlement agreement between the husband and wife. This payment could also have been intended as child support, in the event that the couple had minor children at the time of the divorce.

The payee must include in her or his income any alimony paid by the payer. Although not technically income in the sense of salary or wages, alimony constitutes earned income as characterized by a traditional IRA contribution. This means that a stay-at-home ex-wife receiving alimony from her husband may contribute and deduct up to the specified annual amount for IRA savings and her own eventual retirement.

To qualify as tax-deductible alimony, payments stipulated in the divorce or separation agreement cannot be designated as something other than alimony (such as child support, for example). The payments cannot be scheduled to continue after the death of the payee spouse and must be made in cash or its equivalent. For example, transferring appreciated securities to an ex-spouse does

235

not constitute alimony. However, payments made to a third party on behalf of the payee—such as life insurance premiums payable on the life of the payer—*do* constitute alimony.

For example, assume that a wife receives a sizable alimony award as a result of her divorce from her physically ailing husband. She is very concerned about how these alimony payments will be made if her husband predeceases her. Accordingly, as a part of the divorce decree, she mandates that the husband continue his premium payments on his life insurance policy and retain her as the irrevocable beneficiary. These premium payments constitute qualifying, deductible alimony for income tax purposes.

In this example, what happens if the husband *fails* to make the premium payments on his life insurance policy, leaving the wife without income protection? The husband may be held to be in contempt of court and punished with jail time. This complicates the wife's situation even further, though, since if the husband is in jail, it is extremely unlikely that he will resume making life insurance premium payments. There is a better way.

As a planning technique, always have the *wife* own the life insurance policy and make the premium payments. This prevents changes from being made to the policy without her knowledge. Second, if the wife can afford it, have her buy life insurance that can build cash value on the life of the husband (for example, a whole life, universal life, variable life, or variable/universal life policy). The cash account within this policy is now hers to do with as she pleases, including borrowing against the policy for her own retirement. If any *new* life insurance is needed as a result of her changed financial circumstances after the divorce, the wife should apply for the insurance *before* the divorce is final. Then, if the husband cannot qualify for the life insurance (for example, because of poor health), the wife may still modify the final divorce decree to make up for the loss of the insurance proceeds.

Child Support

Each state has applicable guidelines with respect to the amount of child support that may be appropriate in any divorce agreement.

If you are working with a divorce attorney or financial planner, they will be familiar with these guidelines. But as with any cash flow issue, be sure that you, as the payer, can afford the minimum recommended payment. For most divorcing individuals, the question is not whether child support should be paid, but rather how much, so be sure you are comfortable with the amount specified by the court. And pay it! Although it is against the law for an employer to fire you because you are not current with child support, there is no prohibition against garnishing your wages to pay back-due amounts. If this happens, the employer may use other reasons to terminate your employment, notwithstanding that the real reason was your failure to assume the parental responsibility of supporting your children.

Child support payments are neither deductible by the payer spouse nor taxable as income to the payee spouse. However, sometimes there is a question as to whether a payment is, indeed, child support or is disguised alimony. Here is the standard rule that will permit you to tell the difference: if *any* portion of the agreed-upon payment may be reduced because of circumstances related to the child, *it is child support* for income tax purposes. For example, if the payment is reduced once the child goes to college, it is treated as nondeductible and nontaxable child support. This characterization is likely very important to high-income divorcing couples, where the higher wage earner wants as much of the payment treated as deductible alimony as possible. This is in marked contrast to a lower income earner, who is likely not nearly so concerned with the tax treatment of the payment.

Property Settlements

The overriding issue in finalizing a property settlement agreement is to be fair to both spouses. In **community property** states, where both spouses own a half of an immediate interest in all property acquired during the marriage, an equal division is relatively easy. The notable exception is where one spouse brings an already thriving small business to the marriage, but at the time of the couple's divorce or legal separation, the business is worth considerably more. The question then arises: how is the appreciation of the business during the couple's marriage best handled? The answer varies depending on state community property law, but generally, the founder-of-the-business spouse is awarded the value of the business at the time he or she brought it to the marriage, and then half of the appreciation in the business thereafter. The non-founder spouse receives the other half of the appreciation.

Assume that you live in California and have recently started a computer software business. It is worth $1 million when you marry your spouse. Eight years later, you are divorced. At the time of your divorce, the business is worth $10 million. It is likely that the court would award you a settlement of $5.5 million with respect to the business—your original $1 million in the business when you were married and another $4.5 million worth of appreciation. You now have to come up with another $4.5 million to buy out your spouse's interest or sell the business entirely to make the required payment. (Can you see why divorce can be financially devastating to your accumulated wealth?)

There are currently eight community property states in the United States and a ninth—Wisconsin—has a very similar form of property law known as marital property. The two largest community property states—California and Texas—are relatively well-known to most Americans. The other six states with community property law systems are:

- Louisiana
- New Mexico
- Arizona
- Nevada
- Washington
- Idaho

The state of Alaska allows for the establishment of community property among married couples on an elective basis.

All of the remaining states (forty-one, after accounting for Wisconsin's variation of the community property form) are referred to in property law as **common law property** or *individual property* states. This means that either the husband or wife (even with property acquired *during* the marriage) can title property in his or her *individual* name. However, for those who think this may be advantage when it comes to making an inordinate or unequal division of property at the time of divorce, think again. Most—if not all—common-law property states follow a concept in property settlements known as equitable distribution. Under this concept, each spouse has a legal right during marriage to the other spouse's earnings and to the assets acquired with those earnings. As a result, common-law states end up in essentially the same place as community property states with respect to property acquired during the marriage: it is typically split in half each between the spouses at the time of divorce or separation.

Often, the most contentious part of property settlement negotiations is how to fairly divide one spouse's present or future retirement benefits. Accordingly, if this issue pertains to you, you should obtain a valuation of your (or your spouse's) current 401(k) or other retirement plan balance at the time of divorce. Once you have this valuation, make sure, if you are the payee spouse, that you obtain what is known as a Qualified Domestic Relations Order (QDRO) from the court. This order will award you the same rights that the plan participant would have had under the 401(k) or other retirement plan, including the right to choose your own investments.

As a divorcing spouse, you can receive current or future Social Security benefits based on your former spouse's employment record if the following conditions are met:

- You were married to your former spouse for at least ten years.
- You are at least sixty years old.
- Your former spouse is at least sixty-two years old.

Note that if you remarry *after* you have attained the age of sixty, it does not prevent or terminate your eligibility for Social Security benefits based on your former spouse's employment record. If you remarried before age sixty, you are not forever precluded from receiving Social Security benefits based on the employment record of your ex-spouse, although benefits are not payable unless and until your current marriage ends.

Principal Residence

Typically, the major asset that most couples own at the time of divorce is their house or primary residence. Since most couples are jointly obligated on the home mortgage, half of each mortgage payment may qualify as deductible alimony by the departing spouse. The other half of the mortgage payment is deductible by the remaining spouse under normal mortgage interest deduction rules; in other words, the remaining spouse should itemize his or her deductions on a separately filed return. Proceed carefully. Remember, under the alimony tax rules, any payment that constitutes deductible alimony may *not* be said to be anything other than alimony. Therefore, if you are the departing spouse and will be responsible for half the mortgage, add a sufficient amount to your required alimony payments to cover your portion of the monthly mortgage interest liability.

For example, assume that you and your wife are getting a divorce. You have agreed to pay her alimony of $3,000 per month. Your mortgage payment per month is $1,000, of which $600 is interest. You will remain obligated for your half of the mortgage payment. As such, add or re-characterize half—or $300—of the mortgage interest payment as deductible alimony, resulting in a total alimony payment of $3,300 per month (the $3,000 original amount plus the additional $300 re-characterized amount).

It gets even more complicated if you, as the departing spouse, are *solely* responsible for the mortgage payment. Although you are considered to have paid all the monthly interest on the mortgage, it does not mean you are necessarily entitled to the full itemized interest deduction. Rather, once you have moved out of the house, the house is no longer your *primary* residence (which, as we know from chapter 11, can have serious tax implications if your ex-spouse sells the house immediately or if you did not live in it for at least two years before she sold it). You may be able to claim the house as a *secondary* residence and deduct the mortgage interest in that manner. The catch in this strategy is that you must let your ex-spouse remain in the primary residence rent-free.

In summary, if you are involved in a divorce, do *not* try to represent yourself. The potential damaging consequences to your accumulated wealth are much too significant to forego seeking the assistance of competent legal and financial counsel.

LOSS OF EMPLOYMENT

Beyond the major psychological trauma of losing your job, particularly if you were terminated "for cause," are the financial aspects that should be considered. Chief among these is how to immediately reduce your ongoing expenses of living. For example, if you have not done so already, consider refinancing your current mortgage to obtain a lower interest rate. Although refinancing will extend the life of the mortgage obligation, your monthly payment will be reduced. Refinancing usually frees up cash that can be used for any reason, including the payment of living expenses until new employment can be found.

Another key issue involved in managing job loss is the reevaluation of your and your family's health insurance needs. As discussed earlier, remember that you can exercise your COBRA rights. Upon losing your job, you will have to pay your previous employer's share of the group medical insurance, but this is likely much less expensive than purchasing an individual policy. Alternatively, cost savings may result from funding a health savings account (HSA) and purchasing a high-deductible individual health insurance policy. Under current tax rules, as a former employee, you may also take distributions from your IRA to pay health insurance premiums while unemployed *without* being subject to a 10 percent early distribution penalty. However, unless it is a Roth IRA owned for a specified period of time, you will have to pay ordinary income tax on the distribution.

Should you file for unemployment benefits once you have lost your job? There are several considerations here. The first is psychological: do you feel embarrassed or are you reluctant to file? Many workers, particularly those who have been terminated from a management position, simply cannot bear to file for unemployment benefits. Nevertheless, you should be aware that, in most cases, unemployment is available *regardless* of the position you left and your job status at your former employer. Your former employer has paid a tax under the Federal Employment Tax Act (FUTA) for just this reason.

The second consideration with respect to unemployment benefits is a more practical one: are you eligible to receive benefits? It depends on why you left your former employer. Assuming that you had earned enough money to qualify for unemployment benefits during the previous twelve-month period, you must, then, have left your job for one or more of the following reasons:

- You were terminated (laid off) through no fault of your own
- You voluntarily quit your job for good reason.
- You were involuntarily terminated, but not because of embezzlement, violating the company's drug policy, or anything else unrelated to poor job performance.

The biggest uncertainty in any of these reasons is what constitutes "good reason" for you to voluntarily leave your job? Unfortunately, you do not get to make this determination; your local unemployment agency caseworker does (sometimes along with your former supervisor). As a result, if you left your job voluntarily and file for unemployment benefits, carefully document in writing why you left before speaking with your caseworker and justify that it was for reasons unrelated to personal preference.

DEATH OF A SPOUSE OR LIFE PARTNER

Like job loss, there are psychological and financial issues associated with the premature death of a spouse or life partner. Unlike job loss, however, assuming that the life of the spouse or partner is adequately insured, the psychological aspects of overcoming the loss are probably paramount.

Nonetheless, countless financial questions confront the survivor of the spouse or partner, including

- Do I pay off or pay down the mortgage now while remaining in the house?
- Do I sell the house and move?
- If I am not retired, do I retire now (or as soon as financially possible)?
- Do I continue to work?
- Am I entitled to a retirement or life insurance benefit?
- How do I distribute any retirement or life insurance benefit to which I am entitled?
- Can I afford to live the same lifestyle to which I am accustomed?
- Should I seek the assistance of a financial advisor?

None of these questions is easy to answer, particularly during the grieving process, but they need to be addressed sooner rather than later to avoid damage to your joint lifetime wealth.

Not only is the surviving spouse or life partner the beneficiary of all or most of a decedent's estate, he or she is also often the named executor or administrator of that estate. Legally, the difference between an executor and administrator depends on whether the decedent dies with or without a will. If the decedent dies after having written a will (or dies testate), the individual named to handle the decedent's financial affairs is referred to as the executor. If the decedent dies without a will (or dies intestate), the individual appointed by the court to handle the decedent's financial affairs is said to be the administrator of the estate. Regardless, if the spouse or partner survives, he or she is normally the named executor or appointed administrator.

This raises the question of whether the surviving spouse, as the named executor or administrator, should take a fee for the rendering of services. Under the probate code of most states, the surviving spouse is entitled to such a fee, but he or she should consider the usual circumstances of most estates. In most circumstances, the surviving spouse or executor is also the primary (if not sole) beneficiary of the deceased spouse's property. Under federal transfer tax, property that is inherited by the spouse or any other beneficiary is *not* income taxable. However, if the surviving spouse or executor collects a fee for administration services associated with the estate, that fee *is* income-taxable. As a result, the surviving spouse has now converted nontaxable income into taxable income. The better option is for the executor to receive all (or his or her share) of the decedent's property at death in the form of an inheritance and *not* reduce this amount by an after-tax payment of executor fees.

As will be discussed further in the *distributing* your wealth section of the book, whether a court gets involved in administering your estate depends on whether your estate goes through *probate*. Probate is a legal proceeding administered by the local court to verify title to a decedent's assets and distribute them to his or her heirs at death.

A great number of individuals do not like the potential costs and delay in distributing the decedent's property inherent in the probate process and search for ways to plan around the process. There are three primary means of doing this:

1. Title all your assets jointly (in joint tenancy with right of survivorship) with someone else, such as your spouse or life partner.
2. Use beneficiary designations on as many assets as are permitted by law.
3. Establish and transfer as many assets as you can during lifetime into a revocable living trust.

Titling Assets Jointly

Titling all your assets in joint tenancy with right of survivorship (JTWROS) with someone else is sometimes referred to as the poor man's way of avoiding probate, since it does not involve the drafting of a trust or acquiring any other assets where a beneficiary designation is possible, such as a life insurance policy. Typically, only spouses title assets jointly, although such titling is heavily used by same-sex domestic partners in states where the marital relationship is not legally recognized.

Joint tenancy titling may be both a blessing and a curse. It provides an easy way to dispose of property at death while avoiding probate, but it can be relatively inflexible from a transfer tax standpoint. Specifically, if a surviving spouse already has significant property of his or her own, leaving even more property to him or her by operation of law is only going to add to an already existing taxable estate. Fortunately, under current tax law, it is possible for a surviving spouse (or other surviving joint tenant) to refuse, or disclaim, the receipt of this additional property. However, the survivor must do so within nine months of the decedent's death and in a certain manner, or the survivor will be considered to have made a subsequent gift to whoever receives the property in his or her stead.

For example, assume that you are a joint tenant at your death with your already wealthy spouse. To avoid potential additional estate taxes at her death, your spouse should refuse the property within nine months of your death by making a qualified disclaimer. She must do this *before* accepting any benefits from the disclaimed property and *without* separately directing to whom your property should now pass. If you have children, under state law, they will normally receive any disclaimed property. If you do not have children, your closest blood relative (or relatives) will receive the property.

Using Beneficiary Designations

Beneficiary designations are typically used to leave property by contract at the death of the owner. Common examples of assets where beneficiary designations are used are life insurance policies, employer-sponsored retirement plans such as 401(k) plans, and IRAs.

It is also possible to use a beneficiary designation to avoid probate on brokerage or advisory accounts. While there may be few or no assets to pass in this manner, given that during lifetime, you should access these taxable accounts *before* accessing any tax-deferred accounts, you can avoid the probate process by asking your broker or financial advisor for a transfer-on-death (TOD) form. Fill that form out for each of your brokerage or advisory accounts and ask that it be sent back to the broker-dealer with whom you established the account. If you are investing online, ask whatever company or mutual fund family you are investing with to send you the comparable form. By proceeding in this manner, you should be able to avoid the probate process on those particular assets in the state of residence where your estate is potentially subject to court administration.

Establishing and Funding a Revocable Living Trust

As discussed, revocable living trusts are frequently promoted for several reasons, but the most prevalent is their ability to avoid probate. Be careful: many grantors or creators of revocable living trusts believe that all that is necessary to avoid probate is to purchase the trust document from the promoter. *This is not correct.* Rather, to avoid probate, your assets must be transferred into the name of the trust before your death and while you are still legally competent to know the ramifications of that action. If the assets (or any assets you may have acquired after establishing the trust) are not in the name of the trustee of the trust at your death, they will *not* avoid probate.

If you are electing to establish and pass all your assets via a revocable living trust outside of probate, *you must fund the trust during your lifetime.* Alternatively, if you are not concerned about the delay or cost of probate, you can use the trust only to distribute your assets in a transfer-tax-efficient manner subsequent to your death. As a third option, you may elect to pass all your property using joint tenancy titling or beneficiary designations and use the trust only as a standby document in the event that you become mentally incompetent during your lifetime.

For example, assume that you and your spouse own most of your property jointly, including your house, checking and savings accounts, and investment accounts. In addition, your retirement plans and life insurance policies name your spouse as the primary beneficiary and you are not concerned about having your estate or that of your spouse subject to transfer tax at death. As such, you establish a revocable living trust to standby and be used to manage your assets only in the event of your own mental incapacity. If this event occurs, you name your spouse as the successor trustee and, if he or she is not able to serve in such capacity, your favorite brother. Since you are legally incompetent at the onset of your mental incapacity, you must also give your spouse a durable power of attorney to transfer property to the trust and avoid probate. (Durable powers of attorney are discussed later in this chapter.)

Now let's proceed to a very common issue confronting many members of the baby boomer generation: how to pay for the long-term care expenses of a dependent parent.

DEPENDENT PARENTS

Certainly, there are more issues involved in caring for dependent parents than paying for their long-term care expenses. (Long-term care is defined as daily care provided in a nursing home for a chronic medical condition.) Nevertheless, the payment of the ongoing expenses of a parent who cannot live by him- or herself independently or for whom you, as a concerned child, cannot care for properly is a significant threat to your accumulated wealth. This is not to mention the additional emotional burden that taking care of a formerly able-bodied and responsible parent entails.

As you know from the previous discussion of Medicare and Medicaid, Medicare has only a *limited* benefit for skilled nursing facility care and, while Medicaid does cover long-term care, qualification requirements are extremely difficult. As such, you are faced with the following options:

1. The best option is that your parent or parents are financially educated enough to recognize the need for long-term care insurance and have previously purchased a policy. Unfortunately, many seniors do not recognize this need before they can no longer qualify for the coverage or the protection is so prohibitively expensive that they cannot afford it.

2. The next best option, if your parents are likely to need long-term care but are unable to pay for the cost of the insurance themselves, is for *you* to buy the policy for them. The risk of this approach is that your parents may never need long-term care and the expended premium dollars are now lost forever.

3. A close alternative to the above option is that you set aside money to pay for your parents' long-term care needs. This option gives you more flexibility since you do not lose the money if your parents do not need long-term care, but it means an added monthly or other periodic expense for which you need to budget.

4. The *least* best option is that you do nothing and have the need for long-term care for your parents arise. In this instance, you are likely to see the wealth your parents accumulated slowly depleted over the years, at the end of which Medicaid is the only option.

As noted, the preferable option is that your parent does not place the burden of funding their long-term care on you, but if they do, you should purchase a long-term care insurance policy for your parent while he or she can still qualify for the coverage. You will also need to consider how long an insurance benefit period you should purchase. Remember, the *longer* the benefit period, the *greater* the premium costs associated with the policy.

You may wish to purchase a lifetime benefit period for your parent to be absolutely sure that proper long-term care will be there for them when they need it. You may also wish to purchase a higher-than-normal daily benefit as a part of the policy (currently, the average cost of nursing home care is approximately $200 per day). If you do purchase a high daily benefit (beyond the average $200 per day), it is possible that you can *make* money from the policy. Before you do purchase such a high benefit, check with the insurance company or issuer of the policy since such a motivation may be frowned upon in your particular state.

You also need to consider what Medicare will and will not cover once your parent reaches age sixty-five. Beginning in 2006, Part D of Medicare was fully phased in and now covers the cost of most prescription drugs for your elderly parent, but a privately owned policy may provide better coverage. There are many deductibles and co-insurance payments associated with Medicare Part A (hospital insurance) and Medicare Part B (physician's care). The preferable way to cover these costs is to purchase a supplementary health insurance policy, commonly referred to as a Medigap policy. All Medigap policies are standardized according to federal law, with Medigap Policy A constituting the least expensive and least comprehensive form of coverage, and Medigap Policy J historically constituting the most expensive and most comprehensive. This also means that you or your parent is protected by federal regulation with respect to supplementary medical care, a fact that may be of some comfort to you.

It is also important to note that you may purchase only *one* Medigap policy for your parent at any one time under current law and that your parent may not be turned down for supplemental coverage regardless of any preexisting, potentially disqualifying medical conditions so long as he or she applies for such coverage within six months of reaching age sixty-five.

Claiming Your Parent as a Dependent for Income Tax Purposes

To claim your parent as a dependent for income tax purposes, all of the following tests must be met:

- You must pay for more than half of the financial expenses of your parent for the tax (calendar) year.
- Your parent must not have gross income of more than the annual personal dependency exemption provided for under law (this amount was $3,700 in 2011).
- Your parent, if married, cannot file a joint income tax return with his or her spouse unless the only reason he or she files the return is to obtain a tax refund.
- Your parent must not have claimed a personal exemption individually.
- Your parent must be a U.S. citizen or resident.

Assuming all of these tests are met, you may claim an income tax credit for taking care of your dependent parent of up to $600 annually ($1,200 annually for two dependent parents). The applicable credit equals 35 percent of expenses to a maximum of $3,000 if your AGI is $15,000 or less and is reduced 1 percent for each $2,000 of AGI up to $28,000. The credit is then limited to 20 percent of expenses if your AGI is more than $43,000. Thus, an individual with an AGI over $43,000 may take a credit of $600 ($3,000 times 0.20) for one qualifying parent and $1,200 ($600 times 2) for two qualifying parents.

As a planning technique, if your parent has a small amount of investments that are currently generating income in excess of the annual personal dependency exemption, have your parent use up these investment assets *first* to pay for their support for a short period of time. Depleting those investments should subsequently *lower* your parent's income in the future so that when you pay for his or her expenses, including any necessary long-term care expenses, you will be able to receive a tax benefit through the claiming of the dependent care credit.

For example, assume that your mother, age sixty, has investments in bank certificates of deposit of $80,000 in 2011 that are paying her a 5 percent annual interest rate. This is the only income your mother has since she is not yet eligible to receive Social Security benefits. Because the income of $4,000 ($80,000 times 0.05) is more than the personal dependency exemption permitted for the year ($3,700), consider having your mother *cash in* the CDs and use the proceeds for her living expenses for the remainder of the year. Then, in 2012, you will be able to claim the dependent care credit on your 2011 income tax return, assuming that the other qualifying dependency tests are met for that year.

A DEVELOPMENTALLY DISABLED CHILD

A developmentally disabled child presents special challenges in wealth accumulation and management. Specifically, what is the optimal way to pay for the tremendous expenses associated with raising a developmentally disabled child to independence?

The numerous planning techniques that may be used cannot be fully explained here, but certainly a very prevalent strategy is to establish a **special needs trust** for the benefit of the child. To properly establish and maintain such a trust, the child must first meet the Social Security definition of disability, even though, typically, public assistance benefits are paid at the state or local level rather than from the federal government.

The purpose of the special needs trust is to allow the child to maintain eligibility for certain public assistance benefits, such as Supplemental Security Income (SSI) or Medicaid, while at the same time providing for needed services that are not available from the government. The trust document must state that the trust income and principal are to be used *only* to provide for extra services required to care for, maintain, and educate the child beyond those government-provided benefits. If it does not state this or include similar language, the state may attach the assets transferred to the trust to pay for its cost of providing required care.

At a minimum, if you are the parent of a developmentally disabled child, you should consider the implementation of a special needs trust. But beyond that, you need to consider who will care for the child in the event of your or your spouse's death or incompetency. Under law, parents are the natural guardians of their child only until the child reaches age eighteen or the otherwise-specified state age of legal majority. Hence, if your handicapped child needs care after the age of eighteen, you may wish to seek court appointment as your child's legal guardian. Further, in the event of your death or incompetency, you may wish to have your spouse succeed you in this capacity. In your will, you should provide for the naming of a guardian, likely first your spouse, and in the event of a joint death, a willing and competent family member or members. If you fail to do so, the court will normally appoint a guardian for your child, but you will have no say with respect to who this person is or where your child will live subsequent to your death.

The need for the implementation of a contingent family trust is important in all cases where a minor child may be left without his or her natural parents, but it is even more important where one or more children is developmentally disabled. Likely, the guardian named for your child and the trustee of the contingent family trust will be the same individual, but you should give careful consideration to the different skill sets required for each duty. A *guardian* needs to possess considerable empathy and compassion for your disabled child's ongoing needs, whereas a *trustee* needs to have some financial acumen. Just because a family member may have one set of these skills does not mean that they have the other. Moreover, while your first thought may be that your parent (the child's grandparent) is the perfect choice, do you think it is fair to ask your parent to take on a second family, particularly one involving a handicapped child, so late in his or her life? Only you can gauge the correctness of this situation, but do not overlook considering it.

YOUR OWN PHYSICAL OR MENTAL INCAPACITY

The terms *disability* and *incapacity* are frequently used interchangeably, but there is a difference. Disability refers to a *contractual* status, whereas incapacity is a *legal* status. For example, you are typically disabled if a contract definition, such as that included in a disability income insurance policy, says you are. However, you are incapacitated or incompetent to act only if the *law* says you are. An example of a legally incapacitated person is a minor or child who has not yet reached the age of legal majority. Such a child cannot take legal title to property and can only execute what is known as a voidable contract, meaning that once he or she is eighteen (or the state's legal age of majority), he or she can revoke the terms of any contract that was previously signed. For this reason, financial and other institutions often require a parent's co-signature on any contract entered into with a minor.

Another common form of legal incapacity is an individual who suffers from Alzheimer's disease. Such an individual may be physically fine, at least after the initial diagnosis is made, but mentally does *not* have the legal capacity to act. As such, someone must act on his or her behalf. Typically, this surrogate is a close family member (usually the spouse) who has been granted power of attorney by the Alzheimer's patient while still competent. This leads to a very important point in planning for your own or your parent's possible legal incapacity: *the power of attorney must be executed while the author (or principal) is still legally competent.* How do you determine this? Usually, it is done by asking the author's primary physician to render an oral or written opinion that the author is legally competent at the time of granting the power. Absent a positive affirmation from a physician, or if a power of attorney is never completed, the family must ask the local court to have someone appointed as the legal guardian of their incapacitated loved one.

Is one type of power of attorney preferable to another? Yes. In all cases, you should seek to execute a **durable** power-of-attorney form. Under the property law of every state, the principal's authority to grant someone else the right to act on his or her behalf *terminates* at the date the principal becomes legally incapacitated (for example, becomes so severely demented that the consequences of his or her actions are not readily understood). Practically, when the principal most needs his or her power of attorney (or agent) to act, the power of attorney is legally prohibited from doing so. The legal document that avoids this consequence is a durable power of attorney, which specifically includes in its language that the power of the agent to act continues *even after* the principal is declared legally incompetent. Again, if this language is not included in the power of attorney form, family members will be forced to request court intervention.

If you execute a durable power-of-attorney form for yourself or your parent, you have a choice with respect to the date that you request your agent to act on your behalf. You can grant the agent the right to act immediately (a non-springing durable power of attorney) or postpone this right until you, the principal, are declared legally incompetent (a springing durable power of attorney). While many authors or principals are concerned about giving someone else the ability to act immediately with respect to their financial affairs, as a practical matter, the agent named is almost always a close family member. Typically, if you are married at the time of executing the power, your spouse is named as the agent. Many authors draft a non-springing durable power and continue conducting their own affairs as if the power was never granted. This avoids the inherent problem presented in the drafting of any springing durable power where someone (usually, the concurring opinion of two physicians) must determine *when* you have become legally incompetent.

While you will want to execute a durable power of attorney to plan for your own possible legal incapacity, there is often a practical problem with third-party acceptance of the document. This is particularly the case with financial institutions that either:

(a) want you to execute their own durable power-of-attorney form, or (b) refuse to recognize an outdated form. As a result, you should adopt the following two measures:

1. Have an attorney draft the *broadest* possible durable power-of-attorney form in the hope that all conceivable actions that the financial institution may require of your agent are covered by the power.
2. Periodically (every three years or so) *re-execute* the durable power-of-attorney signature page; this will ensure that the form is executed while you are still legally competent to grant the power.

Most states provide for the execution of *two* durable power-of-attorney forms: a general durable power-of-attorney form for *property* or financial management and a *medical* or health care durable power-of-attorney form. This second form is intended for you to grant authority to an agent (again, usually a close family member) to give informed consent to any needed medical procedure on your behalf if you are unable to do so. Some states also allow the inclusion of living will provisions in the medical durable power-of-attorney form, while others require two separate documents. However, of the two documents (living will and medical durable power-of-attorney), the medical durable power is likely the *more important* since it is much broader and covers additional health care situations in which terminal illness is not the diagnosis.

A sample general durable power-of-attorney form is included in appendix C. You may wish to adopt or discuss adopting it with your attorney.

SECTION V

DISTRIBUTING WEALTH DURING YOUR LIFETIME

CHAPTER 15

PLANNING FOR YOUR CHILD'S HIGHER EDUCATION

We now move to the last step in the PADD process of wealth accumulation and management: *distributing* your wealth. This section focuses on the distribution of wealth during your lifetime and considers the common financial planning goals of saving and planning for your child's higher education, for retirement, and for other lifetime financial goals such as starting your own business. The next and last section of the book and the PADD process takes up the distribution of your wealth at *death*.

When evaluating how to distribute wealth during lifetime, if you are married and have children, one of your first goals is probably to afford them the best opportunity at a profitable career—and that requires, at a minimum these days, a college degree. There are many colleges and universities, public and private, that they may attend and the costs of attendance will vary dramatically based on their eventual choice. The common thread to whatever choice they make will be that the cost of college is *expensive*—and getting more expensive by the year. According to the **College Board**, over the ten-year period ending 2005–2006, tuition at public four-year institutions increased by an average of 6.9 percent a year nationally (tuition increases at private four-year institutions averaged 5.7 percent a year nationally over the same period). This compared to an average annual inflation rate of only 2.5 percent over the same period. For school year 2010–2011, the total annual cost of public college or university for an in-state student was approximately $20,000 ($32,000 for an out-of-state student) and close to $50,000 at a private institution.

Fortunately, the availability of financial aid increased during the same ten-year period, although most of this aid is based on financial need, with the amount necessary to qualify decided by the school and other factors beyond the control of the average middle-class parent. The need to plan for your child's higher education as early as possible is very important.

How Much Will I Need?

As with any financial planning goal that may be quantified, the first question to be answered with respect to planning for your child's higher education is that of how much money you will need.

The answer depends on several factors, including how many children you have and whether you wish them to attend public or private colleges or universities. In 2011, private-college Ivy League institutions such as Harvard and Yale are among the most expensive to attend, with tuition, fees, and room and board costs averaging at least $50,000 per year. Private liberal arts schools throughout the country are not far behind in cost. The cost of attendance at public schools varies greatly, but for planning purposes, using half of the private-school amount—or $25,000 annually—is not unreasonable.

The first step in computing the cost of your child's education is to inflate, or calculate in today's dollars, what the current cost of attendance—say, $25,000 annually—will be when your child is ready to attend college. To do this, we need to assume an annual increase in costs of a certain amount—say, 7 percent annually (this is very close to the current ten-year average increase). We can input these numbers into a web-based calculator (at http://money.aol. com, for example) or we can enter them on a financial function calculator. Here is an example using the Hewlett-Packard 10BII financial function calculator:

1. Enter $25,000 as the present value (PV). Note: With this calculator, you need to enter this amount as a negative number so the calculator can distinguish between the present value amount you are entering and the future value amount (FV) for which you are solving.
2. Enter 7 as the projected annual percentage increase (I/YR).
3. Enter the number of years (N) until your child enters college; for instance, if your child is ten years of age, enter eight, since age eighteen is the typical age for beginning college.
4. Solve for the future value (FV) of the cost of one year of attendance: Here, this would be $49,178 per year.

Once this is complete, you need to determine the present value of the total sum that will be required to fund your child's college education for his or her estimated four years of attendance. Assuming you want to do this computation on a financial function calculator, the steps are as follows:

1. Shift your calculator into BEGIN mode (you will need the money at the *beginning* of the period when your child enters college at age eighteen).
2. Enter $49,178 as a payment (PMT). Note: You may need to enter this amount as a negative number depending on what calculator you are using.
3. Enter four as the number of years (N) of college attendance.
4. Enter an inflation-adjusted annual rate of return (I/YR) on the monies set aside to fund the education; for example, if you believe you can make a 10 percent annual before-tax rate of return on your investments, the number you would enter would be 2.8037 (or 1.10 divided by 1.07 less 1 times 100).
5. Solve for the present value or lump-sum amount needed to pay for the cost of a four-year college education in today's dollars. Using our assumed numbers, this is $188,810.

The third and final step (after you've picked yourself up off the floor!) is to determine the amount of annual savings that is required to accumulate a lump sum of $188,810. The steps are as follows, assuming that you intend to save on a *monthly* basis:

1. Enter $188,810 as a future value amount, since you are solving for the amount of monthly payment needed today, while the child is ten years old.
2. Multiply eight years by twelve months (96) for the payments that you need to make over the period you are saving. Enter this as N.
3. Divide the 10 percent annual assumed before-tax rate of return by twelve to convert to a monthly rate and enter this as I/YR (here, 0.8333).
4. Solve for the monthly payment or savings amount needed—$1,280.96 per month ($1,291.64 if you do not save this amount until the end of each month). This translates into a one-time lump-sum deposit of $85,122.20.

A word of caution as you consider the challenge before you: many people (probably most) do not have the financial resources to achieve this amount of money quickly. The important point is *not* to focus on the *end* of the process, but rather the *beginning*. In other words, begin to save *some amount*, even if it is not the amount that you *should* be saving. Likely, the worst planning alternative is to *do nothing*, since you will quickly find other ways to spend the required savings. As part of the pay yourself first savings strategy, at least do what you can to provide for your child's college education.

Our next concern relates to whose name you should use to save for this education: your child's or your own?

In Whose Name Do I Save?

Before you begin to save for higher education, you need to consider whether your child is likely to qualify for federal financial aid. As you ponder this issue, ask yourself the following questions:

1. What is likely to be your income at the time that the child enters college or, more precisely, when you complete the Free Application for Student Aid (FAFSA) form in the second semester of your child's junior year of high school? Most federal financial aid is need-based and, if the child's parent makes *too much* money, he or she is unlikely to qualify for the aid.
2. Do you believe it is your responsibility or financial obligation to provide the child with a college education? Do you expect the child to assist financially or cover the complete cost of attendance?
3. Do you anticipate that your child will receive an academic or athletic scholarship to cover the cost of college attendance? Be realistic: we all believe our child is uniquely talented; more realistically, this is probably not the case.
4. Do you have relatives or family members such as grandparents who have offered—or expect to offer— financial assistance to the child when he or she goes to college?

Fundamentally, you may be somewhat ambivalent about whether your child attends college or pursues higher education, but remember this: studies have shown that a college graduate will earn in excess of a *million dollars* more than individuals who only receive a high school diploma.

In whose name should you save for college? This is a critical concern if you anticipate that your child will need financial assistance to cover the cost of college attendance. For example, as you complete the mandatory FAFSA form, it will ask you to list your assets and income as well as those of the child. This is necessary so that the federal government can determine an amount of expected family contribution (EFC) toward the cost of college attendance. If your child needs financial aid, you want this contribution to be *as low as possible.* Accordingly, you will want to know the formula that the federal government uses to compute the amount that the family is expected to contribute. The current FAFSA form can be found at www.fafsa.ed.gov.

The most critical component of this formula is the fair market value of the assets that are held in the name of the child versus that of the parent. In other words, what percentage of these assets is expected to be contributed to the cost of a college education and is therefore counted *against* the family in the formula? The answer is 35 percent for the child and less than 6 percent (5.64 percent, to be exact) for the parent. Just from this entry into the formula alone, it is generally much more advantageous to save for college *in the name of the parent* rather than the child. The most predominant example of saving in the name of the parent is a **Section 529 private savings plan**; the most prevalent example of saving in the name of the child is a **custodial account,** such as the Uniform Gifts to Minors or the Uniform Transfers to Minors accounts.

There are other savings strategies that may reap dividends when saving for college. They are as follows:

1. Spend down the student's assets *first.* This may easily be understood when recognizing the disparity in countable children's assets (35 percent) versus parental assets (approximately 6 percent).
2. Maximize contributions to your retirement fund. Whereas annual contributions to your 401(k) (or other) retirement plan are included in the computation of countable parental income, the vested account balance in a retirement plan is *not* counted among available parental assets that may be used to help pay for college costs.
3. If you are going to borrow to help fund the cost of your child's college attendance, do so through a home equity loan or line of credit. As discussed in chapter X 12, this type of borrowing also gives you a tax deduction for the interest you pay on the loan.

4. Pay off as much of your credit card and other unsecured debt as possible before filing the FAFSA. This will *reduce* the amount of cash or other assets that you must list and will be counted against you when applying for federal financial aid on behalf of your child.

5. Try to pay down your original mortgage as much as possible before applying. This yields two benefits: (a) it can free up cash flow that you may need to fund your child's college education, and (b) the amount of equity in your home is not included among parental assets when computing the expected family contribution.

To determine the amount of assistance required, most publicly funded college financial aid offices use a formula determined by the federal government known as the federal methodology. This formula does *not* consider the value of a family's home in arriving at the **expected formula contribution (EFC)**.

Some private colleges or universities use a formula known as the institutional methodology when computing the EFC. In this formula, the amount of equity in your home is *added back* (and is thus counted against you). You will know that the school is using the institutional methodology if it asks you to file the CSS/Financial Aid PROFILE along with the more exhaustive FAFSA form. Unlike the information requested on the FAFSA, the PROFILE form requires the parent's expected income during the child's college years and not just your current or past year's income.

As a parent, be aware of a bait-and-switch tactic used by some colleges or universities in enticing your child to attend their institution. While not as prevalent as it once was, some schools may offer an extremely lucrative financial aid package to a student who they want to see attend the institution, only to reduce the amount of financial aid after the student's first year of attendance. If the student is not comfortable at the school, he or she is then forced to consider transferring to another school (often with the disadvantage of not being able to transfer credit hours) or continuing studies at the same school and trying to resolve acclimation problems. As a result, once your child has obtained a financial aid package from a school, be sure and ask the financial aid officer how long the current aid package will be offered or, absent that, if your child can easily transfer credit hours to another school if he or she becomes uncomfortable at the institution.

Types of Financial Aid

The two most common federal need-based loans are the Perkins and Stafford loans. Unlike grants or scholarships that do not need to be repaid, both Perkins and Stafford loans require repayment by the student after graduation.

The federal Perkins loan is a *campus-based loan*, meaning that the school disburses the loan proceeds to the student through its financial aid office. The loan may be taken out by undergraduate and graduate students, although the annual limit is slightly *higher* for graduate students than for undergraduate study. Financial need must be demonstrated, but repayment is not required to begin until nine months after the student graduates from graduate or undergraduate school. Interest on the loan (at a relatively low rate) does not accrue on the loan principal until repayment is required.

The federal Stafford loan (also known as a direct loan) may be subsidized or unsubsidized. A *subsidized* Stafford loan means that the U.S. Department of Education pays the interest on the loan while the student is in undergraduate or graduate school and during grace and deferment periods. An *unsubsidized* Stafford loan means that the student is responsible for repayment of interest during the life of the loan and should repay the loan interest while he or she is still in school. If the student does not repay the interest as due, it is simply added to the principal of the loan for repayment at a later date. In both subsidized and unsubsidized Stafford loans, financial need by the student must be demonstrated.

There is a third type of federal loan available to the *parent* of a student that is made to the parent in his or her name—the

Parent Loan for Undergraduate Students (PLUS). This is the only type of loan available on behalf of a student where financial need is *not* determined under the FAFSA formula. As a parent who makes too much money or has a significant net worth such that the child cannot qualify for federal financial aid, a PLUS loan is the only recourse offered by the federal government to assist with the child's college education. Good financial planning dictates that you have already planned for the cost of your child's college attendance, but if you have not, the PLUS loan will be offered to you. Interest will begin to accrue immediately on the loan and repayment begins sixty days after you receive the money.

There are also need-based government grants. A grant does *not* need to be repaid. The most prevalent grant is the federal Pell Grant, for which the student is eligible if the family's EFC does not exceed a specified amount as determined annually. Scholarship awards do not affect student eligibility for the Pell Grant, although there is a limit on the amount of grant money that any student may receive annually (the maximum is $5,550 for 2011–2012). The student must be eligible for the Pell Grant on the basis of need before he or she can also qualify to receive federal Perkins or Stafford loans. The Pell Grant is available to undergraduate students only.

HOW DO I SAVE?

Custodial Accounts

Prior to the advent of **Education Savings Accounts (ESAs)** and Section 529 private savings plans, custodial accounts were the primary method of saving for a child's college education. There are still advantages to using this method, although they are likely outweighed by the fundamental disadvantage that the parent or grandparent loses control of the money once the child attains the state's legal age of majority.

Two types of custodial accounts have been established by all states: the Uniform Gifts to Minors Act (UGMA) or the

Uniform Transfers to Minors Act (UTMA). In most states, UTMA accounts are the norm, since that legislation superseded the earlier UGMA law. Operationally, the two accounts are the same, except that the UTMA allows for a broader range of investments to be made on behalf of the child, including a direct or indirect investment in real estate. Ownership of both accounts is vested in the child, with the custodian (usually the child's parent or grandparent) managing the account investments on behalf of the child.

As discussed in chapter 13, anyone can give a child up to $13,000 ($26,000 for married couples who use the gift-splitting planning technique) each year free of federal gift tax. As a result, this number is usually the initially funded annual amount transferred to custodial accounts. Appreciated securities or expected-to-appreciate securities are a common funding mechanism, although as the child approaches college age, the custodian should tend toward more conservative and less volatile investments such as bonds or CDs to preserve the principal of the account. There are disadvantageous taxable implications associated with too much annual unearned income generated from the account on behalf of a child under the age of eighteen (or under the age of twenty-four if a full time-student). Specifically, a separate tax, colloquially referred to as the Kiddie tax, is imposed on such unearned income. An example of unearned income is dividends or interest generated by the investments in the custodial account. The Kiddie tax was introduced by Congress to deal with the perceived income tax abuse of using your child as a tax shelter by shifting income to him or her, presumably to be taxed at a lower marginal income tax rate.

There are two advantages of custodial accounts as compared to ESAs or Section 529 plans:

1. The funds held within the UTMA or UGMA account may be used for *anything* that benefits the child, not just education. However, if the funds are used to pay for expenses that otherwise constitute an obligation of support

of the parent, depending on state law, all or part of the earnings on the account may be taxed back to the parent.

2. There is a nominal income tax benefit to the parent if saving in the custodial account. Specifically, for children under the age of eighteen benefiting from the account, the first $950 of income (in 2011) or other specified annual amount is *tax-exempt*. The next $950 or similar specified amount is then taxed at the child's marginal tax rate—typically, the lowest tax rate of 10 percent. As such, income splitting between the parent and child is possible, to a limited extent.

As mentioned, as attractive as these two advantages of custodial accounts may be, they are likely outweighed by the disadvantages. One has already been noted: at his or her legal age of majority, the child can do with the money in the account as he or she wishes, including *not* going to college if the child chooses to pursue another career. In addition, there are several other disadvantages associated with establishing custodial accounts on behalf of your children:

1. The unearned income tax on minors will apply once a specified annual amount of interest or dividends on the account is generated. Accordingly, once this amount is reached (for example, $1,900 in 2011), any further income is taxed to the child at the *parent's* top marginal income tax rate. This is the taxable result even if the child's grandparent or other relative actually funds the account.

For example, assume that your parent (your child's grandparent) has transferred $50,000 over the years to an UTMA established on behalf of your child. You are in the 25 percent marginal income tax bracket in 2011. Further assume that this $50,000 generates a 5 percent return within the account (or $2,500 of unearned income to the child). Thus, the child incurs a tax of $150 on this income or 25 percent on the amount in excess of $1,900. Note that you received a nominal income tax benefit in avoiding tax on the first $950 of income from the account, with the child subsequently paying only $95 tax on the next $950 of income, for a total tax due of $245.

2. As compared to Section 529 private savings plans, where up to a $65,000 one-time contribution may be made (or $130,000 for married couples who split the gift), the amount that may be contributed annually to the custodial account free of any federal gift tax is extremely limited. For example, currently, no more than $13,000 may be contributed in any one year on behalf of any one child to a custodial account *without* having to report the gift as taxable for federal gift tax purposes.

3. As a general rule, custodial assets are treated as an asset of the *child* when determining his or her qualification for federal financial aid. As a result, these assets are usually counted *against* the child in the amount of 35 percent when computing the EFC.

There is one major exception to the federal financial aid disadvantage incurred in saving for college using custodial accounts. Given the recent introduction of the much more favorable Section 529 private savings plan, many parents are transferring (or should be transferring) UGMA or UTMA monies into Section 529 plans. The resulting account is known is the financial world as an UGMA/Section 529 plan or UTMA/Section 529 plan, depending on which type of custodial account is possible under state law. While current financial aid law states that either an initially established Section 529 plan or a converted UGMA/ or UTMA/Section 529 plan is treated as an asset of the *parent* if the student is dependent, the parent is *not* permitted to change the beneficiary of a converted *custodial account* (as would be possible with the initially established Section 529 plan.

Education Savings Accounts (ESA)

The formal name of this education savings alternative is the Coverdell Education Savings Account (ESA), after Senator Paul Coverdell of Georgia, who sponsored the initial legislation. The ESA account is the successor to the well known (though not well understood) Education IRA.

An ESA is an investment account opened with a bank or other financial institution and is funded with cash. The contribution is not income-tax deductible, but the earnings generated from the contribution grow tax-free within the account. This is the case only so long as distributions made from the account are used in payment of the child's educational expenses. If they are not, the earnings are taxed to the owner—usually the parent—along with a 10 percent penalty. Contributions to the ESA are limited to no more than $2,000 annually for the benefit of a child under the age of 18. The ability to make account contributions were phased out in 2011 for single taxpayers with an adjusted gross income of between $95,000 and $110,000, or between $190,000 and $220,000 for married taxpayers filing jointly. This phase-out does not adjust annually for inflation.

The major advantage to funding an ESA is that distributions or withdrawals from the account may not only be used in payment of college education expenses, but also to cover costs associated with attending public or private elementary or secondary schools. If you are anticipating sending your child to a college preparatory elementary or high school, you may wish to seriously consider saving via an ESA. Preparatory school costs may include the expense of school uniforms, computers, and even tutoring services, all of which may be paid with ESA money. However, given the limitation on annual contributions, you may wish to couple your ESA savings with that of a Section 529 plan that allows a greater one-time contribution.

When the beneficiary of an ESA attains age thirty (unless the beneficiary is developmentally disabled, otherwise has special needs, or dies prior to that age), the account proceeds must be distributed to him or her within thirty days. However, at such time (or before the child attains the age of thirty), the account proceeds may be rolled over, income-tax free and penalty-tax free, into an ESA for the benefit of another younger family member. If the younger family member is a child of the original beneficiary (and is thus in a generation below that of the original beneficiary), the parent is treated as having made a potentially taxable gift to his or her child.

For example, assume that you have established an ESA for the benefit of your child but have never made distributions from this account for any purpose. The child has just turned thirty and is now eligible to receive the proceeds from the account. He or she is potentially subject to income tax on the earnings plus a 10 percent penalty. However, he or she now also has a child (your grandchild). Your child—the original beneficiary—may roll over the account proceeds to his or her child income-tax free, but in doing so, he or she has made a gift of the proceeds. If the ESA account balance is more than $13,000 at the time of the gift, your child must file a federal gift tax return (IRS Form 709) reporting the making of the gift to the government.

Section 529 Savings Plans

There are two types of savings plans described in Internal Revenue Code Section 529 (where the savings plans get their name).

The first type of Section 529 plan is a *qualified prepaid tuition plan* (QTP) that may have been established by your state to assist your child financially when attending college. A QTP allows the contributor (typically the parent) to prepay tuition at a particular school using *today's* tuition price. As such, the parent is protected from future increases in the annual cost of the child attending college. In addition, the earnings made on the prepaid tuition grow income tax-deferred. If the parent withdraws the accumulated contributions and earnings in a QTP (or a private savings type of

Section 529 plan, which we will discuss shortly) only for payment of higher education expenses, the entire distribution is *free of income tax.*

The problem with the QTP plan is that the child is *restricted* in choosing where he or she will attend college. For example, the State of Florida may require that the prepaid tuition feature is only valid if your child attends a publicly funded institution in that state. If your child attends a private school in Florida or another state, or a public college or university outside of Florida, you may not be able to use the money accumulated within the QTP. This is also the result if your child is unfortunate enough not to be accepted to the public school qualifying under the provisions of the state plan. Another problem associated with a QTP is that most plans only cover tuition, fees, and books at the qualifying institution and *not* room and board.

As a result of the disadvantages associated with the QTP, in 2001, Congress adopted a second type of Section 529 plan— the *private savings plan.* This plan is very similar to a private investment account, but unlike the QTP, does *not* lock in future college tuition payment at today's prices. Rather, the private savings plan affords an opportunity for the parent or grandparent to earn a rate of return on funds invested that hopefully exceeds the annual increase in college tuition (currently averaging 6 to 7 percent annually). Earnings within the account grow income-tax free as long as distributions are used to pay college education expenses, including room and board. While contributions to the private savings plan are not federal-income-tax deductible, some states permit a state income tax deduction for contributions offered by their state for state residents. Generally, however, 529 private savings plans are open to investors from *any* state.

In addition to possible state income tax deductibility for contributions, another major advantage of a Section 529 private savings plan is the significant amount that may be contributed on a one-time basis every five years. In 2011, this one-time amount is $65,000 for a single donor (or five times the annual gift tax exclusion of $13,000) and $130,000 if the contribution is made jointly by a married couple. There is also a maximum amount that may be accumulated in each of these plans, usually $300,000, on behalf of each plan beneficiary. A relatively unknown but significant estate planning technique is that the donor may establish a 529 account on behalf of each family member beneficiary and *exclude* as much as $300,000 per family member from the donor's gross estate. This can be achieved *even though* the donor controls the distribution of these funds until the date of his or her death.

Another significant advantage of a Section 529 private savings plan is that *it is your money*. Thus, for federal financial aid purposes, it is counted among parental assets at a much lower percentage in computing the EFC than if a custodial account was established on behalf of the child. Most private savings plans will permit you to change the beneficiary at any time as long as the account proceeds are transferred to a member of the beneficiary's family (a sibling, cousin, grandparent, or even back to the parent). Therefore, you can take money back from a 529 plan, although you must then use it only for your own higher education or you will pay taxes plus a 10 percent penalty. There are no age limits associated with distribution of Section 529 private savings plan money, unlike with custodial accounts or the Coverdell ESA.

If this all sounds too good to be true, it isn't—with one minor disadvantage. In any Section 529 private savings plan, you cannot directly manage the invested money yourself. You must choose an investment manager who then decides where the money is to be invested. This is no different from making a contribution to a mutual fund where you entrust the investment choices to someone else. To minimize this disadvantage, many plans have increased the number of investment choices (typically, mutual funds) in which you can invest. States have been very careful in selecting whom they choose to manage the investors' monies. Usually, only major brokerage houses or mutual fund companies are chosen.

274

So what should you look for when selecting among the many choices offered in Section 529 private savings plans? Here are among the most important factors:

1. Look for a plan that offers a variety of good choices—typically, mutual funds. Ask the same questions you would ask before investing in any mutual fund, such as what is its investment objective, how much investment risk will you assume, and what has been the fund's longer term, risk-adjusted investment performance?
2. Try to choose a plan with relatively *low* expenses. Some of this total amount depends on the mutual fund manager in charge of the assets, but the *higher* the fund expenses, the *more* the manager must beat the market. And remember, the market in this instance is the ever-rising annual cost of attending college.
3. Consider the possible availability of a state income tax deduction for contributions made to the plan. A top-performing fund of another state plan may offset the loss of the deduction when not investing in your own state's plan, but you should at least consider the advantage of the possible state income tax deduction.
4. Approach an investment in a private savings plan as you would an investment in any mutual fund. If you like the manager and the funds within the fund family, you may wish to invest in the plan of the state where the fund company is responsible for managing the plan investments. If not, consider another state's plan (or your own state's plan).

Other Methods of Saving for the Cost of College

There are several other methods of saving for your child's higher education, including establishing a trust on his or her behalf. (See chapter 13 for further discussion of trusts.) All of the trusts that may be used for this purpose are *irrevocable*, meaning that you cannot get the money back and ultimately the trust principal must be distributed to the minor. Perhaps the most popular trust used in planning for the college education of a child is the Section 2503(c) trust, also known as a minor's trust. This trust must be drafted by an attorney, with the trust principal (and any unexpended income) made available to the child at the age of twenty-one. This age of distribution may be extended at your discretion by the adoption of an alternative trust, referred to as a Section 2503(b) trust, but the income from the 2503(b) trust must be distributed annually to the child, thus resulting in additional Kiddie tax concerns.

You can also purchase Series EE and inflation-adjusted Series I U.S. Savings Bonds and dedicate them to the purpose of paying for your child's college education. With both of these alternatives, the bond must be purchased in your name or in the name of an adult who is at least twenty-four. Adjusted gross income limits apply at the time of redeeming the bonds. For example, if you purchase the bond in your name with the intent to use it to pay for the college expenses of your child, and your adjusted gross income is too high (a specified amount under law) when the child attends college, you will have to pay income tax on the amount of bond interest at the time that you redeem the bond. However, if your adjusted gross income is *below* the prescribed amount, there is no tax on the interest as long as the bond is used in payment of qualified higher education expenses.

TAX DEDUCTIONS AND CREDITS AVAILABLE FOR PAYING FOR THE COST OF COLLEGE

This section of the chapter addresses benefits provided by the income tax law to help you or your child pay for costs incurred while in college or some other type of higher education. The deductions available are a deduction for interest paid on student loans and a qualified higher education tuition deduction. Important credits include the Hope Scholarship credit and the Lifetime Learning credit. However, since 2001, these deductions and credits cannot be taken *together* in payment of the same expense. As such, the use of each must be planned for carefully so as to take maximum advantage of everything available.

Deduction for Student Loan Interest

Under current law, the interest paid (never the principal paid) by any individual who is obligated to make repayment on a student loan is deductible whether or not the taxpayer itemizes his or her deductions. However, the deductible amount is limited to a maximum of $2,500 per year and an income phase-out range applies based on the taxpayer's adjusted gross income level. While these phase-out ranges are very high, particularly for a student borrower, they can operate to deny the deduction for high-income taxpayer borrowers, such as parents who opt to take out a PLUS loan to pay for their child's education.

For this deduction to be taken, any debt incurred by the borrower must be *solely* used to pay for qualified higher education expenses, including tuition, fees, books, and room and board. There is no restriction with respect to whether this debt is incurred for study toward an undergraduate or a graduate degree, but as part of the definition of a qualified higher education expense, the debt must be taken out for study at a qualified educational institution.

Qualified Higher Education Tuition and Fees Deduction

Unlike the student loan interest deduction, which may be taken by a parent or child, the deduction for qualified higher education tuition is almost always taken by the *parent*. Also unlike the loan interest deduction, the qualified higher education tuition is *not* a specified maximum amount, but rather is tiered based on the amount of the taxpayer's adjusted gross income (AGI). For example, in 2011, a higher tier $4,000 annual deduction is permitted for married taxpayers filing jointly whose AGI does not exceed $130,000. A lower tier maximum annual deduction of $2,000 is permitted for joint taxpayers whose AGI does not exceed $160,000. Above $160,000 AGI for a joint taxpayer, *no* deduction is permitted.

How does the parent determine how much he or she has paid in qualified tuition? You will have some assistance here. The educational institution your child attends during any part of the academic year must send you those qualifying expenses as reported on an IRS Form 1098-T. In order for you to deduct those expenses, you must be able to claim the child as a taxable dependent. While this is not typically a problem if you are the parent of a child who has not yet completed an undergraduate degree, it is an issue if you are attempting to claim the deduction for graduate school expenses. In part, this is because one of the tests for dependency has an age limit—the child must not have reached the age of twenty-four by the end of the calendar year. It also occurs because most children are financially independent by the time they attend graduate school.

As we will discuss shortly, a parent may also potentially claim a tax *credit* for higher education tuition expenses. However, if he or she does so, the tuition deduction is not permitted for the same expense for the same student. This presents an interesting dilemma if you are a parent with two children in college at the same time. Accordingly, the parent should give some thought as to how to best maximize any tax credit that is allowable for one child and a deduction of up to the maximum limit of tuition for the other. In essence, while a two-student parent may mix and match tax credits and the tuition deduction, he or she cannot double dip when trying to take advantage of both tax breaks for the same student.

Higher Education Tax Credits

A tax *credit* (or a dollar-for-dollar reduction in tax due) is a very valuable tax avoidance technique. In most cases, if a taxpayer can qualify to take advantage of any tax credit, he or she should structure his or her financial affairs to do so.

When a tax benefit is sought in paying for the considerable cost of pursuing higher education, three credits are permitted: the Hope Scholarship credit, the American Opportunity (modified Hope) credit, and the lifetime learning credit.

Hope Scholarship Credit

The first credit that is permitted is the Hope Scholarship credit, which applies for tax years before 2009 (and perhaps once again beginning in 2013). This credit was included in the tax law during the Clinton administration and took its name from President Clinton's birthplace of Hope, Arkansas. The credit is permitted for tuition and fees (*not* books or room and board) paid in the first *two years* of postsecondary education for the taxpayer, spouse, or dependent. The amount of credit available is 100 percent of the first $1,200 of qualified expenses paid in the tax year, plus 50 percent of the next $1,200, for a maximum annual credit of $1,800. It is computed on a *per student* basis; therefore, the two-student parent family may take the credit for each student only if both those students are either freshmen or sophomores in college and the parent does not make too much money. Income phase-outs also apply.

American Opportunity Credit

The American Opportunity credit is a modification of the Hope Scholarship credit for tax years beginning after December 31, 2008, and before January 1, 2013. The credit amount is the sum of 100 percent of the first $2,000 of qualified tuition and related expenses plus 25 percent of the next $2,000 of qualified tuition and related expenses for a maximum credit of $2,500 per eligible student. Thus, a maximum of $4,000 in qualifying annual expenses may be taken into account in computing the credit. What is a qualifying expense for purpose of the credit?

Unlike either the tuition and fees deduction or the lifetime learning credit, where *only* tuition and fees may be considered, the American Opportunity credit also includes such expenses as books, school supplies (including computers), software, and other class materials.

The credit is available for the first *four years* of a student's undergraduate education, but phase out rules apply. In 2011, the credit amount phases out ratably for single taxpayers with annual adjusted gross incomes between $80,000 and $90,000, and for married taxpayers filing jointly, it phases out between $160,000 and $180,000.

Lifetime Learning Credit

In contrast to the Hope Scholarship of American Opportunity credit, the lifetime learning credit is much broader in application and may therefore be used by more parents. This credit is available for tuition and fees incurred for expenses associated with an undergraduate, graduate, or professional degree program. There are no credit hour enrollment requirements, as is the case with the Hope Scholarship credit or the American Opportunity credit, where the student must be enrolled at least half-time. All that is necessary to claim the lifetime learning credit is that the student incur the expense and that you are below an applicable income phase-out range.

The maximum amount of lifetime learning credit that may be taken in any year is $2,000 *per family*. Therefore, depending on the number of children you have attending college at one time and what year of school they are in, the per-family limitation may or may not be an advantage. If you have two children in their undergraduate years of college and you are under the income phase-out range, the American Opportunity credit may afford you a maximum annual credit of $5,000 ($2,500 times two), whereas the lifetime learning credit yields a credit of only $2,000. With this limited exception, if you have to choose between the two credits (remember, you cannot take both credits for the same expense), you are better off claiming the lifetime learning credit. Unlike either the Hope Scholarship credit or the American Opportunity credit, the lifetime learning credit may be claimed for an *unlimited* number of years. Even as an employee looking to improve your job skills by taking a single or several courses not leading to an eventual degree, you may take advantage of it.

THE TAX COORDINATION RULES: WHY CAN'T I DO THAT?

Congress does not want you to take too much advantage of a good thing (the "thing" here is double dipping by using allowable tax credits and deductions in payment of the same expense). But what about withdrawals that you may anticipate making from your college savings techniques—notably, the Section 529 private savings plan? One of the major advantages of the Section 529 private plan is that if you use those withdrawals to pay college tuition and fees, the earnings on them are income-tax free.

Congress has permanently shut down the opportunity to pay college tuition expenses and fees with tax-free Section 529 plan withdrawals and then subsequently claim either a Hope Scholarship, American Opportunity, or lifetime learning credit for the same expenses. Technically, this prohibition is included in the tax law and is called the tax coordination rules. However, if you were reading closely, you know that a Section 529 plan withdrawal may be used to pay room and board expenses, books and school supplies, and tuition and fees. This is in contrast to any of the permitted credits that may only be used in payment of tuition and fees (or related expenses). Therefore, you have your answer for how best to maximize both tax benefits—that is, save for college with a Section 529 private savings plan and subsequently make withdrawals from that plan to pay for college education expenses *other than* tuition and fees. In the same taxable year, then, depending on your AGI at the time your child attends college, you can also claim either the Hope Scholarship or American Opportunity tax credit when you pay for your child's college tuition and fees.

USING A ROTH IRA IN COLLEGE FUNDING

Many individuals think of a Roth IRA only in conjunction with planning for their own retirement (the subject of the next two chapters). However, this vehicle may also be effectively used as a college savings technique.

A retirement savings plan or account such as a Roth IRA may only be titled in the name of the participant or owner, but it is possible to title a Roth IRA in the name of a minor child—therefore avoiding the need to also name a custodian. The account requires that the child accumulate some earned income before contributions are possible. The same rule applies before contributions may be made to either your or a child's deductible traditional IRA.

In planning for your child's college expenses, consider *hiring* your child to perform household duties and pay them at least the maximum amount of annual contribution permitted to a Roth IRA (in 2011, $5,000 per year for taxpayers less than age fifty). Do this at least five years before your child is planning to attend college, and the child can withdraw the after-tax contributions and earnings *income tax-free* for college use. Alternatively, if the child does *not* go to college or if you have otherwise saved to pay those expenses, the child now has a wealth accumulation vehicle that is very powerful. For example, if you contribute the maximum amount of $5,000 per year to a child's Roth IRA between the years that the child is age ten and thirteen and make no further contributions, and assuming you can earn an 8 percent annual before-tax return on that money, the child will have over $1.2 million in the account ($1,232,527, to be exact) when he or she reaches the age of sixty-five.

CHAPTER 16

PLANNING FOR THE FINANCIAL ASPECTS
OF RETIREMENT

There are many opinions with respect to when it is best to start planning for your retirement, although the best opinion is to do so as soon as possible. As part of the PADD process, recognize that accumulating sufficient funds to retire comfortably should be your *number one* financial goal. If you are married with children at the time of your planned retirement, having sufficient retirement funds will help you avoid becoming a burden to your family, and, as a result, will make your retirement years that much more enjoyable. Adequate retirement monies will also prevent you from becoming overly dependent on the Social Security system, which is heading for financial difficulty absent Congressional action.

How Much Will I Need?

Similar to the lifetime distribution of your wealth in planning for your child's higher education, the first question in planning for the financial aspects of retirement is how much you will need. Generally, we can say you will need a lot of money, but a specific computation using a financial function calculator can give you a more approximate amount. Let's use the following example to describe the steps: assume that you are thirty-five and you make $100,000 a year. You should anticipate that you will need approximately 75 percent of your before-tax income in today's dollars to retire comfortably, or $75,000 annually.

As part of your retirement planning assumptions, you anticipate that inflation will average 3 percent annually prior to and during your retirement and that you can earn a 7 percent after-tax return on your investments. You plan to retire thirty years from now at age sixty-five and plan to be in retirement for twenty years. Note: All amounts are calculated using a Hewlett-Packard 10BII financial function calculator.

Step 1: Compute your annual retirement income need in today's dollars until your planned date of retirement:

- PV = $75,000 (Enter this as a negative number if using the HP 10BII calculator.)
- I/YR = 3
- N =30
- Solve for FV = $182,045

Step 2: Compute the lump-sum capital needed to generate this annual income during the period of retirement:

- PMT = $182,045 (You need to be in BEGIN mode if using the HP 10BII calculator and the amount needs to be entered as a negative number.)
- I/YR = 3.8835 (This is an inflation-adjusted rate of return, so you need to enter 1.07 divided by 1.03, less 1, times 100 on your calculator.)
- N = 20
- Solve for PV = $2,596,849

Step 3: Compute the annual amount of savings needed to accumulate this lump sum (assuming you have not already begun a retirement savings program and have not accumulated any invested assets for retirement):

- FV = $2,596,849 (Round to $2.6 million. If using the HP 10BII calculator, you now need to convert back to END mode.

- I/YR = 7
- N = 30
- Solve for annual savings deposit required or payment = $27,524.65

Again, as in education funding, the important action to take here is to *begin to save some amount now*. The amount that needs to be set aside from your salary is intimidating— over 25 percent of your *gross*, and *not* your take-home, pay (where the percentage to be saved would be even greater). Do not fixate on the required annual savings or total lump-sum amount as much as the financial goal of beginning to save for your retirement.

If you do not want to purchase a financial function calculator and do this retirement needs analysis computation yourself, there are a number of financial calculators and worksheets available online (for example, at www.money.msn.com). Some helpful charts are available in financial magazines that, given certain assumptions, tell you much money you will need to accumulate at a certain age in order to retire comfortably.

There are three basic methods to saving for retirement:

1. contributing to employer-sponsored retirement plans, such as Section 401(k) plans
2. contributing to personal tax-deferred savings plans, such as traditional deductible IRAs or after-tax Roth IRAs
3. contributing in the form of payroll taxes to the Social Security system

Even after maximizing all of these methods, to accumulate the necessary amount for retirement, you will likely also have to set aside money in a *taxable* account. If so, follow the investment strategy of dollar-cost averaging discussed in Chapter 3 and, if investing solely or primarily in mutual funds, try to choose funds with low expenses and tax-efficient investments.

OTHER QUESTIONS TO ASK WHEN PLANNING FOR RETIREMENT

There are not only financial questions to answer when planning for retirement, but some that are softer in nature. In other words, you will also need to determine where you will live and what you will do once you stop working. Questions such as these are the focus of the next chapter, but there are two more financially related issues to consider in planning for retirement:

1. Is my mortgage paid off (or at least paid down to a manageable amount)?
2. How will I cover major expenses during retirement, particularly the rising cost of health care expenses?

Mortgage Expenses

The possibility of using a reverse mortgage to generate additional income during the retirement period will be discussed in detail in the next chapter, but studies have shown that individuals who have been able to free up cash by paying off as much of their mortgage balance as possible prior to retirement tend to be much happier. Certainly, if you can remove the monthly mortgage payment from your list of fixed expenses, you will have that much more cash to live on and enjoy during retirement.

There is a debate about whether you should pay off your mortgage early, given the corresponding loss of the mortgage interest deduction if you itemize deductions for income tax purposes. However, you should keep in mind that, at most, you are receiving a 35 percent offset from the ability to deduct any mortgage interest. Further, depending on the type of mortgage you signed, you may be accumulating very little—if any—equity in your home. For example, if you signed an interest-only mortgage, you are likely *not* reducing your mortgage principal (and thus are relying only on the possibility of your home appreciating over time). As a result, paying off as much of your

286

mortgage as possible before you retire will likely prove to be wise financial planning.

There is also the issue of refinancing your mortgage prior to retiring to lower your monthly fixed expenses. While this may prove to be wise, the disadvantage of doing so is that you have likely extended your mortgage payment term to a greater number of years.

For example, assume you have a fifteen-year mortgage and are planning to retire in three years. The remaining term on this mortgage is ten years. In an effort to free up needed cash and reduce your monthly payment, you refinance your mortgage at a lower interest rate and take out another fifteen-year mortgage. Thus, you have an additional twelve years of mortgage payments to make during your retirement period instead of only an additional two years after you retire. Similarly, if you signed a new thirty-year mortgage instead of another fifteen-year one, you would now have an additional twenty-seven years of mortgage payments.

A method of refinancing to avoid this consequence is to sign a mortgage with a *shorter* repayment term, such as ten years, but the tradeoff for doing this is that your monthly mortgage payment will go *up* and not down. Accordingly, unless you have budgeted for this, the increased mortgage amount may result in cash flow pressures throughout the remaining seven years of the mortgage term after your retire.

Health Care Expenses

As almost everyone is aware, there is a health care crisis in the United States. This crisis is particularly acute for retirees, many of who are relying on a fixed income to pay for their retirement years. According to Fidelity Investments, a sixty-five-year-old couple that retired in 2007 will need approximately $215,000 to cover medical costs after they stop working. This amount is in *excess* of Medicare coverage, which will typically cover catastrophic expenses of an age sixty-five or older individual. Further, these needed medical costs are rising at an amount of 8 percent per year—much *faster* than inflation.

What is the best strategy to cover these costs? Short of being fortunate enough to be provided with retiree health insurance from your prior employer, the best plan is to save even more while you are working. For example, the thirty-five-year-old-wage earner noted earlier in this chapter should plan for an additional amount to the $2.6 million lump-sum capital needed—at the very least, he or she needs approximately $200,000 (actually more, since the noted amount has not been inflated for thirty more years of growth) for the cost of health care. Another option is to apply for Medigap coverage within the first six months of qualifying for Medicare to assist with the payment of these expenses. A third option, at least for self-employed individuals, is to establish and save for current and future medical costs via a health savings account (HSA), permitted since 2004.

This estimated $200,000 cost of medical care does not include possible long-term care expenses. Contrary to common knowledge, Medicare does *not* cover the cost of custodial care. As such, it is critical that you consider the purchase of a qualified long-term care insurance policy while you can still afford it and can qualify for coverage. While it is probably too early for a thirty-five-year-old individual to consider purchasing such a policy, unless it is for his or her parent, once he or she reaches the age of fifty or so, investigating the purchase of an individual long-term care policy (or participating in an employer's group policy, if available) should be a top financial planning goal.

THE FINANCIAL RISKS OF RETIREMENT

Similar to the general investment risks discussed in chapter 9, retirees face several special financial risks. Specifically, these may be termed as

- Inflation or purchasing power risk: This is a daily risk of any retiree living on a fixed income. Succinctly, it may be asserted that the purchasing power of fixed dollars is less in the future than it is today.

- Longevity or the risk of superannuation: This is the risk that a retiree will run out of money before he or she dies. It is this type of risk that most frightens the average retiree and is the primary reason that annuities are very important retirement planning vehicles.
- Market risk: This is the general risk of investing in the stock or bond market and is sometimes referred to as volatility risk, since the values of those investments will fluctuate daily.
- Investor behavior risk: This is the risk that investors are irrational and subject to herd mentality. For example, they will tend to purchase today's hot stock at the top of the market and then sell that same stock at the bottom of the market. Thus, many investors are not positioned for optimal, or even average, returns. Indeed, a whole new field of finance has arisen known as **behavioral finance** to study just this type of risk.
- Point-in-time or sequential risk: This is the risk that a retiree begins retirement during a market downturn and then withdraws too much money initially, thus accentuating the risk of superannuation.

The most important of these risks is likely longevity risk—the risk of outliving your money. There is really only one surefire way to avoid this risk, and that is to purchase an immediate fixed or variable annuity). However, many retirees are dubious about purchasing annuities for two reasons: (1) they do not like the idea of spending down the money invested in the annuity, and (2) they fear making such a large investment and then dying shortly thereafter, with the money lost to the insurance company. There are ways to resolve or at least minimize these concerns, but another way of managing longevity risk is to establish a fixed percentage of retirement savings withdrawal and then adhere to that percentage, adjusted for annual inflation, until your death.

Such strategy is the subject of much academic study: what should be the fixed percentage annually that a retiree should withdraw? Many studies have been done attempting to answer this question, but the consensus of most academics and financial planning practitioners is to annually withdraw 4 to 5 percent of your initial account balance, then step up this percentage each year after accounting for inflation. In other words, the actual dollars you spend in any year should be 4 to 5 percent of what you have saved at the time of retirement, adjusted for the effect of inflation in the subsequent years.

Assume that you are sixty-five, have been a diligent saver throughout your working years, and have accumulated retirement savings of $1.5 million. In year first year of retirement, you would withdraw $67,500 (or 4.5 percent of your initial account balance). Assuming that inflation for that year is 3 percent, in the next year, you would withdraw $69,525 ($67,500 times 1.03) and so on throughout your retirement period.

There are two big challenges associated with this strategy:

1. As you enjoy your retirement years, you need to average an after-tax return of *more than* 4.5 percent annually or you will invade the principal of your retirement savings.
2. You have not begun this strategy in a down market and your withdrawal of more than 4.5 percent annually will deplete your account balance much more quickly than otherwise. In other words, you are not living off the interest and will not have as much—if any—money to be left to your heirs at the end of your retirement period. You can make up this deficiency in later years by earning that much more annual investment return than you have otherwise assumed. But what happens if you do not achieve your expected rate of return or even *lose* money? For example, if you lose 2 percent from your portfolio from a previous return of 4 percent, that is a mathematical *loss* of 50 percent. To recover that loss or get back to even, you now need to earn back that lost 2 percent or achieve a mathematical *gain* of 100 percent.

It is critical that you associate point-in-time risk with longevity risk. Practically, this means that the investment climate at the point in time that you retire is very important. You want the first few years of your retirement to be enjoyed in an *up* market or at least a market that is relatively stable. You also do not want to be overly invested in fixed-income securities such as bonds and cash equivalents or you will likely *not* achieve an after-tax return equal to or more than the inflation rate. Accordingly, that is why financial planners and investment advisors recommend approximately a 60 percent equity/40 percent bond and cash mix throughout retirement.

THE "THREE-LEGGED STOOL" OF RETIREMENT SAVINGS

Historically, financial planners have tended to view saving for retirement as consisting of three legs of a retirement "stool":

1. pension income from an employer-sponsored retirement plan such as the traditional defined-benefit plan
2. personal savings income from either a tax-deferred personal savings plan such as an IRA or a taxable mutual fund account
3. Social Security income

Recently, however, given the rapid increase in defined-contribution plans where the investment risk is transferred to the employee or participant, a fourth "leg" of retirement plan earnings is also included among retirement savings. As such, the "stool" is really more like a table—one that needs to be "set" more and more by your own retirement plan contributions.

Employer-Sponsored Retirement Plans

Most medium- to large-size employers now offer their employees an opportunity to participate in a retirement plan, usually a Section 401(k) plan. Nevertheless, according to a recent survey by the Profit Sharing/401(k) Council of America, almost 23 percent of eligible employees do *not* participate in their employer-sponsored 401(k) plans. This is a mistake! Particularly if the employer matches all or some portion of the employee's before-tax contribution, the employee is essentially leaving found money on the retirement savings table. Moreover, even if the employer does not match a portion of employee contribution, the employee contributes to a 401(k) plan with *before-tax* dollars. Not only is the employee saving for his or her retirement, he or she is also reducing his or her current income taxes at the same time.

There are two basic types of employer-sponsored retirement plans: **defined-benefit** plans (also known as pension plans) and **defined-contribution** plans (sometimes lumped together under the heading of profit sharing plans). A Section 401(k) plan is a type of profit sharing plan wherein the employer may choose at its discretion whether or not to make a separate contribution in any given year.

As has generally been well documented, because of their complexity and cost, defined-benefit plans are a dying breed of employer-sponsored plan. According to the Employee Benefit Research Institute, today only about 33 percent of retirees receive a pension check from defined-benefit plan. But for workers now in their twenties, the outlook is even worse: it is likely that only 10 percent or fewer of those workers will receive a monthly pension check. For the employer, this is a positive trend, but for the employee, it is not so favorable since he or she now assumes the responsibility for funding retirement. Hence, in addition to the lack of a promised retirement benefit, the now-predominant defined-contribution plan requires considerable investment expertise on the part of the employee—a trait that many do not possess.

There are defined-contribution plans where employer contributions arc not discretionary. For example, a money-purchase plan requires mandatory employer contributions equal to a percentage of employee salary, plus investment of those contributions on behalf of the employee at his or her direction. Due to a recent law that equated the percentage deduction of a mandatory-contribution employer plan such as a money purchase plan to that of a discretionary-contribution plan such a Section 401(k), profit-sharing plans have become much more popular. You should respond in one of two ways:

1. First, participate and contribute to a defined-contribution plan in whatever amount you can afford. Remember, the lump-sum amount you need to accumulate for a comfortable retirement is substantial.
2. Educate yourself as much as possible about the concepts of investment risk and return. Know the minimum amount of risk you are willing to assume for the maximum possible amount of return you wish to achieve.

Contribute to your employer-sponsored retirement plans *first* and *before* you attempt to separately contribute to any personal savings tax-deferred (such as an IRA) or taxable investments. In this manner, you can best take advantage of any matching contributions that your employer may choose to make to encourage you to save for your retirement.

Personal Savings Plans

There are both tax-deferred and taxable personal savings plans for retirement. Tax-deferred personal savings plans include the traditional deductible IRA, the traditional nondeductible IRA, and the Roth IRA (although Roth IRA distributions, if made properly, are actually *tax-free*). There are also rollover IRAs, which are used as a receptacle for lump-sum distributions from employer-sponsored (defined-benefit and defined-contribution) retirement plans. All of these types of IRAs may be established without the assistance of the employer, although other types of IRAs—notably the Simplified Employee Pension (SEP) IRA and the Savings Incentive Match Plan for Employees (SIMPLE) IRA—must be established and contributed to by the employer on behalf of the participating employee.

The traditional deductible IRA is the oldest and most well known of all the types of IRAs. The annual amount that may be contributed to this type of IRA is established by law, but whether this same contribution amount may be deducted on the owner's income-tax return depends on a number of factors:

- If neither spouse is an active participant in an employer-sponsored plan such as a Section 401(k), or if a single taxpayer is not an active participant, then contributions to the traditional IRA are deductible without regard to the amount of the participant's AGI in the year of contribution.
- If one spouse is an active participant in an employer-sponsored plan but the other spouse is not—for example, a stay-at-home spouse, then the non-participant spouse may deduct contributions to his or her traditional IRA as long as the couple's AGI is less than a specified annual amount in the year of contribution (in 2011, it was $169,000).
- If both spouses are active participants, or if a single taxpayer is an active participant in an employer-sponsored plan, then a deduction is phased out if his or her income exceeds specified annual AGI ranges in the year of contribution (in 2011, for jointly filing taxpayers, $90,000 to $110,000; and for single taxpayers, $56,000 to $66,000).

The important point to take away from these complex rules is that if you are a relatively high wage-earner and participate in a retirement plan offered by your employer, you are likely prohibited from deducting your contribution to the traditional deductible IRA. As such, you have only two other options to personally save—by taking advantage of the traditional nondeductible IRA or the Roth IRA.

Traditional deductible IRA contributions may be invested in any type of asset with three specific exceptions:

1. You cannot invest IRA contributions in collectibles such as stamps, coins, or antiques.

2. You cannot invest IRA contributions in life insurance policies (although annuities are permitted).
3. You cannot write yourself a promissory note and invest in that manner; that is a form of borrowing and borrowing of any type is strictly prohibited from an IRA.

An individual or a married couple may also make traditional nondeductible IRA contributions up to the same specified annual amount as those of the traditional deductible IRA. However, there are no complex rules or AGI limitations associated with nondeductible traditional IRA contributions. If you are a high-income wage-earner and cannot otherwise contribute to a Roth IRA, you should consider contributing to a nondeductible IRA. You should do this only *after* fully maximizing whatever contributions you can make to an employer-sponsored plan, since those contributions are fully deductible from your taxable income without regard to how much you earn.

For example, assume that you are making $200,000 annually and that your employer offers a Section 401(k) plan. Because you make too much money, you are prohibited from deducting your contributions to the traditional IRA. Therefore, you should first contribute as much of your salary as you can afford and is permitted under law on a pretax basis to your employer's Section 401(k) plan. You should then make a contribution to a traditional IRA—in this case, a traditional *nondeductible* IRA—even though you cannot deduct the contribution in the current year.

A second option to consider in the event that you cannot make a deductible contribution to a traditional IRA is to make this same contribution to a Roth IRA. The Roth IRA was introduced in 1998 and for the most part is still an extremely underutilized personal savings retirement plan. It does have its own annual AGI contribution limits, meaning that very high-income wage-earners (like our taxpayer in the above example) cannot contribute. But for most of us, a Roth IRA is a very effective personal retirement tool if you do not distribute those funds until at least five years after you established the Roth and are at least fifty-nine and a half years old. Why? Because if you meet these requirements (a qualified distribution), the withdrawal made from the Roth IRA is completely *income-tax-free*. In addition, unlike either form of traditional IRA, you can make contributions to a Roth IRA *after* you have reached the age of seventy and six months, meaning that throughout your retirement, assuming you are within the AGI limits, you may continue to accumulate wealth.

The major disadvantage to the Roth IRA is that your annual contributions are never income-tax deductible, meaning that you will not see a place to deduct those contributions on your income tax return. However, in exchange for this disadvantageous tax treatment going in, distributions from a Roth IRA owned more than five years are taxed extremely favorably going out. Specifically, not only are the earnings generated from Roth IRA investments income-tax-free at time of distribution, but so are the contributions. This is not the case with the traditional deductible IRA, where only the earnings, not the contributions, are income-tax-free.

Social Security

If you want to get into a disagreement quickly with a business colleague or friend, just ask them their opinion of the Social Security system. Many people, particularly younger individuals, do not believe that Social Security benefits will be available for them when they retire. They believe this even though they have paid into the system for most—if not all—of their working years. To view Social Security in this way is probably a mistake: your ability to receive a benefit under the system is a *contract* between you and the federal government. Thus, despite all the political hand-wringing, Congress is likely to do whatever it takes to shore up the system and make good on their part of the contract.

Who is eligible to receive Social Security retirement payments? Anyone who is *fully insured* under the system is eligible to receive these payments. A fully insured individual is any worker who has earned forty quarterly credits (worked ten years) before his or her full retirement age under the system. There is a nominal amount of income that must be earned each quarter (for example, $1,120 in 2011) for a credit to be awarded, but most of us easily exceed this amount ($1,120 per quarter's worth of earnings equates to only $4,480 of annual earnings).

Once you are fully insured, you—and, usually, your surviving spouse—are entitled to Social Security retirement benefits at a certain age. Many people think the age to receive retirement benefits under the system is sixty-five, but your full retirement age (FRA) actually depends on your date of birth. For instance, if you were born in 1962 or after, your FRA is age sixty-seven, not age sixty-five. The following table, included in Social Security publications, will help you determine what your FRA is and when you and your spouse are entitled to unreduced retirement benefits under Social Security:

FRA for Retired Worker	Year of Birth	FRA for Surviving Spouse
65	Before 1938	65
65 and 2 months	1938	65
65 and 4 months	1939	65
65 and 6 months	1940	65 and 2 months
65 and 8 months	1941	65 and 4 months
65 and 10 months	1942	65 and 6 months
66	1943	65 and 8 months
66	1944	65 and 10 months
66	1945-54	66
66 and 2 months	1955	66
66 and 4 months	1956	66
66 and 6 months	1957	66 and 2 months
66 and 8 months	1958	66 and 4 months
66 and 10 months	1959	66 and 6 months
67	1960	66 and 8 months
67	1961	66 and 10 months
67	1962 and after	67

In the table, the FRA for the surviving spouse is shown when the spouse is entitled to retirement benefits from *your* employment record. It is also possible for the spouse to be entitled to retirement benefits as a result of his or her *own* employment and earned credits under the system. In that case, the spouse is entitled to the *greater of* the retirement benefits computed under your employment record or those determined using his or her own employment history.

Unlike Medicare, it is also possible for a retired worker under the Social Security system to receive retirement benefits before age sixty-five or the otherwise applicable FRA. If you are fully insured, you may elect to receive permanently reduced benefits as early as the first full month after your sixty-second birthday, regardless of your date of birth. However, whether you should elect to do so is the subject of the next section.

WHEN SHOULD I ELECT TO BEGIN RECEIVING SOCIAL SECURITY RETIREMENT BENEFITS?

According to Social Security Administration figures, approximately 70 percent of all beneficiaries are collecting reduced benefits (beginning at age sixty-two) because of early retirement. Is this the correct decision?

The choice to receive Social Security retirement benefits early is a complex one and should take into account several factors. Certainly, if you are in poor health at age sixty-two or have an unfavorable family history with respect to your expected future health, it is prudent to elect to receive Social Security benefits early. Given a number of reasonable assumptions, the break-even point between making an early election and delaying receipt of benefits until your FRA under the system is approximately age eight-one or later. That is, if you believe that you will live beyond age eighty-one, you are generally better off *delaying* the receipt of Social Security retirement benefits until your FRA.

Individuals who are fortunate enough to make the choice between early receipt of Social Security versus delaying may be categorized into two groups: (1) those who can or want to continue working after age sixty-two, and (2) those who do not need to work after age sixty-two and can fund their retirement years through personal retirement savings or an employer-sponsored retirement plan (or both). If you plan to continue working after age sixty-two, you need to be aware that your Social Security benefits will be reduced by $1 for every $2 received in excess of a specified amount (for example, $14,160 annually in 2011). If you anticipate making *more* than this amount, it will prove beneficial for you to delay benefits until your FRA, when no benefit penalty exists.

The actual percentage reduction suffered by sixty-two-year-old recipient depends on his or her date of birth and how far in time he or she is away from the FRA. The reduction in benefit is on a sliding scale, ranging from a total of 20 percent for individuals born before 1938 and retiring at age sixty-two to 30 percent for individuals born in 1960 or later electing to take early benefits. A reference table can be found on the U.S. Social Security Administration website (www.ssa.gov) that lists the percentage reduction you will suffer for early receipt of benefits, depending on your date of birth.

Your other option is to postpone collecting benefits until you turn seventy. If you postpone collection to age seventy and reach your FRA on or after 2011, the increase in retirement benefits for each month of delay is two-thirds of 1 percent of your otherwise-payable normal retirement benefit. This works out to an increase of 8 percent for each year that you delay—a relatively reasonable rate of annual return, particularly in a bear stock market such as at present.

How should you analyze what to do: take benefits early at age sixty-two, delay until your FRA under the system, or postpone receipt until you age seventy? Perhaps the simplest way to make this decision is to ignore alternative uses of the money and plot the percentage reductions and increases based on your monthly retirement benefit payable at FRA. You can determine what the amount of your otherwise-payable monthly benefit is by contacting the Social Security Administration (SSA) or by referencing the projected payment from the statement the SSA is required to send to you each year. Then run the numbers on a spreadsheet and determine which gives you the most gross benefit over your anticipated life expectancy. Once applying actuarial (life expectancy) tables, if you live exactly as long as the tables predict, you should have the *same* amount of gross benefit, regardless of which option you choose.

There is one other factor to consider regarding the receipt of Social Security retirement benefits. Benefits are income-tax-free for the majority of all Social Security beneficiaries, but for taxpayers with higher annual incomes, up to 85 percent of all benefits received must be included as income for federal income-tax purposes. Special step-rate thresholds apply. The first of these thresholds requires inclusion of 50 percent of all benefits and the second threshold mandates an 85 percent inclusion. Currently, these two thresholds of modified AGI, depending on taxpayer filing status, are

- single taxpayer: $25,000 and $34,000
- married couple filing jointly taxpayers: $32,000 and $44,000
- married couple filing separately taxpayers: zero

When computing modified AGI for purposes of Social Security benefit taxation, it is important to keep in mind that you must add back to your regular AGI any tax-exempt interest income. Thus, a retiree whose investment portfolio consists primarily of municipal bonds or municipal bond mutual funds will likely pay more when filing his or her return. This is all the more reason that a retiree should continue to diversify his or her portfolio among equities, corporate bonds, and cash or cash equivalent asset classes.

Understanding Distribution Options from an Employer-Sponsored Retirement Plan

Depending on plan provisions, there are four basic options available to a participant in an employer-sponsored retirement plan such as a Section 401(k) when he or she terminates employment or retires:

1. taking a lump-sum distribution from the plan
2. receiving an annuity or other periodic distribution from the plan
3. rolling over the distribution to an IRA or to his or her new employer's retirement plan
4. leaving the accumulated funds in the employer plan

This last option is infrequently offered, since most sponsoring employers do not want the responsibility of continuing to manage and invest your retirement monies.

Of the three remaining options, if a lump-sum distribution is available, most participants will choose it. Presumably, this is because most participants believe they can invest the retirement monies at least as well as the plan trustee, but also, unfortunately, many people choose the lump-sum option since they think they need the money. However, given the power of tax-deferred compounding, the *younger* the participant's age, the *more advantageous* it is for him or her to roll the distribution into an IRA and continue the tax deferral. Alternatively, if the participant elects to receive the distribution in a lump sum, he or she must first pay income taxes on the total and then may use only the net amount for his or her personal needs.

The annuity or other periodic distribution option is the most common and prudent for a retiring or soon-to-retired participant. The primary advantage of selecting the annuity option from an employer-sponsored plan is that the *participant cannot outlive his or her money* from the plan. However, this does not mean that the employer is actually underwriting the annuity for the participant. Rather, most employers transfer the risk of future investment performance and liability to an insurance company at the time that the participant retires. Thus, they buy a commercial annuity on behalf of the participant to fund their retirement payment obligation.

Given that most employers purchase a **tax-qualified annuity** with the retirement monies of the employee, this raises the issue of whether you are better off taking a lump-sum distribution and purchasing the annuity yourself. This is not a simple question and is the subject of a separate discussion with respect to the use of annuities in retirement, but here are some general guidelines to assist you in making this decision:

- If you are married at the time of taking an annuity payout from most employer-sponsored plans, under law, the plan must provide for at least a 50 percent joint and survivor annuity for your spouse *unless* your spouse waives the survivor annuity in writing. This protection for your spouse in turn *reduces* your monthly annuity payment, although there are alternatives to provide for the spouse while also ensuring that your monthly payment amount is higher.

- If you purchase the annuity yourself, investigate a payment term with at least a *guarantee* of payment to your survivor; for example, a life annuity with a period certain. This ensures that if you die before the end of the period certain (for example, twenty years), your survivor will receive payments for the remainder of the term.

- Consider the purchase of an **immediate fixed annuity** if you need to begin annuity payments as soon as possible; conversely, if you do not need the money immediately, consider a low-cost variable annuity with a lifetime guarantee withdrawal benefit (GWB) rider or guaranteed minimum income benefit (GMIB) rider.

- Try not to annuitize the annuity (use up the principal of the annuity) during your lifetime, but live off the earnings from the annuity's underlying investments. This will ensure that the greater of the annuity's account value or death benefit will pass on to your heirs.

- Annuities can be expensive, so look for as low cost an annuity as possible.

- If the annuity you are considering does not provide as high an annual return as the annuity that your employer will otherwise purchase for you, you are better off letting the employer provide the benefit. Before you make this decision, ask your employer's human resource office the internal rate of return on their annuity will be. In other words, what is the assumed discount rate used to determine the present value of your monthly annuity payment?

Since more and more defined-contribution type retirement plans are being offered by employers, a lump-sum payment option may be your only choice of distribution. If you are fortunate enough to be entitled to a pension from your employer's plan, an annuity payout or other periodic distribution will likely be among your distribution options. If you are concerned about the longevity risk associated with retirement, you should consider the advantages of an annuity payout very carefully.

REQUIRED MINIMUM DISTRIBUTIONS

Once you reach the age of seventy and six months, in the year following the year in which you attained that age, you must begin to take taxable distributions from either an employer-sponsored retirement plan or a traditional IRA (note that there are no required lifetime distributions from a Roth IRA). Since the amount of distribution you must take in a given year is established by tax law, these distributions are often referred to as required minimum distributions (RMDs).

The RMD for any given year is computed by dividing your account balance in the employer plan or traditional IRA as of December 31 of the preceding year by an applicable divisor or distribution period. This divisor or distribution period is determined by referencing your age as of December 31 of the distribution year in an IRS Table known as the Uniform Lifetime Table. Here is a portion of that table:

Participant's Age	Applicable Divisor or Distribution Period
70	27.4
71	26.5
72	25.6
73	24.7
74	23.8
75	22.9
76	22.0
77	21.2
78	20.3
79	19.5
80	18.7

Once you begin distributions, each subsequent divisor goes down by a factor of approximately one. This is because you are getting older and your life expectancy is reduced.

For example, assume you are age seventy-one as of year-end 2011 and that the account balance in your traditional IRA was $500,000 as of year-end 2010 (remember, you have to use the previous year's account balance in computing the necessary RMD). Your RMD for 2010 is $18,868 or ($500,000 divided by 26.5). You may delay this distribution until April 15 of 2012, but you would have to take *two* distributions for that year (one for 2010 and one for 2011). In 2012, you would divide your year-end 2011 traditional IRA account balance by 25.6 (since, by year-end 2011, you will have reached age seventy-two). All things considered, you are probably better off tax-wise taking the first distribution in 2011 and the second in 2012.

The Uniform Lifetime Table is used for all situations and individuals with the exception of one: if you are married and your spouse or beneficiary is more than ten years younger than you, a different table is used. This second table, known as the Joint and Last Survivor Table, is based on the actual joint life expectancies of the respective spouses. While the Joint and Last Survivor Table also reflects a divisor beginning when you turn age seventy and six months (or age seventy as shown on the table), the applicable divisor is a greater number, thus allowing a smaller taxable RMD to be made.

There are also post-death RMDs that must be made when a plan participant or IRA account owner (including a Roth IRA owner) dies and the entire account balance has not been distributed during the participant's lifetime. The application of these rules is based on, among other factors, the individual named as the designated beneficiary of the plan or IRA. If the spouse is named as the beneficiary, he or she is a favored subsequent owner and may therefore roll over the remaining account balance to his or her *own* IRA free of income tax.

Beginning in 2007, a non-spousal beneficiary of an employer-sponsored plan may also take advantage of the rollover provisions to an IRA. Accordingly, as a plan participant, if you name a child as the beneficiary of your Section 401(k) plan, he or she may now transfer the money directly into a properly titled inherited IRA and stretch the distributions over his or her own lifetime. To title this IRA properly, it must read as follows: "John Doe IRA (deceased 00-00-07 or later) for the benefit of Mary Doe, adult daughter."

Be careful. According to recently issued IRS notices, an employer-sponsored retirement plan does *not* have to allow a non-spouse beneficiary to make a direct transfer to an inherited IRA. Further, a non-spouse beneficiary who inherited funds from an employer-sponsored plan before 2006 cannot take advantage of the direct rollover opportunity at all. If you inherit a retirement plan account balance from someone other than your spouse, the first step is to check with the plan administrator to see if the plan has accorded you the opportunity of a direct rollover.

No Loopholes

You may wonder if there is a planning technique you can adopt to avoid making a taxable RMD from your employer-sponsored retirement plan or traditional IRA. In other words, as a higher-income retiree, you may not need the money and do not want to pay taxes on the distribution. Unfortunately, there is no planning technique or tax loophole that will preclude the necessity of an RMD.

One of the most popular alternative planning techniques to avoid making an RMD was as follows: in years where you do not wish to take a RMD, you transfer the traditional IRA previous year-end account balance to a Roth IRA. You do this before December 31 of the required distribution year, and then after January 1 of the next year, you transfer (or recharacterize) the money back to the traditional IRA. Thus, the previous year's traditional IRA account balance is now zero and no RMD is necessary for the distribution year.

Under current federal tax rules, this technique will not work. Rather, as the owner of the traditional IRA, you must make an adjustment to the previous year-end balance of the account to reflect the return of any recharacterized Roth IRA transfers. In other words, you must look back and add the money that you subsequently transferred to the Roth IRA to the traditional IRA account balance of zero. If you refuse to do this, the IRS will penalize you in the amount of 50 percent on any difference or shortfall. Bottom line: do not do this or you will unnecessarily deplete your hard-earned accumulation of wealth.

IRA Rollovers and IRA Conversions

A rollover is direct or indirect transfer from one employer-sponsored retirement plan such as a Section 401(k) to another employer-sponsored plan or IRA of all or part of the participant's account balance *income-tax free*. Thus, continued tax deferral of the plan assets and earnings is achieved, at least until the required beginning date of the participant reaching age seventy and a half. An additional advantage of this planning technique is that if you roll over the account balance to your IRA, you are still in control of the money and can make investment decisions.

The mechanics of an IRA rollover are relatively simple: you take the money or distribution from your employer's retirement plan and transfer it to a previously established or newly established IRA on your behalf. However, these mechanics can be deceiving and troublesome if you do not properly transfer the money. For example, once you receive the distribution from the employer plan, you have only sixty days in which to roll over or deposit the funds in your IRA. If you exceed this time frame, you must pay income taxes on the amount that you failed to roll over. Further, if you have the distribution check made out in your name, under law, the employer must withhold 20 percent from the amount you are due. As such, you only net and roll over 80 percent of the total account balance to which you are entitled. You can get this 20 percent withholding tax back when you file your income-tax return the next year, but why wait? There is a better way.

The way around the 20 percent withholding tax is to ask that your employer *directly* rollover the distribution to your new employer's retirement plan (if the plan will accept the money) or your IRA. The easiest way to do this is to have your employer's human resources department make the distribution check payable to the trustee of your new employer's plan or the custodian of your IRA. In other words, have your employer cut the check *on your behalf*, otherwise known as an FBO check (FBO stands for "for the benefit of"). In this way, you avoid the application of the 20 percent withholding tax.

For example, assume that you are forty-five and have recently changed jobs. You have an account balance of $200,000 in your previous employer's Section 401(k) plan and are entitled to a lump-sum distribution from the plan since you have separated from service. To avoid the 20 percent withholding tax, you have two planning options: (1) if your new employer has a Section 401(k) plan that will accept the $200,000 account balance, have your previous employer make the check out to the new employer's plan trustee on your behalf; or (2) roll over the distribution into your previously established or newly established traditional IRA with a check made payable to the IRA custodian on your behalf.

In the above example, and assuming that you have both choices, which one is preferable? This is a common question confronting many Section 401(k) participants who either do not need the money from the 401(k) plan or wish to continue the tax deferral. Consider this: if you directly roll over the distribution to the new Section 401(k) and you subsequently leave your new employer when you reach age fifty-five, you may take the total 401(k) balance without imposition of the 10 percent premature disposition penalty that otherwise applies to employer-sponsored retirement plans. Alternatively, this is *not possible* if you roll over the distribution to your own traditional IRA; in that case, you must wait until the year in which you reach age fifty-nine and six months to take the money without penalty. If you choose the new 401(k) plan option and you like the investment choices offered to you under that plan, you may self-direct those investments and perhaps achieve a greater return than the IRA.

Whatever choice you make, the *younger* your age at the time of receiving the distribution, the *more advantageous* it will be for you to roll over the money and continue the tax deferral.

IRA Conversions

It is possible to convert your traditional IRA to a Roth IRA. Prior to 2010, it was the law that you could not make this conversion if your adjusted gross income exceeded $100,000 in the year of conversion. However, now and through 2012, there is *no* income limit, providing a potential planning opportunity for those who are willing to pay the income tax due on the proceeds at the time of conversion. There are two reasons for doing this:

1. You believe you will be in a higher income tax bracket at retirement than you are in currently and will pay no subsequent tax when you distribute the account balance from the Roth IRA.
2. You plan to keep the converted assets in the Roth IRA for a considerable period of time (more than five years) and

will make up the dollars expended in payment of taxes due at the time of the conversion. To ensure that this will be the result, you should pay the up-front tax from assets *other than* those in the traditional IRA. This will permit you to invest an even greater amount in the Roth IRA.

Conversion of your traditional IRA to a Roth IRA raises the possibility of a very intriguing—and potentially very profitable—income-tax strategy:

1. If you have not done so already, establish a nondeductible traditional IRA.
2. Make the maximum allowable annual contributions to this nondeductible IRA for as many years as possible before conversion.
3. Just prior to your planned retirement, convert the entire account to a Roth IRA.

What is the result? Well, remember that you have already paid taxes on the money that you have contributed to the nondeductible traditional IRA—in other words, you made those contributions with *after-tax dollars.* Therefore, the only tax you would owe on the nondeductible account when you make the conversion to the Roth IRA is on the earnings generated from the nondeductible account. In return for this relatively small amount of income tax due, your new Roth IRA will now grow income tax-free *forever.* While it does not get any better than this in accumulating and growing wealth, there is one catch. You should have only *one* traditional IRA (deductible or nondeductible) at the time of conversion. If you have more than one IRA, the IRS will assume that the conversion is coming pro rata from each IRA and thus you would owe *more* tax.

For example, assume that at the time you convert your nondeductible IRA to a Roth IRA in 2012, you also own a traditional deductible IRA. The nondeductible IRA has an account balance of $50,000 and the deductible IRA has an account balance of $250,000. Further, assume that you have made after-tax contributions of $40,000 to the nondeductible IRA and must pay tax on $10,000 of earnings ($50,000 less $40,000). However, since you must consider the converted amounts as being distributed pro rata from both the deductible and nondeductible IRAs, you must treat a total of $300,000 ($250,000 plus $50,000) as potentially subject to tax. As a result, you would owe taxes on $42,000 and not just $10,000 in 2012. Note: The $42,000 is determined by multiplying the fraction of ($50,000 divided by $250,000) times $250,000—or $50,000—and subtracting the product of (0.20 times $10,000)—or $2,000—from the $10,000 of earnings—or $8,000.

Fortunately, if you want to contribute to a nondeductible IRA, you are probably not able to take advantage of a deductible IRA because of AGI limitations and active participation requirements. But if you do have a traditional deductible IRA and if you participate in a Section 401(k) or other employer-sponsored plan, ask your employer if you can do what is called a reverse rollover. That is, roll over your deductible IRA account balance to the Section 401(k) plan, leaving you with only the one nondeductible IRA—and *without* the worry of the pro rata rule.

THE USE OF ANNUITIES IN RETIREMENT PLANNING

According to the McKinsey Consumer Retirement Surveys, the proportion of U.S. working-age adults who consider the lack of a guaranteed retirement income to be an extremely important risk increased from 28 percent in 2004 to 61 percent in 2009. As such, immediate fixed or variable annuities with a lifetime guarantee withdrawal benefit (GWB) rider at the time retirement have increased in importance. This reflects the primary advantage of using an annuity in retirement planning: the opportunity to own a safe investment with a *guaranteed lifetime income stream.* In other words, as the annuitant, or person receiving the annuity payments, you cannot outlive your money.

There are also other advantages of annuities in planning for the financial aspects of retirement:

1. If you purchase a **deferred variable annuity,** you have the opportunity to grow your account balance through investment in mutual funds as part of the annuity sub-accounts. It is also possible to purchase a GWB rider with this form of annuity, ensuring a minimum amount of guaranteed investment return on your money:
2. You can plan the timing of income receipt to take advantage of lower tax bracket years.
3. If you have purchased a nonqualified annuity (one purchased with after-tax dollars), like a nondeductible IRA, you only have to pay tax on the earnings accumulated within the IRA at the time of distribution.
4. You never have to make required minimum distributions from a nonqualified annuity and therefore can leave the *entire* account balance to your heirs at your death.

When should you consider purchasing an annuity as part of the lifetime wealth accumulation and distribution process? When you want

- a guarantee that you cannot outlive your money during the retirement period (in other words, you avoid longevity risk)
- an opportunity to grow any invested funds on a tax-deferred basis
- an alternative or supplement to a traditional or Roth IRA permitting unlimited annual contributions
- an alternative beyond maximizing contributions to an employer-sponsored retirement plan or a traditional deductible IRA

However, as a general rule, you should *not* consider the purchase of a nonqualified annuity or any after-tax retirement planning savings vehicle until *after* you have contributed all that you can on a pretax basis annually to your employer-sponsored plan or deductible IRA.

How Much Should I Withdraw Annually During Retirement?

To steal the name of a popular game show of many years back, this is indeed the $64,000 question. Three corollary questions need to be asked before it may be answered:

1. Over what time frame should my retirement money be expected to last?
2. In what assets should I invest to have the least probability of outliving my retirement money?
3. Once I begin making withdrawals, what retirement monies should I access first to most effectively minimize income tax due?

With respect to the first question, several academic studies have determined that a 4.5 percent annual withdrawal rate, adjusted for inflation each year, provides the greatest chance that a retiree will not outlive his or her money. Therefore, you should assume a retirement distribution period of approximately thirty years with a 4.5 percent after-inflation withdrawal rate. Specifically, studies have shown that you have only about a 10 percent chance of outliving your money over that period using the optimal withdrawal rate.

The second question begs the issue of what you should be invested in during the preretirement period to optimize your chances of not outliving your money. Empirically, it has been shown that a constant asset allocation of approximately 60 percent equities and 40 percent bonds and cash or cash equivalents in your retirement savings portfolio will afford you the greatest chance of not outliving your money. Specifically, I suggest that this should be a 40 percent allocation to large capitalization, blended stocks or mutual funds (blended means a combination of value and growth stocks), 20 percent to international stocks, 20 percent to intermediate-term investment grade bonds, and 20 percent to cash or cash equivalents.

Once you begin making annual retirement withdrawals, there is a rule of thumb for minimizing income tax on those withdrawals:

- Withdraw money first from taxable accounts, thus reducing your future tax bills as much as possible.
- Next, withdraw funds from tax-deferred retirement accounts such as a traditional deductible IRA, where RMD requirements apply beginning at age seventy and six months.
- Last, tap Roth IRA monies, since no taxes are paid on qualified distributions made from those accounts.

To summarize planning for the financial needs of retirement: *keep a constant allocation of 60 percent equities and 40 percent bonds and cash or cash equivalents in your portfolio and withdraw only a real rate of 4.5 percent annually from a portfolio of taxable, tax-deferred, and Roth IRA accounts, in that order.* If you follow this rule, you will have a very high probability (approximately 90 percent) of *not* outliving the money you have saved for retirement.

Now let's move on to other, non-financial aspects of planning for retirement, such as where you will live and what you will do to experience a prosperous retirement.

CHAPTER 17

PLANNING FOR THE LIFESTYLE NEEDS
OF RETIREMENT

Now that you have decided how you will finance your retirement, you need to consider where you will live and what you will do. For many retirees, the choice of where to live is actually fairly simple: they just continue living in the home they purchased prior to retirement. But there are many choices of where to live, including what type of facility to live in, as will be discussed shortly. What you will do in your retirement, however, is more complicated.

Many newly retired individuals, who worked for thirty-five to forty years, need to find a new identity once they retire. This is not easy. While you are working, the first thing most casual acquaintances ask what you will do when you stop working. Part of this chapter is dedicated to helping you answer that question once you are retired.

HOUSING OPTIONS FOR RETIREES

There are at least ten housing options for the newly retired individual:

1. single family dwellings
2. town homes
3. condominiums
4. apartments

5. living with one or more of your children
6. independent living communities
7. assisted living communities
8. continuing care retirement communities
9. skilled nursing care facilities
10. traditional nursing homes

Recently, several more have been added, including row homes and lofts, but these are likely to be of more interest to your children or younger generations.

Single Family Dwellings

Many members of the baby boomer generation grew up with plentiful single-family dwelling choices, many in planned communities. As boomers have advanced in their careers, they have typically purchased larger and more expensive houses.

Now, at least some boomers—particularly those with children who are now independent—wish to downsize their homes, meaning that they seek smaller and less expensive ones. Builders are well aware of this trend and are attempting to meet the lifestyle needs of retirees looking to downsize. This strategy may permit boomers and other newly retired individuals to access the equity in their homes, which are typically the single largest financial asset they own. If they are lucky enough to receive sufficient funds for this equity, boomers may even be able to pay off their mortgages, one of the financial keys to a prosperous retirement.

As a retiree, if you choose to remain in a single-family dwelling during retirement, you should determine where you want to live. In addition to the choice of the subdivision or community where you will buy, there is also the choice of the region of the country and state. These decisions are often relatively easy to make, as retirees generally choose to live close to one or more of their children and grandchildren. You should also consider the income-tax status of the state you choose. Some states, notably Florida, Texas and Arizona, do *not* have state income taxes, thus contributing to their allure as retirement havens. Others, including California, are known for relatively high state income taxes. Still others, such as Colorado, provide partial exclusions for income derived from pensions. If the amount of taxes is important to you (remember, inflation and taxes are the two biggest threats to your accumulated wealth), you should consider carefully the state you choose to live in during retirement.

If you wish to live in a single family dwelling, even one you have downsized to, you should be aware that you will need to continue maintaining and improving that dwelling. As you advance in age, depending on your health, this may become a burden. If you are unable to maintain the home, you will have to call on your children for help (if they live close by) or pay someone to do the daily and weekly chores. The next two options—town homes and condominiums—may provide a resolution to this problem.

Town Homes

According to Webster's dictionary, a town home is "usually a single-family dwelling of two or three stories that is connected to a similar house by a common sidewall, thus forming a continuous group." The townhome owner also owns the land on which the townhome sits. In essence, this means that a purchaser of a town home owns his or her own individual unit, but may be surrounded on both sides or above and below by other owners.

This may not be how you envision retirement living, but if it is, be aware that, unlike with an apartment, you *own* rather than rent. If you have a mortgage on your town home, you are entitled to deduct the interest for tax purposes, just as a single-family dwelling owner can. There is also typically a monthly maintenance fee that is paid to a homeowner's association. The amount of this fee varies greatly depending on the location and quality of the property, but it usually covers maintenance of the common areas of the development. A town home is appropriate for a retiree who does not want the burden of property maintenance and does not mind living closely with multiple neighbors.

Condominiums

Condominiums are much like town homes with two significant differences: (1) with a condo, the owner owns not only his or her individual unit, but also an additional percentage of the surrounding property, and (2)the condo unit may be on any floor, not just from the ground up. The condo owner does not own the ground on which the condo is located. Because of the ownership of an additional percentage of the surrounding property, condo owners also typically face more homeowner restrictions.

As with town homes, condo owners also have to pay a monthly maintenance fee, although this fee may cover more property maintenance and upkeep features. For example, balcony and patio repair may be covered by fee payments made by condo owners, whereas town home owners may have to pay for these repairs themselves.

Condos are best for retirees who want others to maintain the exterior of their property and want to reside and interact with other owners.

Apartments

Apartments may be thought of in several ways for retirees (for instance, retirees typically reside in apartments in continuing care facilities), but the important feature to understand is that the apartment dweller rents rather than owns. As such, you are *not* entitled to favorable income tax treatment, such as being able to deduct any portion of your rent as an itemized deduction. Most renters take advantage of the standard deduction when they file their tax returns.

Living with One or More of Your Children

For many retirees, this is the *least* favorable of all the housing options, yet often because of poor health and lack of funds, they have no other choice.

If you live with one or more of your children, try not to be a burden to them. Help out around the house and offer to pay your fair share of the rent or mortgage payment. If you are in poor health, make sure your child can adequately attend to your daily needs. If your son or daughter works, this may be difficult and is one of the reasons you should investigate the option of adult day care.

Another frequently overlooked consequence of living with your child is that if the child is married, his or her spouse must be approve of you residing in the house or apartment. Many marriages of adult children have been strained (some to the point of divorce) if the child and spouse do not agree on how to take care of the parent.

Independent Living Communities

This type of retirement community is for retirees who are fully capable of attending to their daily living needs without assistance. Usually, an independent living community is age-restricted and may even be gated or feature restricted entry. Sometimes, considerable amenities, such as golf courses and tennis courts, may be part of the homeowner's fees paid by residents in the community. Lawn service is usually covered by homeowner's fees.

Assisted Living Communities

This type of retirement community combines attributes of independent living with limited nursing home benefits. Assistance is provided for bathing, dressing, and other activities of daily living (ADLs). Assistance in giving

319

medications to retirees or seniors is also typical. Lodging in such a community varies from small cottages or apartments to larger scale housing.

An important point to understand if you or your parent moves into an assisted living community is that you are likely eligible to receive benefits under a long-term care insurance policy. Long-term care eligibility usually requires not being able to satisfy at least two of six ADLs. For example, not being able to dress or bathe yourself is typically enough to qualify for benefits, as is needing assistance with eating, transferring from bed to a chair, and using the toilet. Medicaid assistance from the state may also be available if you qualify.

Continuing Care Retirement Communities

Continuing care retirement communities combine independent living, assisted living, and a nursing home approach by segregating retirees by the level of care that they require. Generally, there is a fairly hefty entry fee. Ongoing monthly maintenance fees vary in amount based on the level of care needed. Some CCRCs charge a fixed amount rather than a varying fee, although if you require only independent living, you may be disadvantaged by this method. The type of CCRC may be distinguished by whether any portion of the entry fee is refundable as well as whether the monthly maintenance fee is fixed or flexible.

CCRCs are becoming more popular, in part because the retiree does not have to physically move as his or her health deteriorates and he or she requires more care. However, they are not in all states and, if they are permitted, are usually lightly regulated. As with assisted living coverage, individuals who need the assisted living level of care or nursing home care can access the benefits of a long-term care insurance policy, provided that they meet the eligibility requirements of the policy (for example, the inability to perform two or more ADLs).

Skilled Nursing Care Facilities

Sometimes skilled nursing care facilities and nursing homes are used synonymously, although Medicare makes a differentiation. Basically, a skilled nursing care facility provides *acute* care, whereas nursing homes are designed to meet *chronic* care needs. Skilled nursing care and nursing home care provide for twenty-four-hour assistance by a registered nurse or other medical professional, although nursing home care is more long-term in nature and residents do not require as much daily attention as those needing skilled nursing care. Medicare pays a limited benefit for skilled nursing care attention but does *not* cover nursing home or custodial care.

The requirements that must be met in order for Medicare Part A to cover skilled nursing care facility expenses are as follows:

- You must have been hospitalized for at least a three-day period.
- You must enter the facility within thirty days of hospitalization at a physician's direction. You do not need to go directly from the hospital to the facility to be covered by Medicare, but you do need to enter the facility within the thirty-day period.
- You must be making improvement as certified by your doctor or other medical specialists; in other words, if you are not making either mental or physical improvement during the period of Medicare coverage, payment of expenses will not be afforded (for example, payment of expenses for Alzheimer's disease is *not* a qualifying condition, since mental deterioration is inevitable).

If you meet these three requirements, Medicare will pay for 100 percent of your expenses during your first twenty days of residing at a skilled nursing care facility. After that, there is a daily patient co-payment specified each year by the government through day one hundred of the stay. After one hundred days of receiving skilled nursing care benefits, Medicare Part A no longer provides coverage.

Nursing Home Care

Traditional nursing home care is continual or chronic in nature, which is one of the reasons it is referred to as custodial care, and you pay a sizable monthly fee for coverage. For example, as of 2011, the average monthly expense for nursing home care is approximately $6,500 per month or $78,000 per year. Depending on the state in which the nursing home is located, the monthly expense may even be much higher.

There is no precise way to determine when you or your parent should enter a nursing home, but usually there is a progression: seniors may move from independent living to assisted living to a nursing home. Adult children who have to make the decision to move their parent or parents into a nursing home typically experience a great deal of angst before and after the decision is made. Sometimes, if more than one child is involved in the discussion, there is disagreement with respect to when is the best time to take such a step. Furthermore, if the senior is mentally competent, there may be some troubling discussions before he or she enters the nursing home. The living with a child option is frequently tried in the interim.

There are three ways to pay for nursing home care, although impoverishing yourself to achieve Medicaid coverage (the third way) is not much of an option. The other two ways are from your own savings—private pay—or via receipt of long-term care insurance benefits. You should be aware that, at $78,000 annually, it may not take you or your parent long to deplete all private savings and then have to turn to other alternatives, such as the children paying for the parent's care out of their own pockets. If you do not want this to happen and you can qualify, buy a tax-qualified long-term care insurance policy.

USING YOUR HOME TO FUND RETIREMENT: REVERSE MORTGAGES

You likely are familiar with the terms *mortgage* or *mortgage note* since you probably had to execute such a note to help finance the purchase of your house. You might also have mortgage insurance, which lenders generally require if you were not able to make a down payment of at least 20 percent of the sale value of the home. Seniors may now have another option involving a mortgage note: a *reverse mortgage*, with the term *reverse* coming from the fact that instead of you paying the lender the lender pays you.

A reverse mortgage is a means of accessing the equity in your home. Seniors are the most likely candidates for such mortgages since they usually have considerable equity built up in their homes. With a reverse mortgage, the homeowner is able to remain in his or her home and usually receives a monthly payment from the lender based on a percentage of the principal due on the home. In some cases, this payment may be in the form of a lump sum instead of a periodic monthly payment, but if the senior is looking for an income stream during retirement, a monthly payment is the preferred alternative. Typically, the minimum age to qualify for a reverse mortgage is sixty-two, and the senior cannot take a mortgage for more than his or her home is worth at the time of the loan. If there is an existing mortgage on the home, it must first be paid off with the proceeds of the reverse mortgage.

Here is an example of how a reverse mortgage is structured and how you may be able to use it: assume that you are at least age sixty-two and otherwise qualify for a $150,000 reverse mortgage (there are no income or health status requirements with a reverse mortgage). You have an existing mortgage of $100,000 on your house. As such, you will have enough money from the reverse mortgage to pay off your existing mortgage and have $50,000 in cash to use in whatever manner you wish. It is even more advantageous if you have no original mortgage at all because then you would have the total of $150,000 available for your use.

If you do qualify, does this sound too good to be true? There are some facts to consider before entering into a reverse mortgage arrangement:

- No monthly payments are due on the mortgage while it is outstanding. However, when you die or sell the house, the loan must be repaid. If you are married at the time of your death, the loan typically does not have to be repaid until the death of your surviving spouse, but it then must come out of the spouse's estate, thereby, *reducing* the amount that subsequently passes to your children or other heirs.
- Like a home equity loan, you may receive the proceeds from a reverse mortgage over a set term, in lifetime payout, or via a line of credit. If you take the proceeds in a line of credit, there is a growth feature built into most reverse mortgages where you benefit if your home appreciates in value over the year (in other words, your payments from the reverse mortgage may *increase*).
- In general, the amount of money you will receive from a reverse mortgage depends on your age. The older you are, the more money you will receive.
- A reverse mortgage does *not* affect your receipt of Social Security or Medicare benefits, and the payments are not taxable or considered as taxable income (that is, the 50 percent or 85 percent special step-rate thresholds do not apply).
- Because of the closing costs associated with a reverse mortgage, you should *not* enter into the arrangement if you intend to sell your home within two to three years after you begin to receive the proceeds. You will not be able to recover the closing costs in such a short period of time.

The last point speaks to a very important consideration before executing a reverse mortgage. They are relatively expensive. There may be other less expensive ways to access the equity in your home, such as a home equity loan or line of credit.

Do I Need Life Insurance During Retirement?

Once you retire and your children become independent, you may wonder why you need life insurance. This is particularly the case if you are divorced or separated from your spouse. You may need to think again, particularly if you have a high net worth (say, $1 million or more) and are involved in estate planning and estate tax reduction techniques. For example, life insurance remains a very effective way to pay any estate taxes you may owe at death and the final expenses associated with settling your estate, since it is purchased with considerably discounted dollars from what your estate will receive in death benefits.

For example, assume that you purchase a $250,000 annual renewable term life insurance policy and die during the term of the policy's coverage. Depending on a number of factors, including your age and health at the time of purchase, the premiums you paid for coverage may be extremely low. If we assume a total premium payment at your time of death of $25,000, your estate receives a discounted dollar benefit of $225,000 ($250,000 less $25,000). In addition, your heirs receive a total dollar, *income-tax-free* benefit of $250,000 upon receipt of the life insurance proceeds.

Be careful. If you do not title or arrange for the purchase of the $250,000 term life insurance policy properly, the death proceeds will be included in your gross estate for estate tax purposes, thus *adding* to your estate tax problems. The simple way around this is to title the policy in your spouse's or adult child's name. However, if you do this, you add to the spouse's or child's gross estate. Further, what if the new owner does not make the premium payments on the policy? The policy will then lapse and your intended beneficiaries will lose the life insurance protection on your life. The better way to arrange for the titling of life insurance is to establish an *irrevocable life insurance trust* (ILIT).

If you are married at the time that you enter into retirement and are entitled to a pension, you have a different problem, commonly referred to as the pension dilemma. Specifically, under current law, if you are to receive a pension (*not* a lump-sum distribution from a Section 401(k) plan), you must provide for a survivorship payment on the pension to your spouse. When you do this, your own annuity or pension payment is *reduced*, potentially impacting future cash flow.

For example, assume you are sixty-five, married, and entitled to a pension payment from your company's pension (defined-benefit) plan. The amount of this pension payment is $2,000 per month, or $24,000 per year. This amount is payable to you in a single life annuity form, meaning that when you die, the pension terminates, which also means that your spouse must replace $24,000 of lost income. To avoid this, you *must* elect—unless your spouse elects to waive it—a joint and survivor payout so that your spouse is protected. But since your pension payment must be spread over two lives instead of one, it is reduced, sometimes as much as 30 percent. Using the numbers in this example, this means your pension payment is now $16,800 ($24,000 times 0.70). Taken over a twenty-five year life expectancy, you will have sacrificed approximately $180,000 of lifetime benefits that may otherwise have been payable to you (the $7,200 per year difference in payments times twenty-five).

One option in which you would retain those benefits is to have your spouse consent in writing (signed by a notary) that he or she is waiving the joint and survivor benefit. Then you are right back to where you started: leaving your spouse without loss-of-income protection at your death. Therein lies the pension dilemma.

A preferable option is to purchase a life insurance policy (for our example, in the amount of $180,000) and name your spouse as beneficiary. This has the advantage of *converting* potentially taxable pension benefits to nontaxable insurance proceeds. In the financial world, this is known as the pension maximization planning technique, founded on the idea that you use some of the additional pension payment you receive ($7,200 per year, in our example) to pay the premiums on the life insurance policy to keep the policy in force until the time of your death.

Why doesn't everyone entitled to a pension payment from an employer-sponsored plan take advantage of the pension maximization technique? One primary reason is that the sixty-five-year-old, soon-to-be retired individual may not be able to qualify for life insurance coverage because of poor health. Another is that life insurance is simply too expensive at that age. You need to look closely at a number of factors—such as health, age, cost, and whether the pension payment is adjusted for cost of living each year—and see if the pension maximization technique is right for you. Hopefully, you will do this with the assistance of a competent financial advisor or life insurance agent.

Retiree Health Insurance

Health insurance coverage for retired individuals is becoming less common. Among businesses with two hundred or more employees, approximately 30 percent of them provide retiree health insurance. The statistics are even worse among businesses with less than two hundred employees. Studies have shown that no more than 5 percent of small businesses can afford to offer retiree health insurance.

What should you do if you want to be insured against poor health during retirement? It depends on your age and whether you are working enough hours to be eligible for the group health insurance offered by most employers. Once you reach age sixty-five, you are probably not concerned about private health insurance coverage since you become eligible for Medicare. If you are newly retired but not yet sixty-five, you do not have a great deal of options.

Your first option is to exercise your COBRA rights. Under the COBRA law of 1985, once you leave your job—as long as you were not fired for gross misconduct—you may continue your previous employer's group health insurance coverage for a period of up to eighteen months. As noted in chapter X 5, you will now have to pay the employer's share of the group premium as well as your own previous share. However, you should not overlook the opportunity to take advantage of these rights if you retire before age sixty-five. Alternatively, once you reach age sixty-five and qualify for Medicare, if your spouse or dependent children are younger, they may continue group coverage under the COBRA law for a period of up to thirty-six months.

A second option is to begin to fund a Health Savings Account (HSA). HSAs are established much like the traditional or Roth IRA forms of saving for retirement, but they include a high-deductible individual health insurance plan. You may make a tax-deductible annual cash contribution to your HSA and then use this contribution, plus its earnings, to reimburse yourself for medical expenses income-tax-free. Moreover, once you become eligible for Medicare, you may draw on the HSA funds tax-free to pay your share of Medicare Part B monthly premiums and any other co-insurance that you share with the government under the Medicare system.

A third option is to purchase an individual health insurance policy. While these policies are relatively expensive, you can save by being a prudent shopper, remaining healthy, and taking advantage of certain techniques. For example, if you are between ages fifty-five and sixty-four, consider separating your family for coverage at the time of application. Typically, individual health insurance is underwritten by companies according to the age of the *oldest* participant in the plan. Thus, if you have a younger spouse, you may be able to classify him or her for separate coverage under the plan and then combine his or her age with yours for a more favorable overall rating. You may also wish to consider titling the health insurance policy in the name of the younger spouse to ensure that he or she has coverage once you become eligible for Medicare.

If you find the individual health insurance premiums to be so high that they are prohibitive, investigate state-guaranteed policies. Typically, these types of policies are efforts by state governments to cover the uninsured or those who are so unhealthy that no insurance company will provide coverage. To become eligible for state risk pools, you will have to be rated as a high-risk, unhealthy individual and have been rejected by private insurers. If you can withstand the blow to your ego with respect to being classified in such a manner, you may be able to obtain relatively inexpensive coverage.

Another idea similar to paying premiums on individual health insurance coverage is to pay a monthly fee for service to a health maintenance organization. In return for the payment of this fee, you can receive the services of medical professionals for any medical condition that may present as you age. There will be some months (hopefully, many months) when you do not need health-care related services, but it is nice to know that treatment will be provided at little or no additional cost when you do need it.

MEDICARE AND MEDICARE SUPPLEMENTAL INSURANCE (MEDIGAP)

Both Medicare and Medicare supplemental policies (Medigap) were discussed in chapter X 5 as part of the first step in the PADD approach to wealth accumulation and management—*protecting* yourself, your family, and your property. However, it might be helpful to be reminded of the considerable gaps in Medicare Part A and Part B coverage, such as deductibles and co-payments. Once you become eligible for Medicare, you should purchase one of the standardized Medigap policies most relevant to your needs and health status at the time. Hopefully, you have heeded the advice of this book with respect to your possible long-term health needs and have been paying the premiums on a long-term care insurance policy. Remember, neither Medicare nor private Medigap policies will cover long-term care expenses, except in a limited manner, so it is up to you to provide for such coverage.

SO, I AM RETIRED! NOW WHAT?

You experience a significant life change when you retire, no matter the age. Among the issues that you need to consider when you retire is the need to establish a new *identity*, but there are also other lifestyle-related issues. Among these are

1. Are you going to continue to work, even if it is only part-time?
2. Do you plan to pursue educational opportunities that you were too busy to consider while you were employed full-time?
3. Do you plan to travel? What will you do for recreational activities?
4. Perhaps most importantly, how do you accommodate the change from an employment career to retirement?

Let's consider these issues in more detail.

Future Work

In recent surveys, over 70 percent of baby boomers (individuals born between 1946 and 1964) said that they planned to continue working in some capacity during retirement. While this statistic may be somewhat misleading since in many instances boomers will *have* to continue working due to poor savings habits and lack of planning, there is no doubt that they are going to be more active in their retirement than previous generations. Employment of some kind, even if part-time, may be useful because it eases the transition from a working career to the more leisurely time of retirement.

If you are going to continue to work once you are retired, you need to consider the impact of your earnings on your eligibility to receive Social Security benefits. For example, if you elect to receive Social Security retirement benefits early (beginning at age sixty-two), be aware that an earnings limit applies until you are sixty-five or until your otherwise specified full retirement age (FRA) under the Social Security system. If you are *under* FRA throughout a given calendar year and you earn *above* a specified amount ($14,160 in 2011), then $1 of Social Security benefits is withheld for every $2 you earn in excess of this limitation. Further, this earnings limit is separate and apart from any income tax requirements; in other words, between the age of sixty-two and your FRA, not only will your Social Security retirement benefits be reduced, but you will have to pay income taxes on those benefits if your income exceeds either of the special step-rate thresholds.

You should also consider the possibility of *self-employment* during retirement. As part of their desire to stay active, many boomers already started their own businesses. According to a recent survey by *Business Week* magazine, boomers are *twice* as likely to pursue self-employment than the generations that retired before them. This is particularly true for boomers with professional skills, such as medical doctors, lawyers, accountants, and financial planners. Moreover, it is generally advantageous from an income-tax perspective to become self-employed since the ability to benefit from certain tax deductions and credits is more available to self-employed individuals than to salaried employees.

There are also many risks to self-employment. Chief among them is the willingness to *assume* the financial risk associated with becoming self-employed. Most businesses do not generate a profit until at least three years from when the business was started. These businesses have to cover expenses during the years when a profit is not generated. Hence, many self-employed individuals seek financial assistance from banks and other sources of capital to run the business in the formative years. Typically, banks will require a *personal guarantee* of repayment on any monies loaned. This often means that if you become self-employed and require the bank's financial assistance, you must pledge personal assets such as your house as collateral for the loan. Venture capitalists—private money lenders—are even more demanding: they may not only require a personal guarantee, but may also want a percentage of the profits once the business becomes profitable.

Unless you consider yourself a risk-taker—the primary attribute of any entrepreneur—you may wish to remain in the employ of a larger company. For instance, Walmart has become known for aggressively seeking senior workers, and other companies are quickly doing the same, given the wealth of experience that today's retirees bring to any business.

Education

Under current tax law, a taxpayer's educational expenses may be deducted as a miscellaneous itemized deduction *if*

1. the education maintains or improves a skill required in the taxpayer's employment or other trade or business
2. the education meets the explicit requirements of the taxpayer's employer, imposed as a condition of employment

Collectively, these requirements may be characterized as the business expense educational deduction. However, this deduction is not available for educational expenses that are *personal*, which is likely the case if you are retired and not working for another firm or company.

What should you do if you are retired and want to pursue a degree or the college coursework you always wanted? Normally, if you withdraw money from a traditional or Roth IRA before you reach the age of fifty-nine and a half, you pay a 10 percent early distribution penalty in addition to regular income tax (you would pay tax on the contributions and earnings from a traditional IRA, but likely only on the earnings from a Roth IRA). There is an *exception* to the penalty when using this money in payment of qualified higher educational expenses, however. The expenses incurred must be for the education of you, your spouse, your children, or your grandchildren, and must include only tuition, fees, and books used in a degree program. The exception is there for retirees younger than fifty-nine and a half.

A second suggestion is to do what increasing numbers of traditional college students are doing: request financial aid. There is no age maximum on financial aid packages offered by schools or the government. If you have a need for the money to attend school, just like your children or grandchildren, you may be awarded financial aid. In addition, if you are attempting to fund the education from your traditional IRA, the assets accumulated within that account are sheltered from the financial aid need analysis; in other words, they are not counted against you.

Also, consider borrowing from an employer-sponsored retirement plan such as a Section 401(k). In practical effect, you are borrowing from yourself to fund your education, but at an extremely favorable interest rate—usually only a percentage point or two above the prime rate. The funds you borrow from a retirement plan are still tax-deferred and are not subject to income tax when you borrow them. Then, when you pay the funds back, they return to your retirement account and all that you sacrifice in the meantime is any earnings that could have been made on the account if you had not taken the loan.

Travel and Recreation

As mentioned earlier in this chapter, the standard rule of thumb in saving for retirement is to attempt to replace approximately 75 percent of your pre-retirement gross income during your retirement years. This amount comes from a presumption that you will be saving less, paying a lower amount of taxes, and not commuting (or commuting very little) during retirement. But what if one of your retirement goals is to travel extensively or spend considerably on recreational activities that you postponed while working, such as golf or tennis? In this event, should the 75 percent of pre-retirement gross income number be even higher?

Studies have shown that even with increased expenses for travel and recreation, the most that you should budget for is probably 90 percent of your pre-retirement gross income. Still, if your pre-retirement gross income averaged $100,000 per year, you need to save for an amount of $90,000 per year in today's dollars (*after* accounting for the effects of inflation). This is not an insignificant sum, but travel and recreation do not usually add substantially to the total amount of retirement dollars needed. The expense that most retirees typically underestimate is the cost of health care during their retirement years.

Under the tax law, there is a possibility that some of the travel costs you incur may be income-tax deductible. However, these travel expenses must be primarily for and essential to medical care. Thus, a trip to an out-of-state specialty facility, such as the Mayo Clinic in Minnesota or Sloan-Kettering Medical Center in New York City, may be deductible within limits. These limits mean that you cannot deduct meals on the trip and the deduction for lodging is restricted to an amount that is not lavish or extravagant. Even if you can pass these tests, you still may not be able to claim a deduction *unless* the aggregate total of medical expenses exceeds 7.5 percent of your AGI *after* any health insurance reimbursements. As a result of these limitations, this pretty much eliminates a travel expense deduction incurred for most noncatastrophic medical care.

Some taxpayers have tried to deduct the cost of living in a warm locale, such as Florida, during the winter after getting a note from their physician that it is advisable for their good health. Nice try, but the U.S. Supreme Court has ruled that such expenses are primarily personal and not medical, thus denying the claim for the average taxpayer.

Accommodating Change

For many retirees, the most difficult part of retirement is not what we have discussed so far, but rather the simple fact that their daily life has changed. For example, before retirement, when you got out of bed each morning, you had somewhere to go and something to do. This routine changes considerably when you retire.

Just as with the financial aspects of preparing for retirement, you also need to prepare for the lifestyle change. There are many seminars or workshops available to help you deal with retirement issues and retirement life, but the most important task upon retirement is to establish a new *purpose* for your life. This may be as simple as just being there for your children or grandchildren or may involve working part-time. Whatever you do, you should strive to maintain good physical health and keep mentally active. Keeping mentally active does not necessarily entail writing the great American novel, but it does mean that exercising your mind is an integral part of a fulfilling retirement.

If you can accept change and, hopefully, thrive on it, you will probably find yourself among the 90 percent of Americans who say they are very pleased with their retirement and are very happy with the lifestyle decisions they have made while in it.

CHAPTER 18

PLANNING FOR OTHER LIFETIME FINANCIAL GOALS

Whereas most people's number-one financial goal is planning for a comfortable retirement, there are other financial goals that are sometimes part of the wealth distribution process. Among these are starting your own business (and perhaps subsequently selling that business), buying and selling a personal residence, purchasing a second or vacation home, and investing a windfall such as lottery winnings or a substantial inheritance. This chapter considers all of these goals and, to the extent possible (you cannot really *plan* to win the lottery), discusses how to achieve their attainment.

STARTING YOUR OWN BUSINESS

The term *entrepreneur* is defined in Webster's Dictionary as "someone who organizes, manages, and assumes the risk of a business." Does that sound like you? If it does, you are not alone, since many individuals of all ages (particularly baby boomers who are just beginning retirement) harbor the dream of starting their own business.

However, the sad fact is that according to the Small Business Administration, approximately 56 percent of start-up businesses fail within five years. Another 33 percent fail within *two* years of beginning operation. Therefore, your business has approximately a 40/60 chance of being successful.

Numerous books have been written about how you can avoid becoming a failed business owner. Summarizing all of these ideas, success in starting your own business comes down to the same initiative that applies throughout the financial planning and wealth management process: you have to *plan* to be successful.

Here are five commonly agreed-upon steps that you can use to help ensure success in the starting of a business:

1. Begin a business in a trade, skill, or service that you know
2. Write a business plan
3. Consider your form of business operation. Do you wish to operate as a sole proprietor, partnership, corporation, or limited liability company?
4. Recruit individuals to the business who possess strengths different from your own.
5. Give some thought up front to how you will pass on the business to others—usually family members—if that is important to you.

Begin a Business with What You Already Know

According to a study by the Kaufmann Foundation, a center for research and education for entrepreneurs based in Kansas City, Missouri, people ages fifty-five to sixty-four are more likely than anyone else to start their own business. In part, this is because these individuals are retiring or getting close to retiring from the workforce and are preparing for their retirement years. It is also because people of this age group have readily transferable skills in starting and growing their own business.

For example, if you have worked for all or the majority of your career in product development, who knows more than you about that particular product and how it may be adapted to the broader consumer market? Alternatively, if you have worked in sales, who knows better than you how to sell this or some other product? In any business, having a quality product and being able to convince others that they need it—in other words, being able to *sell it*—is the key to its future success. If you are younger than fifty-five, it is likely that starting your own business will be more difficult since you have probably not accumulated sufficient financial resources and expertise.

All successful entrepreneurs possess several common characteristics. Among these are a take-charge attitude, organizational skills, and enormous self-confidence in their own abilities. In addition, for lack of a better description, although it is now a cliché, an ability to think outside the box is very important. This means an ability to be creative and think of other potential uses for your product or service. For instance, Bill Gates was told many times that consumers would have no need for personal computers (PCs), yet he persisted in his vision that consumers would accept and subsequently demand the ability to improve their daily lives. In essence, what Bill Gates saw was not the physical box that was to become the PC, but rather what that box could do for people to make their lives easier. As such, he proved his ability to think outside the box and is among the richest men in the world because of it.

Write a Business Plan

A critical mistake made by many young entrepreneurs is the failure to write a business plan *before* they open the doors of the new business. Just like writing a forward-looking budget when structuring your personal finances, it is terribly difficult to operate a business profitably if you do not anticipate where that business is going—and what risks you have to assume in taking it there.

Not only is a well-thought-out business plan a key to operational success, it is also an important document for raising business capital. It is very unlikely that, particularly if you are young, you will be able to finance the start-up and first few years of business operation out of your own pocket. You will probably have to seek capital from friends or family or—more likely—a bank. Most banks will not lend you the necessary money before they have seen and analyzed your business plan. If you seek financing from a venture capitalist or private equity group of investors, they are exceedingly likely to ask you to prove to them in writing how you intend to grow the business and what niche your product or service will fill in the marketplace that is not already there. A business plan forces you to think about these questions and how you intend to answer them.

The components of a business plan are up to you, but among the more common parts are

- a detailed description of your product or service
- a marketing plan and strategy
- the management team that you plan to assemble
- financial plans and projections
- an analysis of the potential problems and risks you will encounter in bringing your product or service to market, including a competitive SWOT (strengths, weaknesses, opportunities, and threats) analysis

Estimates of start-up costs, profit, and loss projections for the next three to five years should also be included, as well as a break-even financial analysis. Many websites and books are available to assist you in drafting and implementing a business plan, so refer to them often and *before* you begin business operations.

After taking the time to write a thorough and complete business plan, you may decide not to start the business. In that case, the business plan served its purpose: it convinced you that the time is not right to begin your business and that perhaps you should think again before pursing your entrepreneurial dream.

Consider the Form of Business Operation

Often, the form of business operation is included in the business plan. This is particularly true if you plan to start the business with others. Under law, if a business is to have two or more owners, it cannot be a sole proprietorship, the most common form of business operation today. Rather, a multiple-owner business must be a partnership, a regular (also known as a "C") corporation, an "S" corporation, or the increasingly popular limited liability company (LLC), which is now permitted in all fifty states.

Commonly, there are three primary formational issues that any potential business owner should consider before beginning business operations:

1. the possibility of incurring personal liability for any business acts and operation
2. the ease of formation of the business entity and its ability to assist the owner in raising capital
3. the income tax consequences of operating the business in a particular form

Briefly, here are some concepts to think about with respect to each of these issues.

1) Possibility of Personal Liability

The regular or S corporation form of doing business, as well as the LLC form, limit the business owner's liability only to the amount he or she has *invested* in the business. Conversely, in the sole proprietorship or general partnership form of conducting business, the owner or partner retains unlimited *personal* liability for all acts of the business. In other words, in the sole proprietorship or general partnership business form, there is no distinction made between the business entity and the business owner or owners. As a result, the creditors of the business (including the bank) may foreclose on the owner's *personal* assets to satisfy any obligations.

It is possible in some states to operate the business like a sole proprietorship but otherwise limit your personal liability. This may be done by structuring a one-owner business as a single-member LLC. The LLC entity may be formed rather easily by filing standard documents with your Secretary of State or other prescribed office and declaring that you wish to operate as a single-member LLC. Alternatively, a business attorney can advise you of the consequences of conducting your business in this form.

2) Ease of Formation and Ability to Raise Capital

The sole proprietorship type of conducting business is the easiest to form. No formal documents are required by the state and you may simply hang out a sign and begin business (although, in some cases, you may need a state license to conduct the business). This ease of formation should be balanced against the assumption of personal liability that is inherent in operating your business as a sole proprietor.

There is also no written agreement necessary to conduct your business in the general partnership form. Nonetheless, it is generally prudent to spell out the obligations and capital contribution of each partner before the partnership. At some point in the future, the partnership may dissolve and dispose of partnership assets and obligations. It is usually much easier for this process to proceed smoothly if the possibility was considered at the time of commencing business operations.

The regular and S corporation forms of doing business both require the filing of articles of incorporation with the state. Note that an S corporation is simply a regular corporation that has elected to be taxed as a partnership for income tax reasons. If you plan to do business as a corporation, you will need to seek the services of an attorney. While it is possible to form a corporation or LLC on your own without legal assistance, consulting with an attorney before you do so is generally prudent.

With respect to raising capital, there is one clear winner: the regular or C corporation. This is because this form of corporation may issue both common and preferred stock shares and solicit financing from the public in the buying of such shares (an initial public offering or IPO). Nonetheless, given the complexity of forming a business as a regular or C corporation, most start-up businesses shy away from corporate organization, at least initially.

3) Income Tax Consequences

All business forms, for income tax purposes, may be categorized as flow-through entities or separate taxable entities.

Fortunately, all business entities, with the exception of the regular corporation, may be categorized as flow-through entities. This means that all business income and losses are reported on the owner's individual tax return—in other words, the filing of a separate tax return is not necessary. While the income part of the flow-through consequence may not be significant, since most start-up businesses experience losses in their first few years of operation, the attribution of tax losses that may be taken by a business owner on his or her tax return assists greatly with cash flow needs. Remember, in many cases, the cash flow of the business and of the business owner is one and the same. Unlike capital losses, which are restricted to no more than a $3,000 income-tax deduction in any one calendar year, ordinary businesses losses are fully deductible *without limitation*. As such, a loss may be incurred by the business in one year and offset against the business owner's other taxable income in that same year.

For example, assume that you have elected to conduct business in the sole proprietorship form and in the first year you have a business loss of $10,000 (after considering any income you received from the business). You would report all of this loss on Schedule C of the IRS Form 1040 and offset any other non-business income by the $10,000 loss. You can do this *regardless* of whether or not you itemize your deductions for income-tax purposes.

The one exception to flow-through tax rules is the regular or C corporation form of doing business. If you conduct business this way, a separate tax return, with the application of a separate set of tax brackets, is required. As with individual tax rates and brackets, corporate tax rates are progressive in nature. As such, it is possible to have some corporate income taxed at a *lower* marginal tax rate than that of the corporation's shareholders. Similarly, however, business losses may only be taken by the separate corporate taxable entity and may *not* be applied against the owner's individual taxable income.

Recruit Individuals with Different Strengths

Having a quality product or superior service and then being able to convince others of this quality or superiority is critical to the success of any business. Operational strengths are also important.

It is very unlikely that you or any potential business owner possess the myriad of skills necessary to conduct and grow the business to the level you anticipated when you first drafted your business plan. You will likely need the services of others to ensure the success of the business. As such, you should try to recruit individuals your business with strengths and skills different from your own to fill in any gaps that may arise in business operation or development. For example, if you possess strengths in product development, you should hire someone with the marketing skills to sell that product. If you can sell, you need to ensure that the product you are selling is of the utmost quality. Perhaps strength in product development should be sought. Although the need for operational skills is often neglected by small business owners, the more *efficient* your business, the more it will be reflected in the amount of *net profit* generated by the business.

Business Succession

It is estimated that 70 percent of family businesses do not survive the transition from the original founder or founders to a second generation of family members. Why? Usually it is because most founders of a business fail to plan for their succession. While some of this failure to plan is due to the founder's temperament (for example, many entrepreneurs act as if they are immortal), perhaps the major reason for the lack of business succession planning is simply because the founder just does not wish to talk about the possibility of his or her eventual death.

A way to address the succession issue is to include provisions for possible successor owners in your business plan before you begin operations. This has the advantage of forcing you to think about how you will pass on the business to others without the attendant pressure of developing a formal estate plan. The most probable successor owner is a family member who has either previously worked in the business or has indicated an interest in taking it over. However, a trusted non-family-member employee with many years of experience in the business is also potentially a worthy successor.

Regardless, if you want the business to continue after your death or disability, you must develop a business succession plan. This should be accomplished in as tax-efficient a manner as possible for the sake of the business seller (usually a senior family member) and the buyer (usually a junior or younger generation family member). Accountants and tax attorneys may provide an invaluable service in this regard and should be consulted as early as possible in the business succession process.

Buying a Personal Residence

The tax aspects of buying and selling a personal residence were addressed in chapter 11. The discussion here focuses on the money you need to save to buy a home (particularly a first home) and the types of mortgages available to finance this purchase.

As everyone who has ever purchased a home knows, buying a personal residence is expensive. While the actual cost of the home depends on local market conditions, you should attempt to save at least 20 percent of the purchase price so as to avoid the additional cost of private mortgage insurance. Let's consider an example.

Assume that you are considering the purchase of a starter home for $150,000. You should attempt to save at least $30,000 as a 20 percent down payment. How long will it take you to accumulate $30,000? The answer depends on how much money you can save each month as well as the rate of return you can earn on those savings. If you can put away $500 per month and earn a 6 percent before-tax rate of return, you would have $30,000 after approximately fifty-three months of saving. However, if you can earn a 12 percent before-tax rate of return (in other words, *double* your rate of earnings), you would achieve $30,000 in savings six months earlier, after approximately forty-seven months. If you can save more than $500 per month, you can achieve the needed down payment even sooner.

There are mortgages that allow you to put down *less* than 20 percent of the home's purchase price, but the conventional mortgage marketplace (at least until subprime mortgages were introduced) requires 20 percent as a minimum.

Just as with any other financial goal, to achieve the funds necessary to buy a home, you have to plan for it. This goes back to the financial planning fundamentals discussed in the first section of the book: *you must establish a savings strategy and then implement it.* If you need to prepare a budget to allow you to accumulate the necessary savings, then you should do so. One of the reasons to prepare a budget is to monitor your future spending in the hopes of accumulating a cash surplus at month's end. Another word for this cash surplus is savings, and you must have the discipline to save or you will not accumulate wealth.

Mortgages

Historically, there were four primary types of mortgages, although recently a fifth—the interest-only mortgage—has also been offered to home-buyers. All demonstrate a primary advantage of investing in real estate: the use of borrowed money to leverage an investment and thereby achieve a greater return on your money.

Here are the five types of mortgages available in the marketplace, along with some factors to consider before choosing which is most appropriate for you:

1. Conventional mortgages: These are fixed-rate mortgages for the term of the loan—usually fifteen or thirty years—that give the borrower a guarantee that the interest rate (and therefore the monthly payment) will not increase.

These types of mortgages are for individuals who have a stable cash flow and anticipate this stability in future years.

2. Adjustable rate mortgages (ARMs): With this type of mortgage, the interest rate charged may change on a monthly or yearly basis according to some specified index or benchmark, such as the current yield on the ten-year U.S. Treasury note. ARMs are for individuals who want *lower* monthly payments and do not anticipate remaining in the home for a considerable period of time.

3. Federal Housing Administration (FHA) mortgages: The payment of this mortgage is guaranteed by the federal government and as such will normally have a lower interest rate than conventional mortgages. A low down payment is also a feature of the loan. FHA mortgages are usually available only to lower-income homeowners.

4. Veterans Administration (VA) mortgages: This type of mortgage features the same federal guarantee of repayment as that for FHA mortgages but is for veterans of the armed services only. A feature of the loan is that *no* down payment is required.

5. Interest-only mortgages: In this form of mortgage, the borrower only pays the interest on the loan for a specified number of years. Little reduction of loan principal is possible, thereby effectively preventing the borrower from building much, if any, equity in the home. When executing an interest-only mortgage, the borrower is anticipating that the fair market value of the home will appreciate from the purchase price, allowing a payoff of the mortgage balance from any sale proceeds. By their very nature, interest-only mortgages should only be executed by relatively *risk-aggressive* individuals.

PURCHASING AND USING A VACATION HOME

Purchasing a vacation home is a *direct* form of real estate investment. Although sometimes a vacation or second home is rented out and generates rental income for the purchaser, more times than not such a home is purchased as a private getaway for the purchaser and his or her family. If so, treating the home as an income-producing investment in lieu of an income stock or fixed-income bond portfolio probably is not foremost in the purchaser's mind. Moreover, if the purchaser does rent out his or her vacation home for more than fourteen days a year, the IRS will tax it as a rental. This could push the purchaser into the next marginal income tax bracket, resulting in higher income taxes overall.

Presuming that you, as the purchaser, are buying the vacation home for your own private use or that of your family, there are several techniques you can use to take maximum advantage of the tax laws. The first, known colloquially as a like kind exchange, may allow you to defer taxes on the gain from a sale of the home. The second is an estate or transfer tax planning technique whereby if certain conditions are met, you can exclude the fair market value of the home from taxation in your gross estate. This second technique is known as a **qualified personal residence trust (QPRT)**.

Under Section 1031 of the income tax code, it is possible to do a nontaxable exchange of one investment property for another investment property. However, it is *not* possible to do this same exchange if either property is held for personal use. If you plan to use your vacation home for more than fourteen days during the year (which is likely since you probably bought the home for personal use anyway), you are definitely out of luck. It will *not* qualify as a nontaxable or like kind exchange. Alternatively, let's say that, for whatever reason, you only plan to use the vacation home for one week during the year. You could argue that the vacation home is strictly held as an investment property and nontaxable exchange treatment should be possible. The key word here is "possible," since the law is unclear with respect to the taxable result of an exchange of vacation homes where each home is used by the owner for less than fourteen days out of the year (and is not rented out for more than fourteen days). While this is certainly aggressive tax planning, it may work if the facts are right.

Section 1031 nontaxable exchange treatment is much more clear-cut if you rent out the vacation home instead of using it for personal use. In that case, assuming that you keep your personal use during the year to fourteen days or less, it likely *will* qualify as a like kind exchange and any realized gain will be deferred. However, remember, the tradeoff for the deferral of gain is the annual reporting of all income from the home as a rental property.

Now let's move to the second planning technique involving a vacation home: the QPRT. In a QPRT, the vacation home must definitely be used as a *second* personal residence. As such, you cannot rent out the vacation home for any period of time during the year. As a result, if you subsequently establish a QPRT and make the vacation home part of its corpus, you may potentially exclude the fair market value of the home from your gross estate and avoid estate tax on that value.

The mechanics of the QPRT technique are as follows:

1. Establish a QPRT with the assistance of an estate-planning attorney.
2. Re-title the vacation home in the name of the trustee of the QPRT.
3. Provide for your right to use the home for a period of years. Be careful here: if you die during the period of time that you have the right to use the home, the value of the home at your death will be included and taxed as part of your gross estate.
4. Transfer the title to the home at the end of this period of reserved use to a separately named trust beneficiary or beneficiaries (typically, your adult child or children).

Note that it is also possible to have the trust beneficiary *lease* the vacation home back to you at the end of the reserved period. In this instance, while the value of the home is still excluded from your gross estate, the trust beneficiary must now report taxable lease income, but you will further reduce your gross estate by the amount of the lease payments that are made.

For example, assume that you are sixty-five, in a high marginal estate tax bracket, and establish a QPRT, funding it with a vacation home as the corpus of the trust. You reserve the right to use the vacation home for a period of fifteen years, or until you turn eighty. If you die before age eighty, the fair market value of the home is included in your gross estate. However, if you survive the term of the trust, the value of the home is totally *excluded* from your gross estate. In addition, if you still wish to use the home, you can enter into an arm's-length rental arrangement with a family member as the trust beneficiary when you turn eighty.

Consider the practical consequences of establishing a QPRT carefully. If you establish the trust and do not outlive the trust term, you are in no worse taxable shape than you would be if you had done nothing. Therefore, for only the cost of establishing the trust, you can possibly enjoy a sizable potential estate tax savings. In addition, you have also defended your wealth from one of the often-cited primary threats: the imposition of taxes.

INVESTING A WINDFALL: SO YOU WON THE LOTTERY!

There are ways you could come into some unexpected money or experience a windfall other than winning the lottery. Among these is the receipt of a substantial inheritance, an unexpected bonus, or the settlement of a sizable lawsuit in your favor. Still, when most people hear the term windfall, they think of winning the lottery. What do you do after you learn that you hold the lucky winning numbers resulting from an investment of only a dollar or two?

Following are three commonsense tips to be used in managing unexpected wealth:

1. Do not tell anyone—most of all, do not tell the media! This will allow you to make important financial decisions about how to invest the windfall without everyone telling you what you should do with the money. The obvious exception to this rule is that you *do* want to consult with

financial and legal professionals about how best to invest the money.

2. Decide how best to receive the money—that is, in a lump sum or over time. If you tend to be a spendthrift, structure the payment so that is received over time; alternatively, if you consider yourself a pretty good investor and saver, you may wish to take the lump sum. Regardless, both forms of payment will be immediately income-taxable, so you will receive a greatly reduced after-tax amount.

3. Invest the money, at least for the time being, in a money market mutual fund or savings account that you can easily access without fear of any loss of principal. This will enable you to meet with a financial expert with respect to how you should invest the money for both your short-term and long-term needs. Further, it should help you to avoid the making of any immediate bad investment decisions when your judgment may be clouded by the excitement of coming into so much money.

Remember a basic rule of debt management: pay off high interest debt immediately, such as credit card interest. With such a significant windfall of money, you should be able to get rid of your credit cards entirely and pay cash for all future expenses.

SECTION VI

DISTRIBUTING WEALTH AT DEATH

CHAPTER 19

ESTATE PLANNING

We have now reached the last stage in a person's financial life (and physical life, for that matter): death. In this chapter, we will discuss how to distribute wealth to your spouse, family members, or other specified individuals or charities when you die. Estate planning and the distribution of an individual's assets at death may best be thought of as the second component in the last step of the PADD process: *distributing* your lifetime accumulation of wealth at death so as to benefit others.

Most people think of estate planning as lifetime planning to avoid the possible imposition of sizable (some would say punitive) estate taxes. But estate planning is actually much more than that: more properly, the process can best be described as the efficient distribution of an individual's property to his or her heirs in the proper amount at the proper time. The *proper amount* means generally whatever distribution among your heirs is the most preferable; however, the term takes on special meaning for high-net-worth individuals who must plan in a transfer-tax-efficient manner. The *proper time* is not only at the decedent's death, but also when he or she is still alive. Lifetime gifting is a very prudent and effective way to distribute one's wealth on a trial basis to see how your intended heirs manage and use the property you give them. If you do not like the way your intended beneficiaries are using the assets you have gifted them, in most cases you have the opportunity to amend your estate plan.

As a general rule, everyone should prepare certain estate planning documents *regardless* of whether they believe they will owe any estate taxes at death. Among the estate planning documents that almost all individuals should have are

- a last will and testament
- a financial durable power of attorney
- a medical or health care durable power of attorney
- a declaration as to medical and surgical treatment (commonly referred to as a living will)

We begin our discussion of these documents specifically and the estate planning process generally with the last will and testament.

Do I Need a Will?

The short answer to this question is yes. Regardless of your personal and financial circumstances, a last will and testament permits you to express how you wish your property to be distributed at death. The writing of a will permits you to name an individual of your own choosing to administer your estate at your death. If you do not do either of these things, your estate will likely be distributed according to how the state in which you reside when you die wants the property to be distributed and by whom. This is known as the process of **intestate succession** and can be summarized as the will that the state has already written for you. If you do not like the state's will—to the extent you even know what that is—the private writing of a will to carry out your personal wishes is a prudent estate planning technique.

The writing of a will is particularly critical for a young married couple with minor children. This is because a will is the only document that allows them the opportunity to name a guardian for their minor children. It is not necessary to name a guardian if one of the natural parents is still living at the death of the other. But what about in the unfortunate circumstance where both natural parents die in a common disaster or accident? In that event, without a will, the court (known here as the probate court) will name a guardian. If either set of the grandparents of the children is alive, they may be a likely choice. However, what if your parents (the child's grandparents) are in poor health or do not reside close to you at your death? In this instance, the court will likely look to a sibling to assume the guardianship role. If neither a grandparent nor a sibling (or any other family member) is close by or even exists, the court will look to a trusted friend or perhaps a foster family. Regardless, as a young married individual, if you do not wish for the court to decide, be proactive and write a will providing for a guardian.

The naming of a guardian for minor children by a parent is really only half of what needs to be done. While your parent or sibling may be able to assume the guardianship role, what if this individual is not very good in handling the money that is left to him or her for the child's care? If this is the case, you may wish to consider including a trust in your will for the purposes of receiving and investing the money on behalf of the child for later distribution. You will need to name a trustee for this trust—and the skills that are necessary to perform the legal duty of a trustee effectively are *not the same* as that of a guardian. For example, the empathetic skills of a person suited to be a guardian, and the financial skills most important for a trustee, may not be present in the same person or family member. As such, you may wish to name two separate individuals for each role. If you do, make sure these individuals can work together effectively. Remember, you are not there to serve as a go-between if your two guardians do not get along, and your minor child (or children) will suffer the consequences.

If you do include a trust in your will for the benefit of your children (known in estate planning as a **contingent trust**, since it only takes effect on the contingency of the simultaneous death of both parents), you need to change *all* your beneficiary designations to include the name of the trustee. It is particularly important to name the trustee as the contingent or secondary beneficiary of a life insurance policy on your life; otherwise, the insurance company will need to get a probate court order allowing it to pay out the proceeds to the trustee. Moreover, under the laws of all states, a minor cannot take title to property in his or her own name. If you have left property to a minor child in your will and have not named a guardian, the court will have to appoint a guardian to receive the property on the child's behalf. All things considered, it is much easier to complete the necessary estate planning while you are alive so as to avoid these consequences altogether.

Given its importance, why do many individuals never write a will? For two primary reasons:

1. The writing of a will reminds us of our own mortality, a topic that many people do not wish to consider.
2. Many people believe the writing of a will is prohibitively expensive.

With respect to overcoming the first objection, consider the situation in which you may leave your survivors if you do *not* write a will. More than likely, your survivors will want you to make your passing as easy as possible on them—and knowing that they have been provided for in your will give them great comfort. Further, if you have gone so far as to establish a trust in your will, you may direct the disposition of your property at a time when you believe it will be most appropriate for your survivors. This is colloquially known as speaking from the grave, and the more direction you give in your estate planning documents, the louder you speak.

The cost objection is often resolved by investigating your alternatives. For example, most attorneys charge a flat fee for drafting a will, with this charge varying according to the amount of drafting that must be done. A simple will—or one that does not involve any estate tax planning—may not cost you any more than several hundred dollars or even less, if it is part of a package of estate planning documents drafted by the attorney. Any number of websites now have standardized wills and other estate planning documents that you may wish to consider using, but you should use these only *after* you have spoken with a competent estate planning attorney in the state where the documents will be effective.

LEAVING PROPERTY VIA BENEFICIARY DESIGNATIONS AND TITLING OF PROPERTY

It is possible to avoid the probate process and leave your property to others via beneficiary designations, such as those included with your life insurance policy, IRA, and retirement plan at work. Many educated consumers are aware of this possibility. But what about that property where a beneficiary designation is *not* possible—for example, your checking or savings accounts, brokerage accounts, and articles of personal property? Unfortunately, each of these must be considered separately when it comes to disposing of property to others.

1. Checking or savings accounts may only be left to others by a will (or your state's laws of intestate succession). If you are married, you may wish to consider titling these accounts in joint tenancy with right of survivorship. By titling the accounts in such a manner, they will pass directly by operation of law to the other named joint tenant, and not under a will, at your death. However, be aware that during lifetime, each spouse owns 100 percent of the monies in the accounts and can do with them as he or she wishes—*without* the consent of the other spouse. If you are not married, but nevertheless want a second name on the account, ask your bank to establish a joint account for convenience only (otherwise referred to as a convenience account). In most states, account titling in this form means that the second party to the account may withdraw monies from the checking or savings account but *only* for the benefit of the primary joint tenant. At death, a convenience account may or may not be left to another without the necessity of writing a will, depending on the law of the particular state.

2. Brokerage accounts are usually easier to title in a way to pass directly to others without a will. Specifically, if you are working with a stockbroker, ask him or her to title the brokerage account using a **transfer on death** (TOD) form. Like an IRA or retirement plan, you need only to name a beneficiary for the account and fill out the requisite form for the broker or mutual fund family to honor the request. However, be aware that if you have not completed a TOD form during your lifetime for a brokerage account, your will or state law will dictate its disposition at death. Note that a bank has a similar form, known as a **payable on death** (POD) form, to provide for the passing of bank accounts directly to a named beneficiary.

3. The disposition of personal property articles at death may not be of much concern to many decedents. This is either because they do not have significant articles to value, or they simply wish to leave it to others to sell or dispose of. However, if an article is an antique or has been passed down through several generations of family members, you should attach to your will a statement of personal property memorandum. All states provide for this statement and, so long as it is incorporated by reference at the time of executing your will, and so long as default provisions are included in the will, you do *not* need to complete the statement at that time. Rather, you may subsequently describe the articles you wish to leave to others and sign the statement at a later date. In other words, you have time to consider future circumstances in deciding how best to dispose of valuable items.

We now move to what is known as the poor man's will in estate planning—titling all or most of your property jointly and having it pass by operation of law in the state where you die. This means that you may not have to write a will at all, although, as just discussed, you may wish to do so for other reasons. Although titling property jointly with another is a simple and effective method of transferring your property at death, for estate tax reasons, you may need to reconsider. For example, leaving property via joint tenancy to a surviving tenant who already owns significant amounts of property in his or her own name may add to the potential estate tax liability of the survivor.

For example, assume that you own property with a fair market value of $2 million jointly with another at your death. Depending on when the survivor dies and the estate tax exemption amounts at that time, if the survivor already owns $2 million of property in his or her own name prior to receiving your property, he or she may owe a sizable amount of estate tax. Note that this may be a concern for spouses and non-spouses who are the surviving joint tenants of another's property.

If you do not believe that you will have an estate tax problem at your death, owning property jointly with another may substitute for the beneficiary designation that is possible with other assets. In this case, even if you do write a will and leave your property to someone other than the surviving joint tenant, the will provision is generally ignored and the property passes by operation of law to the surviving tenant.

SHOULD I AVOID THE PROBATE PROCESS AT DEATH?

Very simply, the probate process can best be described as the act or process of proving a will. However, this entails numerous steps and court intervention, which may lead to both excessive cost and delay in distributing your property to heirs. For these reasons, among others, many decedents wish to avoid the process entirely. There are three primary methods by which individuals can avoid probate:

- using a beneficiary designation whenever possible to leave specific property to a named individual or individuals
- titling property with survivorship rights. In most states, this means titling property jointly with another, but even in community property states such as California and Texas,

it is possible to elect rights of survivorship with respect to property acquired during the marriage.

- establishing and transferring assets to a revocable living trust

Due to its popularity, the **revocable living trust** (RLT) deserves additional explanation.

In order for the assets within a RLT to avoid probate, they must be transferred out of the individual names of the owners and re-titled in the name of the trustee. It is possible, however, and very common, for the original owner to also name him- or herself the trustee of his or her RLT. As a practical matter, what is required is simply the preparation and filing of a quitclaim deed transferring title to property from the owner's individual name to his or her name as the trustee. For this to occur, there must be a trust document in existence at the time the title is transferred. If not, the re-titling from individual owner to trustee is not legally valid, and all such property must be probated.

In addition to the need to write an RLT document, only the property that is actually re-titled in the name of the trustee may avoid probate. Accordingly, many individuals couple the drafting of an RLT with a **pour-over will**. Such a will is executed for the express purpose of transferring forgotten and after-acquired property into the RLT—in other words, the will "pours over" this property to the RLT at the decedent's death and distributes it according to the terms of the trust. Since, at the moment of the trust grantor's death, there is still property owned by the decedent in his or her name, the property passing via the will is subject to the probate process. Nonetheless, the fair market value of this property is typically so nominal that many state laws provide for an exemption.

We have now discussed the reasons for avoiding probate and the primary methods available to individuals who wish to do so. This begs the question: *should* you avoid the probate of assets at your death?

There are several advantages to probate. It provides a mechanism to clear title to the decedent's property. It also implements the provisions of the decedent's will. A frequently overlooked advantage of the probate process is that it also protects the decedent from an untimely filing of claims by his or her lifetime creditors. For example, let's say you own a small business at your death and potentially have many creditors at your death. If your interest in the small business undergoes probate, the business creditors must file their claims against the estate within nine months of your death or *they are forever barred*. Moreover, should you anticipate the filing of some unknown creditor's claim at your death, forcing these creditors into a time-specific period to make their intentions known is prudent estate planning.

Ultimately, the only person who can make a decision about whether the avoidance of probate is preferred is you. You should recognize the advantages to having your property probated at death and that probate's frequently cited disadvantages—cost, the potential for delay, and the public nature of the process—may not be so important that you skip the process altogether.

ESTATE TAXES

Estates taxes may be assessed at the federal and state level (for example, New York has an estate tax), but typically only the *federal* tax rates are of concern to most decedents. If federal estate taxes are likely to be due in your estate or that of your spouse, you may want to include some tax-planning measures in your will or trust. The inclusion of these measures will initially make the writing of a will or trust more costly, but the planning will pay for itself many times over in estate taxes saved.

Estate taxes at the federal level are part of what is known as the unified transfer tax system. In practical effect, this means that the tax rates and brackets are the *same* whether you make a lifetime gift of property to others or transfer this property to others at your death. Thus, operationally, any lifetime taxable gift that you make *reduces* the amount of property that you can leave to your heirs or beneficiaries at death.

Assume that you make a taxable gift of $1 million in 2011 to someone other than your spouse (when an unlimited deduction applies). Although you pay no federal gift taxes—remember, an allowance of $5 million is permitted before any gift tax is due—you have reduced your current aggregate $5 million estate-tax exemption to only $4 million. Accordingly, if you die with a taxable estate of $5,000,001 in 2011, that $1 of additional property is taxed at a marginal tax rate of 35 percent.

Note that in this example, the reduction of your exemption amount for estate-tax purposes does *not* mean you should avoid lifetime gifting. Rather, in most instances, you should engage in as much lifetime gifting as possible. This means, first, that you should take advantage of the annual gift tax exclusion ($13,000 per person in 2011), since such exclusion is applied *before* you begin to calculate tax liability on a taxable gift. Second, and perhaps even more important, is the possibility of excluding the subsequent appreciation on gifted property from your estate. For instance, in our example, let's say you did not die until 2013 and the property gifted in 2011 appreciated 50 percent over the course of those two years. Since you previously gifted the property, you avoided estate taxes on $500,000 (or the 50 percent of appreciation).

Once your taxable estate has been computed at death, your executor may apply a specified amount of credit—known in estate tax language as the unified credit—against your tentative estate tax due. Since, as with in income tax, a credit is a dollar-for-dollar reduction against taxes, what you should really be concerned about is the *amount* of that credit in the year of death. In turn, that credit equates to an amount of property that may be transferred estate-tax-free to others at your death (hence the term *exemption equivalent*). For example, in 2011, the amount of allowable unified credit is $1,730,800, which is equivalent to an exempted property amount of $5 million.

Let's look at another example: assume that you die with a taxable estate of $5 million in 2011 and have made no previous lifetime taxable gifts that operate to reduce this amount. When you refer to the applicable unified transfer tax table, you will find that the estate tax liability on this $5 million of property is $1,730,800. Since you have an allowable credit equal to that same amount, you may reduce your tax liability by the allowable credit, resulting in an actual tax due of zero ($1,730,800 tentative tax liability less the $1,730,800 unified credit amount).

Accordingly, when you hear estate planners say that you do not pay any estate tax until you die with property in excess of $5 million or the otherwise applicable exemption equivalent, what they are really telling you is that you have a unified credit that is equal in amount to the estate tax due on that $5 million.

You need to understand how the federal estate tax system works and what measures you may adopt to reduce the amount of your taxable estate at death. This is in part why you should contact a financial planner or estate-planning attorney. Nevertheless, the more you can educate yourself with respect to the estate and gift tax laws, the better off you will be in understanding the planning techniques that may be undertaken to minimize those taxes.

To that end, following are two very important tables that relate to estate tax transfers and estate tax planning. The first table reflects the tax brackets and marginal tax rates that apply to taxable transfers through 2009–2012 (for decedents who died in 2010, the estate tax was repealed). The second table specifies the amount of applicable unified credit and exemption amounts for those same years. You should be aware that the higher exemption amount of $5 million and the unified credit of $1,730,800 (first taking effect for transfers made during 2011) only apply through the end of 2012, when the transfer tax rates—if the tax applies at all—will be revisited by Congress.

Unified Federal and Gift Tax Brackets and Marginal Tax Rates

If the amount is:

Over (Column 1)	But Not Over (Column 2)	Tax on Column 1	Excess Tax on Column 2 (Marginal Tax Rate)
-0-	$10,000	-0-	18%
$10,000	$20,000	$1,800	20%
$20,000	$40,000	$3,800	22%
$40,000	$60,000	$8,200	24%
$60,000	$80,000	$13,000	26%
$80,000	$100,000	$18,200	28%
$100,000	$150,000	$23,800	30%
$150,000	$250,000	$38,800	32%
$250,000	$500,000	$70,800	34%
$500,000	$750,000	$155,800	37%*
$750,000	$1,000,000	$248,300	39%*
$1,000,000	$1,250,000	$345,800	41%*
$1,250,000	$1,500,000	$448,300	43%*
$1,500,000	$2,000,000	$555,800	45%*
$2,000,000	$3,500,000	$780,800	45%*
$3,500,000	$5,000,000	$1,455,800	45%*
$5,000,000	Excess	$1,730,800	45%*

* For 2011 and 2012, taxable transfers above $500,000, whether made during life or at death, are taxed at a maximum marginal rate of 35 percent.

Unified Credit and Applicable
Exemption Equivalent Amounts for Estates

Year of Death	Unified Credit	Applicable Exemption Equivalent
2009	$1,455,800*	$3,500,000*
2010	Not applicable; estate tax repealed*	Not applicable; estate tax repealed*
2011	$1,730,800	$5,000,000
2012	$1,730,800	$5,000,000

*Gift tax applicable exemption equivalent for transfers made during 2009 and 2010 was $1,000,000 with a unified credit amount of $345,800.

THE IMPORTANCE OF DURABLE POWERS OF ATTORNEY

Statistics show that at any age, you are more likely to become disabled or incompetent than to die. Disability and incapacity are not the same thing, but many people use the terms interchangeably. However, in understanding and applying powers of attorney, it is important to recognize that their use is only triggered in the event of legal *incapacity* (or *incompetency*). The individual granting the power may be physically disabled and still be legally competent to conduct his or her financial and health-related affairs.

There are two parties to a power of attorney: the *principal*, or the individual granting the power, and the *agent* or *attorney-in-fact*—the individual responsible for carrying out the duties of the power. It is essential when granting a power of attorney to someone else that the principal is legally competent when granting the power; if he or she is not, the power cannot be effective. Moreover, unless the power of attorney is specifically written to continue in the event of the principal's incompetency (a *durable* power of attorney), the power of the agent to act on behalf of the principal will terminate on the date of the principal's incompetency. In other words, a nondurable power of attorney is *not* effective just when it is needed most—on the date of the principal's inability to act.

There are two types of powers of attorney. The first is used for the management of the individual's *property*, including financial accounts, subsequent to the principal's incompetency. This is frequently referred to as a financial or general durable power of attorney, since it covers a multitude of financial situations in which the agent may act on behalf of the principal. It is also possible to limit the power of the agent to act through the writing of a special or limited durable power of attorney. The second type of durable power of attorney provides for a surrogate or substitute to make decisions with respect to the principal's health. This type of power commonly goes by the name of a *medical durable* or *durable power of attorney for health care*, although it may have a different name in your state (for example, a medical proxy).

A general durable power of attorney (DPOA) becomes effective in one of two instances: either *immediately* at the time that the principal grants powers to the agent, or *in the future*, when the principal becomes legally incompetent. If the power becomes effective immediately, it is referred to as a regular or non-springing DPOA, whereas if it does not become effective until the principal becomes incompetent, it is referred to as a springing DPOA. If the power is springing, there must be some method of determining *when* the principal is legally incompetent. Normally, this is determined by the mutual agreement of at least two physicians that the principal cannot act on his or her own behalf and needs the assistance of the agent. Since the principal may derive some comfort in knowing that he or she has not relinquished immediate control over his or her property, many times he or she will execute a springing DPOA. However, this concern is likely exaggerated in the majority of cases, since typically the designated agent is a trusted family member and is exceedingly unlikely to act until it is clear that the principal cannot do so.

In contrast to the general DPOA, the durable power of attorney for health care (DPOAHC) is *always* springing in effect. In other words, so long as the principal is able to give informed consent with respect to his or her own health care, the medical community will look to the principal. It is only in the event that the principal is *not* able to give consent that the advice of the agent will be sought.

The selection of an agent to make medical decisions on a principal's behalf should be considered even *more* carefully than that of the general DPOA. While some individuals may not be overly concerned about their financial affairs in the event of incompetency, or about who takes over these responsibilities, the same cannot likely be said about their health. It is essential that the principal give considerable thought to the individual whom he or she chooses to make medical decisions on his or her behalf. The individual named as the power of attorney for a principal's health may be different from the individual named to manage the principal's money or property.

How should you proceed with planning for your own possible incompetency? Do you need one or both of these powers of attorney? Yes, and preferably *both* documents. This is the case even if you do not see the need for a last will and testament. Again, the chances of your becoming incompetent at any given time is much *greater* than the chances of your death. The importance of writing durable powers of attorney cannot be stressed enough. To assist you in the writing and implementation of these documents, samples of the general DPOA and DPOAHC are included in appendixes C and D. Alternatively, you should seek out the assistance of an estate planning or elder care law attorney to draft these documents.

While durable powers of attorney are a simple and are by and large effective way to plan for incompetency, there are several potential problems with their use. First, if the powers are dated (say, over three to five years old), the third party to whom the power is presented may not recognize their validity. Moreover, this third party (typically a financial institution) may ask the principal to execute its own durable power of attorney form to protect itself from possible liability in honoring the power. This is particularly a concern if, between the time of writing the original DPOA and the time the power is needed, the principal becomes incompetent. As a general rule, before executing a general DPOA for property management, you should ask the third party how long they are likely to recognize its validity.

The other problem with a DPOA, whether related to a principal's finances *or* to health care, is that, under law, the power terminates on the death of the principal. For example, where minor children depend on the principal to act on their behalf, and the principal dies, this could present a problem. Fortunately, one of the advantages of writing a revocable living trust (RLT) as part of your estate planning is that it may also serve as a very effective method of planning for your own incompetency. Specifically, in contrast to a DPOA or DPOAHC, the power of a successor trustee to act on behalf of the grantor of a RLT does *not* terminate on the death of the grantor. A successor trustee may continue to act without impunity. Note: In some states, because of this feature, many financial institutions prefer to recognize the legal validity of a RLT rather than that of a DPOA.

For example, assume that you granted a general DPOA on behalf of your oldest son ten years ago, and you now die. The power of your son to act on your behalf terminates on the date of your death. Moreover, given the datedness of the general DPOA, some financial institutions may refuse to recognize its validity while you are alive. If you became incompetent during the ten-year period, your son may not have been able to act on your behalf as power of attorney. Both of these problems may be avoided if instead of, or in conjunction with, the DPOA, you execute a revocable living trust naming your son as the successor trustee.

Living Wills

A living will (actually, the absence of one) was much in the news several years ago with the Schiavo case in Florida. If Terri Schiavo had executed a living will before her massive decline in health, it is likely that much of the dispute between her parents and ex-husband could have been avoided.

Unlike a DPOAHC, which can take effect in a variety of medical situations, a living will only takes effect in the event of a *terminal illness*. In other words, you must be in a terminal condition and not expected to recover. Due to medical advances, a hospital or other patient care facility can keep you alive for a number of days or months by having a respirator breathe for you or feeding you intravenously or sometimes both. As a result, in most states, you are permitted to make one of three choices:

1. to maintain an artificial means of life for an indeterminate amount of time
2. to immediately discontinue the artificial means of life after you are pronounced terminal by two or more physicians
3. to maintain the artificial means of life for a period of days—usually seven to ten days—at your discretion

While many individuals opt for the third choice, there is no magic number of days or weeks that, if you survive, you will partially or fully recover. Usually, the result is *the opposite*: if you have not recovered after a specified period of time, you are likely *not* to recover. This makes the execution of a living will that much more difficult, as most people do not wish to consider that they may find themselves in a terminal condition.

Unlike a DPOAHC, which names a substitute decision maker with respect to health care matters, a living will is a personal directive from you to your physician specifying how you wish to be treated if you are terminally ill. As a matter of procedure, after executing a living will, you should give a copy to your family or other physicians. Fortunately, the process of writing a living will is made easier by the publication, in most states, of a pre-printed form that you can fill out prior to entering the hospital. Early completion of this form permits you to discuss with your physician the ramifications and possible unintended consequences of your decision.

Should you execute a living will? If you have not written a DPOAHC or medical proxy, you should. If you have already written a DPOAHC, you should check to see if any living will provisions are already included in the document. Some states permit an individual to include *both* living will directions and powers given to a medical power of attorney. This means that only one document, instead of two, needs to be completed to address any conceivable medical decision that may need to be made. However, it also may make it more difficult for your physician to determine the preferable course of treatment. This fact makes it all the more important (whether you have both a living will and DPOAHC or one all-inclusive document) that you also communicate orally to your spouse or other close family member what should happen in the event of a life-threatening condition.

A sample copy of a living will—sometimes referred to by its proper name of Declaration as to Medical or Surgical Treatment—and a DPOAHC are included in appendix D.

PERSONAL LETTER OF INSTRUCTIONS

A final, often overlooked document that you can use in the distribution-of-wealth process at death is a personal letter of instructions. This letter is an informal writing from you to the executor of your will reminding him or her to contact certain individuals and to perform certain tasks at your death. Such a letter also often includes directions with respect to where the executor may find the originals of your last will and testament, any trusts you have executed, powers of attorney, and living wills. The letter should also specify how you wish to have your body handled subsequent to your death and any other special wishes, such as organ donation.

It is important to understand that you do not have to draft a personal letter of instructions in any particular form or consult an attorney to draw one up for you. Rather, the form of and the inclusions within the letter are limited only by your current and anticipated circumstances, as well as your own creative skills. A sample personal letter of instructions as used by an attorney in his financial and estate planning practice is included in appendix C.

When Should I Change My Estate Plan?

We conclude this chapter with a list of important events that may cause you to consider changing your estate plan, amending your current will or trusts, or rewriting those documents entirely.

You should periodically review your estate planning documents to consider whether your objectives have changed. Here are some events that will likely result in the amendment or changing of your estate plan:

1. if you have moved from one state to another, it is good practice to have your will or any other estate planning document reviewed by an attorney who is licensed in your new state of residence.
2. if you have had a significant change in family circumstances, such as the birth of a new child or the death of a named or intended beneficiary to your estate.
3. if the executor or guardian you have selected for your estate can no longer serve
4. if there has been a substantial change in the estate or gift tax laws subsequent to the implementation of your estate plan
5. if you have come into a substantial inheritance (or another significant change in the amount of property that may be taxed) after the writing of your estate planning documents
6. if any other important distribution or estate planning objective has changed since you first implemented your plan

In amending your plan or documents, it is prudent to seek the assistance of a financial planner or estate planning attorney or both.

Now, let's move on to a common estate planning objective of some individuals, particularly high net worth couples or individuals: to provide for charities or engage in philanthropy.

CHAPTER 20

PHILANTHROPY

We conclude our look at wealth accumulation and management by considering a common financial planning goal of many individuals, particularly unmarried individuals or married couples without children—to benefit, at death or during lifetime, the charity of their choice.

Before we begin this important discussion, a note of caution: most taxpayers are aware that the government provides an income-tax deduction for charitable gifts made during lifetime. While taking advantage of this deduction is a valuable tax-avoidance technique, you should not let your desire to reduce taxes outweigh practical cash flow management. In other words, just because the charitable income tax deduction is permitted does *not* mean you should make a transfer to charity if this transfer will jeopardize your ability to maintain your standard of living. Your analysis should be quite the contrary: *if you cannot afford to make a gift to charity during any given year, do not make such a gift.*

Although you might consider it unfair tax policy, it is the law that you must be able to *itemize* your income-tax deductions before deducting any contributions to charity. If you are unable to itemize deductions (frequently the case, unless you have a mortgage on your house), then you must take only internal satisfaction in giving to the charity of your choice.

Choosing a Charity to Benefit

For income-tax purposes, there are two types of qualifying charitable organizations: a *public* (also known as a 50 percent) charity and a *private* (also known as a 30 percent) charity. Each of these charities gets its percentage name from the respective maximum limitation that you, as the donor, may deduct in the year of contribution as a percentage of your adjusted gross income (AGI).

For example, assume that you have decided that during the current tax year, you wish to make a sizable gift of $50,000 to the American Red Cross to benefit the victims of recent hurricanes. However, your AGI for this year as reported on your IRS Form 1040 is only $80,000. Thus, you are limited to an allowable itemized deduction of only $40,000 for this gift ($80,000 times 0.50) in the year of contribution. The remaining $10,000 must be carried over and deducted in a subsequent year, for up to a period of five years, when your AGI for that year is at least $20,000 ($20,000 times 0.50).

However, for *transfer tax* purposes, it makes no taxable difference with respect to which type of charity you benefit. Regardless of whether the charity is public or private, you will receive an *unlimited* deduction equal to the amount of property that passes to the named charity at death or during lifetime. If you care to also benefit a noncharitable beneficiary, such as yourself, before transferring the property to charity, it must be in a specific form under tax law or the transfer tax charitable deduction will *not* be permitted.

For example, assume that you are interested in benefiting your alma mater with a charitable gift of income-producing property at your death. However, during lifetime, you need the income from this property to maintain your current standard of living. Under current law, you must structure this split-interest transfer in one of only a few allowable ways, including a private transfer in trust (commonly known as a charitable remainder trust) or via a fund that has been previously established by your alma mater (commonly known as a pooled income fund).

Public Charities

A *public* charity is one that receives broad public support and is not established by a private individual. Examples of public charities are the American Red Cross, the United Way, the Salvation Army, and the American Heart Association.

Public charities also include local churches, educational institutions, and hospitals operated by a religious order or municipality that are not-for-profit for income-tax purposes. Given the amount of tuition and fees that many of us pay for higher education, we may not immediately think of our alma mater as a qualifying *charitable* institution, but that is indeed the case. It makes no difference whether the college or university is publicly supported or privately operated; the educational institution to which contributions are made will be considered a public charity.

All public charities will afford the donor an income-tax deduction of up to 50 percent of his or her AGI in any one year. But depending on the type of property given to the charity, this percentage amount may be further limited. For instance, if you make a gift of appreciated stock to a public charity, you *may* be limited to a deduction of no more than 30 percent of your AGI in the year of contribution. The word *may* here is emphasized because the amount of your actual deduction depends on whether you choose to ultimately deduct the full fair market value of the stock or to deduct only your cost basis in the stock. As such, there is a tradeoff: if you choose to deduct the full fair market value of the stock from your taxable income, you are limited to 30 percent of your AGI in the year of contribution. Alternatively, if you choose to deduct only your cost basis in the stock, you may deduct up to 50 percent of your AGI (depending on whether this basis in fact equals 50 percent of your AGI for that year).

For example, assume that you previously paid $40,000 for five hundred shares of XYZ stock. The value of these shares has appreciated to $50,000, a potential capital gain of $10,000. You wish to give the shares to the Salvation Army in a year in which your AGI is $90,000. You have two choices:

1. You can subsequently deduct the appreciated fair market of the shares ($50,000), and deduct now $27,000 ($90,000 times 0.30). You can carry over the remaining $23,000 of allowable charitable deduction ($50,000 less $27,000) to a period not exceeding five years from the date of the contribution.

2. You can deduct currently (in the year of contribution) your cost basis of $40,000 in the shares. If you make this choice, you are not permitted to deduct *any* additional, appreciation amount with respect to the shares or the remaining $10,000 ($50,000 less $40,000).

In most instances, it is to your benefit to elect the first option, since you will avoid the capital gains tax that would have been imposed if you had sold the appreciated stock rather than gifting it to charity. The exception to this is where the gifted stock has not experienced much appreciation from the time you bought it until the time you donated it to charity. In that case, the basis election is preferable for income-tax purposes.

There are also restrictions on the income-tax deduction you may take for any tangible personal property, such as a painting, once given to charity. These restrictions are not only based on the *type* of property given, but also on the *use* that the charity makes of the property once they receive it. These are known as the use-related and use-unrelated income-tax rules. For example, if the charity's use of the property is the same as for which it was intended, it is said to be use-related property and a deduction is permitted for the full fair market value. Nevertheless, in the year of contribution, the 30 percent AGI limit also applies unless the taxpayer elects to deduct only his or her basis in the donated property.

What if the charity does *not* use the property in the way it was intended? In that case, the property is considered to be use-unrelated and the donor is limited to a total charitable deduction of no more than he or she paid for the property. If you are an artist and created a painting yourself before gifting it to charity, you are not permitted any income-tax deduction whatsoever, save for the cost of the materials that you expended to create it in the first place.

For example, assume that you are a collector of fine art and that you gift a painting you purchased to a local university. Although the university has an art museum, it intends to show the donated painting in its administration building. The university is making use of the painting in a use-unrelated manner. Accordingly, as the donor, you are limited to a charitable deduction of no more than you what you paid for the painting. Alternatively, if the university featured the painting in its art museum, you would be entitled to a charitable deduction for the current fair market value of the painting since the university featured the painting in a use-related manner. Note that if you were the original painter of the painting, you would be entitled to a charitable deduction only for the cost of the materials you used to create the painting. This is the tax result *regardless* of the use that the university made of the painting.

The tax rules with respect to charitable income-tax deductions are extremely complex and you should only make gifts to charity after consulting with a tax advisor or financial planner.

Private Charities

A private charity is best described as any charity that is *not* considered to qualify as a public charity. In actual practice, a private charity or private foundation is any charity *other than* a church, educational organization, hospital, or governmental unit. Examples of well-known private charities include the Bill and Melinda Gates Foundation, the Ford Foundation, and the Rockefeller Foundation. Private foundations often support the arts or other community activities through advertising notices of their activities, such as on public television.

The tax rules permitting an income-tax deduction for contributions to a private charity are similar to those for public charities, except that the percentage limitations are even further restricted. For example, a gift of appreciated stock to a private foundation is only subject to a 20 percent-of-donor's-AGI deduction in the year of contribution, instead of 30 percent if made to a public charity. This is also the case where a gift of use-related tangible personal property is made and the donor did not elect to claim only his or her basis in the property as the allowable total deduction. A gift of cash to a private charity is restricted to a contribution-year deduction of only 30 percent of AGI, instead of the 50 percent that applies to a public charity donee.

In table form, here are the most important deduction limits with respect to the making of a gift to charity during the lifetime of a donor:

Charitable Contribution Deduction Limitations

Type of Property	Allowable Total Deduction Amount	Percentage AGI Limitation if Public Charity	Percentage AGI Limitation if Private Charity
Cash	Fair Market Value (FMV)	50% of AGI	30% of AGI
Appreciated Stocks and Bonds (Securities)	FMV Election Basis Election	30% of AGI 50% of AGI	20% of AGI 20% of AGI
Tangible Use-Related Personal Property	FMV Election Basis Election	30% of AGI 50% of AGI	20% of AGI 20% of AGI
Tangible Use-Unrelated Personal Property	Basis in property only	50% of AGI	20% of AGI

Substantiation Requirements

As a taxpayer, once you have determined what type of property to give to which form of charity and in what amount, you need to be concerned about proving what you gave or substantiating the amount to the IRS.

The law used to be that donor only had to obtain a written request from the charity if his or her cash gift was in an amount exceeding $250 in the year of contribution. For gifts of property, the donor did not need a qualified appraisal establishing the actual fair market value, unless it was reasonably estimated that the property exceeded $5,000 in value.

Beginning with charitable contributions made in 2007, these rules changed. Now, all contributions of *any* amount, whether in cash or property, to a public or private charity must be substantiated. In practical terms, this means that unless you can produce either a bank record or written communication from the charity indicating the amount of the contribution, the date of the contribution, and the name of the charity, your charitable income tax-deduction may be disallowed. To date, it is a bit unclear how the IRS intends to enforce this rule, but at a minimum, offering-plate cash contributions to your local church or synagogue may need to be re-thought—you may need to ask your church or synagogue for a written receipt at the time you make the offering.

GIFTS TO CHARITY USING TRUSTS AND ANNUITIES

A distinction needs to be made between trusts that are established solely to benefit a charity at the donor's death and trusts for which there is a lifetime noncharitable beneficiary, with the gifted property then passing to a qualified charity at the donor's death. Income tax deductions for this remainder type of trust are measured by means of a table used to determine the present value of the future bequest to charity. Subsequently, an unlimited amount of estate tax charitable deduction is afforded the donor's estate when the gifted property actually passes to charity.

There are two prevalent types of charitable trusts: (1) trusts that leave property at death in a remainder form to a qualified charity, and (2) trusts where the qualified charity receives the income interest *first* and then a noncharitable beneficiary succeeds to ownership. This second form of trust, commonly referred to as a **charitable lead trust**, is sometimes written into a will in an attempt to zero out any estate taxes that may be due on the eventual transfer to a non-spousal, noncharitable beneficiary.

For example, assume that you have established a charitable lead trust as part of the provisions of your last will and testament. At death, you direct that $1 million be placed in this trust to benefit, first, the American Humane Society, and subsequently your two adult children equally. From this bequest of $1 million, the Humane Society is to receive a payment of $80,000 for the next twenty years. Using the applicable table, the executor of your estate determines that the estate is entitled to a charitable deduction of approximately $997,000. You have effectively zeroed out the value of the subsequent transfer of the trust property to your two children and any potential estate tax that may be assessed on this same transfer. In other words, your two children receive the trust property estate-tax-free.

Charitable Remainder Trusts

The more popular form of charitable trust is one in which you or your spouse benefit from the transfer of property to a charity during lifetime, while still benefiting the charity of your choice at death. This is a charitable remainder trust (CRT) and it comes in two basic forms: a CRT that provides a fixed annuity payment to you throughout your lifetime (otherwise known as a charitable remainder annuity trust or CRAT), and a CRT that provides a fixed percentage of the trust assets, as revalued annually, to you during lifetime (otherwise known as a charitable remainder unitrust or CRUT).

There are additional requirements for each of these remainder-type trusts to qualify for income, gift, and estate tax deductions, but it is important to recognize that if you, as the donor, establish either trust during your lifetime, you are afforded *two deductions*: an *income* tax deduction for the present value of the future property that goes to charity and an *estate* tax deduction at death for the property when it actually is left to the charity. If you intend to benefit a qualified charity anyway at your death, you should establish the remainder trust now and take advantage of the double tax benefit for income and estate tax purposes.

Although both types of remainder trusts must be established as irrevocable trusts—in other words, you cannot get the property back once you transfer it to the trust—there is one basic difference. If, as the donor, you are concerned about the eventual decline of your purchasing power by reason of the fixed annuity payment of the CRAT, you will want to instead consider establishing the unitrust form of remainder trust. A major advantage of the CRUT derives from its ability to keep pace with or exceed the annual inflation rate. Specifically, since the CRUT guidelines include an annual income payment as based on a fixed percentage of trust assets, *as revalued annually*, you may be able to keep ahead of inflation and preserve the future purchasing power of trust payments. In addition, unlike a CRAT, where no additional contributions of property may be made once the trust is established, a CRUT permits subsequent gifts of property.

The implementation of either a CRAT or a CRUT involves some out-of-pocket costs. Since both of these trusts are customized, privately drafted documents, it is necessary to seek the assistance of a competent estate-planning attorney to draft them. You should ask the attorney to estimate the amount of income and estate tax savings that will be generated and compare them on a present value basis to the amount of his or her fee. In most instances, the present value of the tax savings will more than exceed the cost of establishing and maintaining the trust throughout your lifetime.

Charitable Gift Annuities

It is possible to obtain the same benefits of the charitable remainder trust by instead having the charity purchase a commercial annuity to pay you income during lifetime. While this annuity payment is often a predetermined, fixed amount, and thus suffers from the same lack-of-purchasing power disadvantage of the CRAT, it is also possible to have the charity purchase a cost-of-living rider on the annuity to keep pace with inflation. However, a big caveat associated with the purchase of a charitable gift annuity (CGA) is that you need to ensure that the present value of the annuity payments coming back to you in the form of income is *less* than the amount of the property that eventually passes to the qualified charity. If these amounts are equal, or if the present value of your annuity payments *exceeds* the present value of the future property passing to charity, you will not be entitled to a charitable income-tax deduction.

For example, assume that you have determined that the present value of the annuity payments received by you as a result of the American Diabetes Association purchasing a CGA on your behalf is $500,000. The present value of the future property received by the American Diabetes Association must be *more* than $500,000 or you will not be entitled to a charitable income-tax deduction, even if you itemize your deductions.

Be aware that, as with other charitable transfers, the transfer of assets in exchange for an annuity is *irrevocable*, meaning that once you begin to receive benefits, there is no turning back.

Hail, Hail to Your Dear Old Alma Mater

In contrast to the private charitable remainder trust, many educational institutions offer a **pooled income fund** to alumni who wish to contribute endowment funds. Such a fund is created and maintained by the educational institution, which then commingles your contribution with that of other donors. The investments made by the institution and fund manager cannot include tax-exempt securities such as municipal bonds, but other than that, the pooled income fund operates much like a standard mutual fund.

The mechanics of participating in a pooled income fund are relatively simple. First you are contacted by your alma mater's planned giving office, which explains to you the terms and restrictions of the fund. Next, you transfer property (usually cash) to the fund, retaining an income interest for life, with the remainder interest in the cash or property passing to the educational institution. Your actual payment to the fund is determined by your pro rata share of the annual earnings generated by the fund manager. You are then entitled to a charitable income-tax deduction based on the annual return of the fund for your particular age and actuarial life expectancy.

For example, assume that you are fifty-five and transfer $100,000 in cash to your alma mater's pooled income fund. The fund, as managed by the university, generates an annual return of 6 percent. When consulting the applicable table, you find the approximate value of the remainder property that passes to your alma mater to be 33 percent. As such, you are entitled to a charitable income tax deduction of $33,000 ($100,000 times 0.33). As long as your AGI in the year of contribution does not exceed $66,000 ($66,000 times 0.50), you are entitled to deduct your entire contribution. Note: If your AGI in the year of contribution is less than $66,000, you are entitled to carry over the difference and deduct it in the future, up to a maximum period of five years.

The planned giving office of your alma mater or other educational institution of choice can also discuss with you the possibility of purchasing a CGA or structuring some form of CRT in which it is the named remainder beneficiary.

PRIVATE FOUNDATIONS

A private foundation is usually established by an individual or family either as a not-for-profit corporation or as a charitable trust to support a particular scientific, educational, health, or other community cause. The most common form of private foundation is a family foundation where family members work together toward common goals to instill in future generation family members a sense of community service. Another possible option to further the common philanthropic goals of an individual or family is to establish a donor advised fund (DAF) at a community foundation, which will be discussed shortly.

Typically, a private foundation is established by the individual or family creating a principal fund of money—commonly referred to as an endowment—that is subsequently invested, with the income paid out annually to the charity. Only the income from the fund and not the principal itself is spent, leaving the principal to grow. The foundation must not pay dividends to its shareholders, although it may pay reasonable compensation for services rendered by its directors, officers, and employees. Under current law, after a certain period of time, the foundation must make qualifying annual distributions totaling at least 5 percent of its net investment assets.

A private foundation may be either operating or nonoperating in nature. An *operating* foundation uses the bulk of its income to actively run its own charitable functions. Examples of an operating private foundation include the operation of a museum, library, or historical property with the foundation's money. In contrast, a *nonoperating* foundation does not engage in or actively run any charitable activity directly, but rather only disburses funds to other charities for their own use.

A major advantage to contributing to a private foundation is that the donor is entitled to an income-tax deduction in the year that the contribution is made. However, like the charitable deduction income tax limitations previously discussed, the donor's tax deduction is generally limited to no more than 30 percent of his or her AGI in the year of contribution. Additionally, the deduction for contributions of appreciated stock or any other type of long-term capital gain property is limited to the donor's cost basis in the stock, not exceeding 20 percent of his or her AGI.

Wealthy donors are primarily interested in establishing a private foundation because of the considerable flexibility that is afforded to them with respect to investment management. For example, the donor of a private foundation may control the investment and distribution of the foundation's assets, as well as train other family members to eventually manage the wealth that is accumulated within the foundation. The donor may also customize the investments of the foundation to meet any specific charitable objectives that he or she believes are not being adequately addressed by other public or private charities.

Perhaps the most well known private foundation today is the Bill and Melinda Gates Foundation, whose objective is stated to be "bringing innovations in health and learning to the global community." It is particularly dedicated to caring for individuals in Africa who have been afflicted with HIV or AIDS. The foundation is an operating foundation, since the Gateses personally engage in the day-to-day operations of the foundation and use their own money to further its charitable activities. Relatively recently, the foundation attracted a pledge of $30 billion from mega investor Warren Buffett to assist in its day-to-day operation and stated mission.

Is the establishment of a private foundation right for you or your family? Unless you have substantial funds at your disposal to create and operate the foundation, it probably isn't, but that does not mean you are precluded from making a contribution to such a foundation if you agree with its objectives. If you make a contribution and the foundation has been approved by the IRS as a qualified charity, you are entitled to a charitable income-tax deduction in the year of contribution, although in a somewhat reduced amount than afforded by a contribution to a public charity.

DONOR ADVISED FUNDS

A donor advised fund (DAF) is an arrangement where a donor makes a gift to a giving account, which is managed by a commercially available mutual fund. Currently, the largest DAF is the Fidelity Charitable Gift Fund, created by Fidelity Investments in 1991, with fiscal year 2011 assets of $5.6 billion. After contributing to such a fund, the donor then makes future recommendations of its disbursements to any qualified public charity. However, since the donor can only make recommendations, the sponsoring mutual fund is under no legal obligation to actually carry out or implement the donor's requests. Nevertheless, most DAFs do implement their donor's wishes.

A DAF offers the opportunity for a donor to create a low-cost, flexible vehicle for charitable giving that is structured as an alternative to a direct charitable gifting or creating a private foundation. Unlike the minimum 5 percent disbursement requirement applied to a private foundation, there are no mandatory distribution rules with a DAF. Additionally, there are no set-up costs to establish a DAF. Annual fees currently run at approximately 0.60 percent for the DAF and an additional 1 percent or so for expenses associated with management of the mutual fund or funds.

Because the DAF is technically an extension of the public charity, a donor receives the maximum income-tax deduction otherwise available to a 50 percent organization. Current tax law affords the donor of appreciated securities an income-tax deduction for their full fair market value, if an election waiving basis as the allowable deduction is made. By donating appreciated securities to a donor-advised fund and then advising the fund to make donations to several charities, a donor may obtain tax advantages without the necessity of transferring these securities in kind to the charity. Moreover, the DAF can afford a vehicle for the donor to save capital gains taxes that would otherwise be due on the conversion of the securities to cash before gifting to the charity.

For example, assume that you are the owner of 1,000 shares of ABC stock, which has appreciated over the years from $20 per share to $100 per share. You are in the highest marginal income tax bracket of 35 percent, which means your capital gains tax rate is 15 percent. Since you are aware that your public charity of choice is likely to cash in those shares after receipt, you make the tax mistake of selling the securities yourself first and subsequently gifting the cash to the charity. Your net cost in making this charitable gift is $77,000, computed as follows:

$100,000 Cost of donation

+$ 12,000 Capital gains tax due (($100,000 less $20,000) times 0.15)

$112,000 Total cost

- $ 35,000 Income tax saved ($100,000 times 0.35)

$ 77,000 Net cost of gift

Suppose that instead of making the gift to the public charity in this manner, you take advantage of a DAF and then advise the mutual fund to transfer the cash proceeds to the same charity of your choice. Accordingly, your net cost in making the charitable gift using the DAF as a tax-exempt intermediary is only $65,000, computed as follows:

$100,000 Cost of donation/Total cost (no capital gains tax due)

- $ 35,000 Income tax saved ($100,000 times 0.35)

$ 65,000 Net cost of gift

You have effectively saved $12,000, without the administrative and tax cost of making a gift of the appreciated securities directly to the public charity.

There is one important tax planning principle to reiterate in the making of a gift of property to a qualified charity. If the property appreciates in value from the time you purchased it until you plan to gift it to charity, let the charity subsequently sell the property. In that manner, since the charity is a tax-exempt entity, no taxes of any kind will be paid. Alternatively, if the property has depreciated in value from the time of purchase to the time of gifting, *you* should sell the property before gifting it to charity. This will permit you to take advantage of the loss in property value on your income-tax return. If you do not claim the loss before gifting, the allowable loss is lost forever, since the tax-exempt charitable entity cannot take it either.

If you are interested in establishing a DAF, shop the idea around first. Different mutual funds charge different annual fees to operate, which reduces the amount of monies that can go the charities you wish to benefit.

In summary, here are the planning techniques you may wish to consider in accomplishing your philanthropic objectives. In all cases, at least one tax deduction, and in some cases two or three (income, gift and estate tax) deductions, may be permitted:

1. an outright or direct gift to charity
2. a charitable remainder annuity trust
3. a charitable remainder unitrust
4. a charitable gift annuity
5. a pooled income fund
6. a private operating foundation
7. a private non-operating foundation
8. a donor advised fund

SECTION VII

SUMMARIZING THE PADD PROCESS

CHAPTER 21

REAPING THE REWARDS

This book has, hopefully, introduced you to a new method of ordering your financial life and planning for your financial future. It has also developed a novel definition of the term "wealth": a definition that goes *beyond* the traditional meaning of accumulating financial riches to a lifestyle accommodation or, at the very least, ensuring that your current (or desired) standard of living is *maintained* throughout your working years and, subsequently, retirement.

So, how do you go about ensuring that you are "wealthy" in the fullest sense of the word? This book has suggested that this most-sought-after status may best be achieved by following a wealth accumulation and management strategy referred to here as the P.A.D.D. process:

*P*rotecting Yourself, Your Family, and Your Property;

*A*ccumulating Wealth;

*D*efending Your Wealth; and

*D*istributing Your Wealth (both during lifetime and at death)

Broadly, this process may be thought of as the financial planning steps, respectively, of:

1. Insuring yourself, your family, and property against the possibility of significant loss;
2. Taking advantage of benefits that are offered to you by your employer;
3. Investing in financial or real assets or both;

4. Minimizing the effects of inflation on your portfolio as much as possible:
5. Practicing effective tax planning and management techniques;
6. Preparing for your children's higher education;
7. Planning for your own retirement years; and
8. Distributing your estate at death to your intended beneficiaries in as transfer-tax- efficient manner as possible.

Of course, maximizing the implementation of these steps to the greatest extent possible is not easy. (If it were, this book, as well as many others written describing proper personal financial planning, would not be necessary). However, it should be comforting that you are not alone in meeting this challenge! Indeed, a number of professional advisors, among them the Certified Financial Planner ™ , Certified Public Accountant (CPA), securities and/ or insurance professional, and estate planning attorney, stand ready to assist you in meeting your financial planning and wealth accumulation goals. Alternatively, if you believe that you are skilled and disciplined enough to take on this challenge yourself, by all means you should do so!

Still, attending to one's financial life and affairs is analogous to Scarlett O'Hara's famous line in the novel and movie *Gone with the Wind*: "Oh, fiddle-dee, I'll think about it tomorrow!" That is, the *longer* we put off thinking about the financial planning process, the *longer* it will be before we become "wealthy" (and the sooner a financially-challenging tomorrow likely arrives)!! Thus, if this book has accomplished nothing else, it has, hopefully, provided you with some basic principles and knowledge with which you can begin to take control of your financial life. If you do so, and adopt the process described within its pages, you will reap the greatest reward of all: a financially worry-free and independent life that you can enjoy to the fullest with family and friends!!

I wish you good planning!

APPENDIX A

SAMPLE DATA GATHERING FORM		
Personal Information		
	Client	Spouse
Full Name		
Gender(male/female)		
Maiden Name (if applicable)		
Current Marital Status		
(single, married, divorced, separated)		
Prior Marriages (yes/no)		
(If yes, date of dissolution)		
U. S. Citizen (yes/no)		
Current Adddress		
Phone Number		
Cell Number		
Prior Residence (by State)		
Birthdate		
Current Age		
Birthplace		
Social Security number		
Occupation		
Employer		
Length of Current Employment (years)		
Work/Business Phone		

Family Members Who Depend on Your Support			

List any family members or individuals you wish to provide/plan for			
Parent/Child/Grandchild	Birthdate	Birthplace	Social Security Number
Other Individuals/ Dependents	Birthdate	Birthplace	Social Security Number
Family Health Issues			

Are there any major health problems with any members of your family? If yes, please explain			
Family Member		Health	Issues(s)

Family Advisors and Representatives

	Name	Phone Number
Attorney		
Banker		
Doctor		
Executor(s)		
Financial Planner		
Guardian(s)		
Insurance Agent		
Investment Advisor		
Minister/Rabbi		
Tax Preparer		
Other:		
Other:		
Other:		

Family Planning Goals

List all of your financial planning goals (e.g. retirement, travel, large purchases) and a timeframe for when you wish to begin implementing them.

Family Goals	Time Horizon (immediate, within 3-12 months, or 1 year or later)
Client's Individual Goals	
Spouse's Individual Goals	

Family Objectives

Indicate which of the following objectives are important for your family.

Objective	Important to Client (yes/no)?	Important to Spouse (yes/no)?
Saving for education (yourself, children, grandchildren, etc.)		
Saving for retirement		
Being able to retire early (age 55 or earlier)		
Minimizing income taxes		
Minimizing estate taxes		
Providing support for an aging parent/relative		
Improving investment returns		
Improving insurance coverage		
Supporting a favorite charity		
Planning for your estate		
Improving your standard of living		
Changing or improving your employment situation		
Other:		
Other:		

Taxable Assets

List the current value for each of the following and provide the latest account statement available.

Account/Investment	Client	Spouse	Joint
Cash on hand			
Checking account			
Savings account			
Certificates of deposit (CDs)			
Money Market			
Life insurance cash surrender value			
Stocks			
Bonds			
Mutual funds			
Closely held business interest			
Limited partnership interest			
Other:			
Other:			

Retirement Accounts

List the current value for each of the following and provide the latest account statement available. If account statement does not list designated beneficiary, please add beneficiary.

Account	Client	Spouse
IRAs		
401(k)/403(b)		
Pension plan		
Profit-sharing plan		
Stock options		
Deferred compensa-tion		
Other:		
Other:		

Real Estate

List the current value (in dollars) for each of the following.

Type	Ownership (client, spouse, or joint)	Cost	Market Value	Loan Balance	Monthly Payment
Primary residence					
Vacation home					
Rental property					
Other:					
Other:					

Personal Property

List the current value (in dollars) for each of the following.

Type	Ownership (client, spouse, or joint)	Market Value	Loan Balance	Monthly Payment
Aircraft				
Art and antiques				
Automobile				
Automobile				
Automobile				
Boat				
Collectibles				
Fur(s)				
Household goods				
Jewelry				
Other:				
Other:				

Insurance Coverage

List the following types of coverage you currently have.

Type	Amount	Owner	Insured	Beneficiary
Life				
Group term				
Term				
Universal life				
Whole life				
Disability				
Short term				
Long term				
Medical				
Health care				
Long-term care				
Liability				
Umbrella				
Professional				
Property				
Auto				
Homeowners				

Are you or your spouse engaged in any professional activities, paid or unpaid, outside of your main employment (e.g., moonlighting, board memberships, volunteer work, professional association memberships, etc.)? If so, please explain.

Client or Spouse	Professional Activity

Liabilities

List the current balance for each of the following.

Type	Ownership (client, spouse, or joint)	Balance Due
Alimony/child support		
Bank loans		
Charitable pledge		
Credit cards		
Home equity loan or line of credit		
Installment loan		
Insurance policy loan		
Investment debt (margin)		
Personal loan		
Retirement plan loan		
Student loans		
Other:		
Other:		

Credit Ratings

What is your current credit rating or score?	
When was the last time you pulled a copy of your credit report?	
Have you ever filed for bankruptcy? If so, when?	
What is the date when you last prepared a family balance sheet?	

Income

List the following sources of income in annual amounts.

Type	Client	Spouse	Joint
Employment Income			
Annual salary			
Bonus			
Commissions			
Self-employment			
Other:			
Investment Income			
Dividends			
Interest-taxable			
Interest-tax-free			
Rental income (net)			
Annuities			
Other:			
Miscellaneous Income			
Alimony			
Trusts			
Child support			
Estates			
Gifts			
Retirement accounts			
Sale of property/investments			
Social security payments			
Other:			
Other:			
Do you expect a significant change in income over the next two to three years? (if so, estimate amounts)			

Expenses

List the following current estimated expenditures in annual amounts.

Type	Amount
Charitable contributions	
Clothing	
Education	
Employment-related	
Food	
Gifts	
Home improvements/repair/maintenance	
Income and other payroll taxes	
Insurance	
Auto	
Homeowners	
Disability income	
Life	
Medical	
Long-term care	
Personal liability	
Other	
Medical expenses (unreimbursed)	
Mortgage/rent	
Personal expenses	
Recreation	
Dining out	
Vacations	
Other	
Savings	
Taxes	
FICA	
Income	
Property	
Telephone	
Transportation	
Auto fuel/repairs/maintenance	
Auto payments	
Utilities	
Other:	
Other:	

What is the date when you last prepared a family budget?	

APPENDIX B

SAMPLE BUDGET

CASH BUDGET: ESTIMATED INCOME

Name(s) _____

For the _____ Ending _____

Sources of Income		Jan	Feb	Mar	Apr	May	Jun	Jul	Aug	Sept	Oct	Nov	Dec	Total for the year
Take-home pay	Name													
	Name													
	Name													
Bonuses and commissions														
Pensions and annuities														
Investment income	Interest													
	Dividends													
	Rents													
	Sale of securities													

Other Income	Other											
TOTAL INCOME												

CASH BUDGET: ESTIMATED EXPENSES

Name(s) _____

For the period ending _____

Expense Categories	Jan	Feb	Mar	Apr	May	Jun	Jul	Aug	Sept	Oct	Nov	Dec	Yearly Total
Housing — Rent/mortgage payment													

Category		(empty columns)
	(include insurance and taxes, if applicable)	
	Repairs, maintenance, improvements	
Utilities	Gas, electric, water	
	Phone	
	Cable TV and other	
Food	Groceries	
	Dining out	
Autos	Loan payments	
	License plates, fees, etc.	
	Gas, oil, repairs, tires, maintenance	
Medical	Health, major medical, disability insurance (not provided by employer)	

	Doctor, dentist, hospital, medicines
Clothing	Clothes, shoes, accessories
Insurance	Homeowner's (if not covered by mortgage payment)
	Life (not provided by employer)
	Auto
Taxes	Income and social security
	Property (if not included in mortgage)
Appliances, furniture, and other	Loan payments
	Purchases and repairs
Personal care	Laundry, cosmetics, hair care
Recreation and entertainment	Vacations

	Other recreation and entertainment												
Savings and Investments	Savings, stocks, bonds, etc.												
Other expenditures	Charitable contributions												
	Gifts												
	Education loan payment												
	Subscriptions, magazines, books												
	Other:												
	Other:												
Fun Money													
TOTAL EXPENSES													

APPENDIX C

DURABLE GENERAL AND FINANCIAL POWER OF ATTORNEY

I, _____, currently of _____, do hereby execute this durable general (and financial) power of attorney with the intention that the attorney-in-fact hereinafter named shall be able to act in my place in all matters.

SECTION 1: Designation of Attorney-in-Fact

1.01: I constitute and appoint _____ , currently of _____, to be my attorney-in-fact to act for me, in my name and for my benefit.

1.02: In the event that _____ for any reason shall fail to act or continue as my attorney-in-fact, I constitute and appoint _____ currently of _____ to act as my attorney-in-fact.

SECTION 2: Effective Date of Power of Attorney

2.01: This General Power of Attorney shall be effective immediately, and shall not be affected by my disability or lack of mental competence, except as may be provided otherwise by an applicable state statute.

2.02: This General Power of Attorney shall <u>not</u> be affected by my incapacity or disability, it being my specific intention that my attorney-in-fact shall continue to act as such, even though I may not be competent to ratify the actions of my attorney-in-fact.

2.03: Third parties may rely on the representations of my attorney-in-fact as to all matters relating to any power granted to my attorney-in-fact, and no person who may act in reliance upon the representation of my attorney-in-fact, shall incur any liability to me or my estate as a result of permitting my attorney-in-fact to exercise any power. Further, I authorize my attorney-in-fact to indemnify and hold harmless any third party who accepts and acts under this document.

2.04: This power is revocable, provided that insofar as any governmental agency, bank, depository, trust company, insurance company, other corporation, transfer agent, investment banking company or other person is concerned, who shall rely on this power, may justifiably rely on the power. This power may be revoked only by a notice in writing executed by me or my attorney-in-fact and delivered to such person or institution.

2.05: This power shall not be revoked or otherwise become ineffective in any way by the mere passage of time, but rather shall remain in full force and effect until revoked by me or my attorney-in-fact in writing, as provided in paragraph 2.04 hereof.

SECTION 3: Powers

3.01: My attorney-in-fact shall have all of the powers, discretions, elections, and authorities granted by statute, common law and under any rule of Court. In addition thereto, and not in limitation thereof, my attorney-in-fact shall also have the powers set forth below.

3.02: My attorney-in-fact may collect and receive, without the institution of a legal cause of action, all debts, monies, gifts, objects, interest, dividends, annuities and demands that now are due or may hereinafter become due, owing or otherwise payable to or belonging to me. My attorney-in-fact may use and take all lawful actions in my name or otherwise to recover the same or to compromise the same.

3.03: My attorney-in-fact may sell, convey, lease, exchange, mortgage, pledge, release, or otherwise deal with, dispose of, exchange or encumber any of my property, either real or personal. This shall include the power to borrow money or otherwise obtain credit, upon such terms, conditions and covenants as my attorney-in-fact considers as appropriate.

3.04: My attorney-in-fact may appear on behalf in any litigation in which I am or may become a party during the duration of this General Power of Attorney.

3.05: My attorney-in-fact may give discharges, releases, consent and receipts on my behalf.

3.06: My attorney-in-fact shall have the power to deposit funds in my name in any banking or savings institution or in any money market account, whether or not insured.

3.07: My attorney-in-fact shall have the power to pay any and all bills, accounts, claims and demands now due by me or becoming due by me subsequent to the execution of this General Power of Attorney.

3.08: My attorney-in-fact may endorse all checks drawn to my order for deposit in any account in which I have funds on deposit or in any new account opened in my name.

3.09: My attorney-in-fact shall have the right to make gifts of cash or property in kind to any person or institution in connection with any estate planning that needs to be completed or to carry out any beneficial intent of mine as he may understand it.

3.10: My attorney-in-fact shall have the power to transfer or surrender any securities that I may own. In connection therewith, my attorney-in-fact may execute in my name or on my behalf any stock power or other instrument in order to implement any such transfer or surrender.

3.11: My attorney-in-fact shall have the power to enter into or renew any agency or custodian agreement with any bank or trust company at my expense for the investment or safekeeping of any property.

3.12: My attorney-in-fact shall have unrestricted access to, and the right to enter into, any safety deposit box, vault, or other depository that I may own or may be registered in my name.

3.13: My attorney-in-fact shall have the power to prepare, make, execute and file any and all Federal, State, local or other tax returns, claims for refunds or declarations of estimated tax. This power shall include the power to represent me (directly or indirectly through other agents) in any matter before the Internal Revenue Service or any other Federal, State, or local agency.

3.14: My attorney-in-fact shall have the power to execute, seal, acknowledge, and deliver any instruments, documents or papers deemed necessary, advisable or expedient with respect to any property.

3.15: My attorney-in-fact shall have the power to hold, invest, reinvest and otherwise deal with and manage all property in which I may have any interest and wherever situated.

SECTION 4: Ratification; Use of Photocopy; Revocation of Prior Powers: Construction of Instrument

4.01: I hereby ratify, allow, acknowledge and hold valid all acts taken by my attorney-in-fact pursuant to this power.

4.02: I hereby authorize the use of a photocopy of this General Power of Attorney, in lieu of the original copy executed by me, for the purpose of effectuating the terms and provisions hereof.

4.03: I hereby revoke, annul and cancel any and all durable general and financial powers of attorney previously executed by me, and the same shall be of no further force and effect. However, the preceding sentence shall not have the effect of revoking any powers of attorney that are directly related to my health care that have been signed and executed by me.

4.04: This General Power of Attorney is executed and delivered in the State of _____, and the laws of the State of _____ shall govern all questions as to the validity of this power and to the construction of its provisions.

4.05: This instrument is to be construed and interpreted as a general power of attorney. The enumeration of specific powers herein is not intended to, not does it, limit or restrict the general powers herein granted to my attorney-in-fact.

4.06: Pursuant to _____, any person or organization that "arbitrarily or without reasonable cause" fails to honor this Power of Attorney, or fails to comply with the directions of my attorney-in-fact, shall be subject to costs, expenses, and reasonable attorney's fees required to effectuate the terms and provisions of this instrument.

IN WITNESS WHEREOF, I have executed this General Power of Attorney this _____ day of _____, 20xx.

_____
PRINCIPAL

WITNESS:

_____
Witness

_____
Witness

STATE OF _____)

COUNTY OF _____)

The foregoing instrument was acknowledged before me this _____ day of _____, 20xx by _____,

Principal, and the above stated witnesses, for the purposes therein stated.

Witness my hand and official seal.

(SEAL)   _____

                      Notary Public

My commission expires:_____

SPECIMEN SIGNATURE OF ATTORNEY-IN-FACT:

_____
ATTORNEY-IN-FACT

SPECIMEN SIGNATURE OF SUCCESSOR ATTORNEY-IN-FACT:

_____
SUCCESSOR ATTORNEY-IN-FACT

APPENDIX D

DECLARATION AS TO MEDICAL OR SURGICAL TREATMENT AND MEDICAL DURABLE POWER OF ATTORNEY

I. DECLARATION AS TO MEDICAL OR SURGICAL TREATMENT

I, _____, currently of _____, being of sound mind and at least eighteen years of age, direct that my life shall not be artificially prolonged under the circumstances set forth below and hereby declare that:

A. LIFE-SUSTAINING PROCEDURES

If at any time my attending physician and one other qualified physician certify in writing that:
I have an injury, disease, or illness which is not curable or reversible, and which, in their judgment is a terminal condition, and I have been unconscious, comatose, or otherwise incompetent, so as to make or communicate responsible decisions concerning my person, then I direct that, in accordance with _____
law, life sustaining procedures shall be withdrawn and withheld pursuant to the terms of this declaration. It is understood that life-sustaining procedures shall not include any medical procedure or intervention for nourishment considered necessary by the attending physician to provide comfort or alleviate pain.

Moreover, it is my request that the term "terminal condition" be interpreted to include a state of permanent unconsciousness (permanent vegetative state).

B. ARTIFICIAL NOURISHMENT

If the only procedure that I am being provided is artificial nourishment, I direct that artificial nourishment shall also be immediately discontinued when it is the only procedure being provided. Notwithstanding any direction with respect to the discontinuance of artificial nourishment, if my attending physician has determined that pain results from such discontinuance, such physician may order that artificial nourishment be provided to me, but only to the extent necessary to alleviate such pain.

C. OTHER SPECIFIC REQUESTS:

II. MEDICAL DURABLE POWER OF ATTORNEY

A. DESIGNATION OF HEALTH CARE AGENT.

I, _____, currently of _____, do hereby appoint:

Agent Name: _____
Address: _____
Phone: _____
Relation, if any: _____

as my Agent to make health care and personal decisions for me if I become unable to make such decisions for myself, except to the extent I state otherwise in this document.

The term "health care" as used in this document includes all medical treatment, the provision, withholding or withdrawal of any health care medical procedure, including surgery, cardiopulmonary resuscitation, or service to maintain, diagnose, treat or provide for a patient's physical or mental health or personal care, unless such authority is otherwise limited by this document.

B. CREATION OF MEDICAL DURABLE POWER OF ATTORNEY.

By this document I also intend to create a Medical Durable Power of Attorney. This Durable Power of Attorney shall take effect only upon my inability to give informed consent, disability, incapacity, or incompetency, and shall continue during such inability to give informed consent, disability, incapacity, or incompetency. I have prepared this document while still legally competent and of sound mind. If these instructions create a conflict with the desires of my relatives, with hospital policies or with the principles of those providing care, I ask that my instructions prevail.

C. GENERAL STATEMENT OF AUTHORITY GRANTED.

Subject to any limitations in this document, I grant to my Agent full power and authority to make health care decisions for me to the same extent that I could make such decisions for myself if I had the capacity to do so. This authority shall also include all acts related to my personal care and any residential placement and/or medical treatment. In making any decision, my Agent shall attempt to discuss the proposed decision with me to determine my desires if I am able to communicate in any way.

In exercising this authority, my Agent shall make health care decisions that are consistent with my desires as stated in this document or otherwise made known to my Agent. If my wishes regarding a particular health care decision are not known to my Agent, then my Agent shall make the decision for me based upon what my Agent believes to be in my best interests.

D. ACCESS TO MEDICAL RECORDS.

My Agent shall have complete access to my protected health information, as the personal representative of my estate, for all purposes under the HIPPA Act of 1996 (45 C.F.R. Sec. 164.502 (g) (1) and (2), and pursuant to _____ state law (State Statute _____). There is no limitation on the information I authorize to be disclosed and there is no limitation on the period of time for which information may be requested or disclosed.

E. ADVANCE MEDICAL DIRECTIVE: My Agent shall be permitted to execute an advance medical directive with respect to the administration of cardiopulmonary resuscitation (CPR) in accordance with the provisions of ___(State statute)_____ if determining, after conferring with my attending physician, that a CPR directive is appropriate.

F. AUTOPSY, ANATOMICAL GIFTS, DISPOSITION OF REMAINS. I authorize my Agent, to the extent permitted by law, to make anatomical gifts of part or all of my body for medical purposes, authorize an autopsy, and direct the disposition of my remains.

G. DESIGNATION OF ALTERNATE AGENT. If the person designated as my Agent is not available or unable to act, I designate the following person to serve as my Alternate Agent to make health care decisions for me as authorized by this document.

Alternate Agent: _____

Address: _____

Phone: _____

Relation, if any: _____

H. NOMINATION OF GUARDIAN AND CONSERVATOR. If a Guardian of my person is to be appointed for me, I nominate my Agent (and, then, Alternate Agent) to serve as my Guardian. If it becomes necessary for a court to appoint a Conservator for my estate, the same nomination and order as for Guardian is hereby made.

III. GENERAL PROVISIONS

A. HOLD HARMLESS AND THIRD PARTY RELIANCE.
All persons, including attending physicians, or entities who in good faith endeavor to carry out the terms and provisions of this document shall not be liable to me, my estate, my heirs or assigns for any damages or claims arising because of their action. However, if any person shall endeavor to challenge the authority of my attorney-in-fact in bad faith, or intentionally contradict any provision of this document, my estate shall not be liable and is not obligated to pay any fees or expenses arising out of the action or actions of my attorney-in-fact acting on my behalf.

B. SEVERABILITY. If any provision of this document is held to be invalid, such invalidity shall not affect the other provisions, which can be given effect without the invalid provision, and to this end the directions in this document are severable.

C. STATEMENT OF INTENTIONS. It is my intent that this document be legally binding and effective. If the law does not recognize this document as legally binding and effective, it is my intent that this document is taken as a formal statement of my desire concerning the method by which any health care decisions should be made on my behalf during any period in which I am unable to make such decisions. This power of attorney is intended to be valid in any jurisdiction in which it is presented.

D. INCONSISTENCY IN PROVISIONS. In the event of an inconsistency in provisions between the Medical Durable Power of Attorney and My Declaration as to Medical or Surgical Treatment (Living Will), the Medical Durable Power of Attorney shall control.

E. REVOCATION OF PRIOR POWERS. I hereby revoke any prior power of attorney for health care and restate my intentions as specified above.

F. APPLICABLE LAW: All questions pertaining to the validity, interpretation, and administration of this document shall be determined under the laws of the State of _____.
I have read and understand the contents of this document and the effect of this grant of powers to my Agent. I am emotionally and mentally competent to make this declaration.

Signed on this _____ day of _____, 20xx.

Signature: _____

PRINCIPAL

Name of Principal: _____

Address of Principal: _____

SSN of Principal: _____

Birth date of Principal: _____

STATEMENT OF WITNESSES

The foregoing instrument was signed and declared by _____, **PRINICIPAL,** to be his Declaration as to Medical or Surgical Treatment and Medical Durable Power of Attorney in the presence of us, who, in his presence, in the presence of each other, and at _____'s request, have signed our names below as witnesses, and we declare, that at the time of the execution of this instrument, _____, according to our best knowledge and belief, was of sound mind and under no constraint, fraud, or undue influence. Neither of the witnesses is _____'s attending physician or any other physician, an employee of the attending physician or health care facility in which _____ is a patient, a person who has a claim against any portion of the estate of _____ at his death at the time the declaration is signed, or a person who knows or believes that he/she is entitled to any portion of the estate of _____, upon his death, either as a beneficiary of a will in existence at the time the declaration is signed, or as an heir at law. Neither witness is a person appointed as agent by this document. Neither witness is a provider of health or residential care or an employee of a provider thereof.

Witness Signature: _____

Name: _____

Address: _____

_____

Date: _____

Witness Signature: _____

Name: _____

Address: _____

_____

Date: _____

State of _____   )

)

County of _____   )

On this _____ day of _____, 20xx, _____, known to me (or satisfactorily proven) to be the person named in the foregoing instrument, personally appeared before me, a Notary Public, within and for the said State and County, and acknowledged that he freely and voluntarily executed the same for the purposes stated in the document.

My commission expires: _____

(SEAL)

_____Notary Public

GLOSSARY

A

Accelerated Death Benefit Rider: An additional provision to a life insurance contract that permits the owner/insured to receive all or a portion of the proceeds of the contract before death: so as to cover, for example, the costs of a last illness.

Accidental Death Benefit (ADB): Also known as a double indemnity benefit; a provision in some life insurance contracts that pays twice the face value of the policy in the event of the accidental death of the insured.

***American Demographics* magazine:** A U.S. magazine covering the marketing and advertising business. *American Demographics* ceased publication in November, 2004, and became a part of *American Advertising* magazine, owned by Crain Communications, Inc.

Annuity: An insurance product that features an equal stream of payments over the owner/annuitant's lifetime. An important retirement planning technique since the product ensures against the risk of "superannuation" or the risk of a retiree outliving his or her accumulated retirement monies.

Asset allocation: A method of allocating or dividing up an individual's collection of assets or portfolio among several asset classes, usually cash or cash equivalents, stocks, and bonds. Such allocation also includes specified or agreed-on percentages of assets among specified asset classes and is a staple of a properly prepared investment policy statement used by many financial advisors.

B

Basis: An income tax term meaning, first and foremost, the amount of money contributed by a taxpayer in the purchase of any real or financial asset. Sometimes alternatively referred to as an individual's "cost basis" in property; used to determine the amount of taxable gain or loss in the sale of assets.

Behavioral fiuance: A branch of finance that studies the interrelationship of psychology and investor behavior; an alternative to traditional theory of corporate finance that assumes efficient markets and rational investor behavior. An important precept of behavior finance is "prospect theory", which essentially posits that investors fear losses more than they value gains.

Beneficiary: The individual named in a legal document, such as a trust, that benefits in the event of the writer or creator's death.

Bonds: A type of financial instrument commonly issued by corporations or governments to raise capital for needed projects or functions. Sometimes just referred to as "debt" or "debt obligations" since the issuer borrows money from the holder of the bond and must repay the bond holder at the time of maturity of the debt obligation.

C

Capital gain: An income tax and financial term meaning the increase in value or appreciation of the asset from the date of purchase to the date of sale. If such asset is owned for a requisite period of time, currently more than one year from the date of purchase before it is sold, a favorable tax rate is awarded by the taxing authorities.

Capitalization rate: A percentage rate or number applied to the future income from property (typically, real property) to determine its current value. For example, if the net operating income from an apartment complex was $500,000 and a capitalization rate or 20% was applied or divided into that income, the current value of the complex would be estimated at $2,500,000.

Cash value insurance: A type of life insurance that builds a cash reserve on behalf of the owner, which amount may be accessed by the owner during his or her lifetime. Common types of such insurance include whole life insurance, universal insurance, variable insurance, and variable universal life insurance.

Charitable lead trust (CLT): An irrevocable trust used in estate planning designed to provide either a fixed or variable income stream annually to a qualified charity for a certain period with the remainder of the property left to a non-charitable beneficiary, usually the donor's child or children.

Charitable remainder trust (CRT); An irrevocable trust used in estate planning designed to provide either a fixed or variable income stream annually for a certain period to a non-charitable beneficiary (typically, the donor) with the remainder of the property left to a qualified charity.

Child tax credit: An income tax credit or dollar-for-dollar reduction against a taxpayer's income tax liability because of having a child or children currently under the age of 17. The maximum amount of the credit is established by tax law; for example, $1,000 per eligible child.

College Board: A not-for-profit membership organization committed to excellence and equity in education, particularly higher education. Such organization also provides students an avenue to college opportunities, including financial support and scholarships.

Commissioner's Individual Disability Table A: A 1985 table published by the government that provides data on the probability of an individual becoming disabled during his or her lifetime.

Common law property system: One of two property law systems (with the other being the community property system) that permits the titling of property individually even in the event of marriage; currently, the system of property law in 41 of the 50 states.

Community property system: One of two property law systems (with the other being the common law property system) that does not permit the titling of property individually while married; that is, any property acquired by either spouse during marriage generally belongs to "the community" and not to the individual separately. Currently, the system of property law in 9 of the 50 states, most notably the states of California and Texas.

Contingent trust for minors: A trust created in each parent's will specifying a trustee and provisions for the parent's property in the event of a simultaneous death of the parents. It is important that the trustee work in concert with the parent's named guardian for the children of the parents who benefit from the trust property.

Correlation: A measure of the movement of two variables, such as financial assets, in relation to each other. For example, if one financial asset declines in value, while another increases in value at the same time, the assets are said to exhibit "negative correlation". The use of correlation is a key factor in the proper diversification of a portfolio of assets.

Custodial account: A type of account, commonly used in planning for a children's higher education, where monies are set aside on behalf of a minor child, but managed by the child's parent or "custodian". Such account is permitted in all fifty states, either in the form of a Unified Gifts to Minor's Act (UGMA) account of Unified Transfers to Minor's Act (UTMA) account.

D

Defined benefit retirement plan: A tax-qualified employer pension plan that guarantees a specified benefit amount or level at the date of the participant's retirement; commonly offered only by large corporations or government entities.

Defined contribution retirement plan: A tax-qualified employer profit-sharing (or other type of) plan that establishes an individual account for each plan participant with plan benefits consisting of the amount accumulated in each account at the participant's retirement or termination of employment; the most common and popular type of defined contribution plan is a Section 401(k) retirement plan.

Dependent care credit: An income tax credit or dollar-for-dollar reduction against a taxpayer's income tax liability because the taxpayer has incurred child care expenses for a child under the age of 13. The maximum amount of credit is determined by tax law on a "sliding credit" basis, with the maximum capped under law regardless of the number of children receiving dependent care.

Disclaimer trust: A type of trust used in estate planning which allows individual(s) to benefit from property that is otherwise refused or "disclaimed" by the named beneficiary or heir.

Durable power of attorney: A type of power of attorney (granted by the principal to the agent) which continues even in the event of the principal or author's legal incapacity or inability to act; currently permitted by all fifty states in some form.

E

Education Savings Account (ESA): Properly known as the Coverdell Education Savings Account and the successor to the previous "Education IRA"; a trust or custodial account created exclusively for the purpose of paying qualified educational expenses of the designated beneficiary of the account. Currently, taxpayers may deposit cash of up to $2,000 per year into the account for a child under the age of 18.

Expected Family Contribution (EFC): The amount of money that a family is expected to contribute to pay for a child's higher education as determined from completing the Free Application for Student Financial Aid (FAFSA) form provided by the federal government.

F

401(k) Plan: A type of tax-qualified profit sharing plan that provides for before-tax salary reduction contributions to be made by the employee. Such plan must not only be generally non-discriminatory (all eligible employees must be permitted to participate), but also must meet special non-discrimination rules if the employer matches employee contributions with additional monies.

Flexible Spending Account (FSA): A type of "cafeteria plan" – a plan under which employees may choose between cash and non-taxable fringe benefits- that is funded through salary reductions elected by employees each year.

Floater: An insurance term used to describe personal property that travels with the insured and remains insured wherever the insured is currently traveling; commonly used in conjunction with the term "personal articles" and indicates insurance on property such as jewelry or personal keepsakes.

G

Grantor: The individual that creates or establishes a revocable or irrevocable trust; also used in tax terminology to mean the possible individual that is taxed on income generated from trust property, determined under a series of rules collectively referred to as the "grantor trust rules".

H

Highly Compensated Employee (HCE): A specific definition of certain employees that are the focus of the non-discrimination rules determining, in part, whether a retirement plan is "tax-qualified" or granted certain tax advantages. Specifically, the plan, to be qualified for tax purposes, cannot discriminate in favor of HCEs. An HCE is an individual who owns either a certain nominal percentage of the business (such as more than 5 percent) or an employee that makes in excess of a specified amount of annual salary.

I

Immediate fixed annuity: A popular form of retirement product where the retiree turns over to the insurance company a given lump sum of money in exchange for a fixed annuity payment that begins immediately (or typically within 30 days).

Intestate Succession: A series of state laws that specifies who inherits property at a decedent's death where the decedent dies without having written a last will and testament.

Irrevocable Life Insurance Trust (ILIT): A trust whereby the owner of a life insurance policy irrevocably relinquishes those ownership rights to a designated third party, the trustee of the trust. As a result, the death proceeds from the life insurance policy are removed from the owner's gross estate and a trustee is chosen that can provide needed liquidity to pay taxes and other expenses incurred in the administration of a decedent's estate.

J

Joint Tenancy with Right of Survivorship (JTWROS): Also referred to as owning property "jointly"; a type of property ownership (most commonly found in common law property states) that is distinguished by automatic survivorship rights on the death of the first joint tenant to die. The primary advantage of JTWROS property is that title passes automatically to the survivor and without the necessity of the probate process.

L

Lloyds of London: A specialist insurance market, located in London, England, where members join together as syndicated to insure risks; most commonly known for insuring hard-to-insure or unique risks, such as Betty Grable's legs or famous baseball pitchers' throwing arms.

M

Managed care health insurance plans: A certain type of health insurance plans noted for their emphasis on preventative medicine and characterized by such features as a network of physicians and copayments by insureds; examples of managed care plans as health maintenance organizations (HMOs) and preferred provider organizations (PPOs).

Marginal income tax bracket: The rate on a specified amount on the taxpayer's *next* dollar of income; very important for income tax planning purposes since it affects tax decision-making.

Master Limited Partnerships (MLPs): A type of limited partnership investment that is publicly traded (as contrasted to a private limited partnership that is not publicly traded and does not have an active market if the owner wishes to sell his or her interest in the partnership).

Mutual funds: More properly known as an "open ended investment company"; a type of company that pools money from shareholders and invests in a variety of securities, including stocks, bonds, and money market securities. Mutual funds generally continuously offer new shares to investors and redeem old shares.

N

Net Unrealized Appreciation (NUA): A very favorable income tax advantage given to the distribution of employer shares in a qualified retirement plan; specifically, tax is not imposed on the appreciation of employer shares from the date of contribution to the date of distribution until the date of sale of those shares and, then, tax is imposed only at favorable long-term capital gains rates.

O

Ordinary income: A term used in income tax to distinguish the taxation of salary and wages from that on the sale of assets (or capital gains or losses). Currently, the tax rate on salary and wages (ordinary income) is 35 percent but, historically, has been as high as 90 percent.

Overfund: A generic term used in the context of estate planning meaning that improper use of the transfer tax marital deduction has occurred. For example, if the second spouse-to-die estate's is "overfunded", it means that too much property has been transferred to him or her from the first spouse-to-die to engage in efficient estate tax planning for the couple as a unit.

P

Payable on Death (POD) form: A form or account that is used with bank checking and savings account specifying who is to receive such individually-titled account at the death of the owner; the form's primary advantage in estate planning is that is permits the transferred monies to pass automatically to the named beneficiary and without the necessity of the probate process.

Personal Automobile Policy (PAP): The most common form of automobile policy issued by insurance companies as based on Insurance Services Offices (ISO) forms. It includes parts such as liability, bodily injury, property damages, medical payments, and collision.

Pooled Income Fund (PIF): A trust generally created and maintained by a public charity, such as a public or private university or not-for-profit hospital; used in estate planning to provide both a lifetime charitable income tax deduction and to benefit the public charity at the donor's death.

Portfolio diversification: A fundamental investment technique used to reduce the risk associated with capital market investing; technique is characterized by the purchase of securities both within and across asset classes, such as stocks and bonds or stock and bond mutual funds.

Pour-over will: A will used in conjunction with a revocable living trust that distributes or "pours over" to the trust any assets that have not been titled in the name of the trust during the grantor's lifetime or any assets that the grantor may have acquired after the trust re-titling first occurred.

Price-to-Earnings (P/E) ratio : The number by which the expected earnings per share on a stock investment is multiplied to estimate the stock's proper value; also sometimes referred to as the "earnings multiplier".

Q

Qualified charity: A charity that is "qualified" for income tax purposes, meaning that is has met certain requirements to allow the contributor to take advantage of an income tax deduction once a contribution is made to the charity; can be either a public or private charity.

Qualified Personal Residence Trust (QPRT): An irrevocable trust where the grantor of the trust transfers ownership of his or her personal residence (or vacation home) to another, but retains the right to occupy the residence for a period of years, at which time title to the residence passes to the beneficiaries of the trust.

R

Rabbi trust: A trust that is established to hold property used for financing a deferred compensation plan, where the funds set aside are subject to the employer's creditors. As a result, the trust achieves an income tax deferral of funds set aside on behalf of the beneficiary/ corporate executive.

Real Estate Investment Trust (REIT): An investment (usually in the form of a publicly- traded- trust) that holds portfolios of real estate investments.

Recognized: An income tax term that means that all events have occurred from an economic standpoint requiring the taxpayer to pay tax on the sale of the asset or income.

Revocable living trust: A very important estate planning technique that permits the grantor to avoid the probate process at death while still controlling and enjoying the benefits from his or her lifetime property; to be contrasted to an irrevocable trust, which may achieve transfer tax savings but at the loss of control of the grantor's property during lifetime.

Roth 401(k): A relatively recent type of retirement plan that features the advantages of 401(k) contributions and the Roth account at time of distribution. The Roth contributions are included in the participant's gross income when made, but are generally not included in the participant's gross income when distributed.

Roth IRA: A type of individual retirement account (IRA) under which contributions may be made up to a specified limit on an after-tax or non-deductible basis, but withdrawals are tax free presuming certain requirements are satisfied. A Roth IRA is a second form of personal savings plan for retirement with the other being a traditional deductible IRA.

Rule of 72: A simple rule that may be used to estimate how long it will take for a given sum or deposit of money to double in value by dividing the rate of return into the numerator of 72. For example, if an investor achieves a before-tax rate of return of 8 percent compounded annually, it will take approximately nine years for the given sum of money to double in value (72 divided by 8= 9).

S

Section 529 private savings plan: A form of college savings plan, governed under Section 529 of the Internal Revenue Code, where the account owner contributes cash to a plan account for the beneficiary, and the contribution is invested according to the terms of the plan. When the beneficiary attends college, the funds in the account plus all of the earnings may be used to pay for the beneficiary's tuition and other college expenses income-tax free.

Special needs trust: A type of trust established by clients who have children who are mentally or physically disabled and are entitled to receive supplemental Social Security Income (SSI) benefits or other types of governmental assistance. If structured properly, such trust may permit the parents to furnish some benefits to the developmentally disabled child without disqualifying the child from receiving governmental assistance.

Standard homeowner's (HO) policy: A type of homeowner's policy, following Insurance Service Offices (ISO) format, which is written on an "open perils" basis, meaning that losses to the home are covered, regardless of the peril or cause of the loss, unless specifically excluded under the terms of the policy.

Stock: An evidence of ownership of a corporation; a major attribute is the ability to vote for the Board of Directors of the corporation.

T

Tax-qualified annuity: A tax term referring to the purchase of an annuity by the sponsor of a qualified retirement plan on behalf of the plan participant; such annuity is characterized by the lack of any tax basis in the plan, thus making the entire annuity payment income-taxable to the participant at the time of payment or distribution.

Term insurance: A type of life insurance characterized by its temporary nature, that is, for the insured's beneficiary to receive the insurance proceeds or death benefit, the insured must die within the stated term of the policy.

Time value of money: A finance theory that posits a "dollar is worth more today than in the future" given that this dollar can be invested to generate additional monies.

Traditional IRA: An individual retirement account or individual retirement annuity under which deductible contributions, up to certain limits, and investment earnings are tax-deferred. Interest earned and gains received while inside the protection of the traditional IRA are free of federal income tax until withdrawn. IRA can also be offered on a non-deductible basis for individuals that cannot qualify for a deductible contribution.

Transfer-on-Death (TOD) form: A form or account that is used by securities firms specifying who is to receive such individually-titled account at the death of the owner; the form's primary advantage in estate planning is that is permits the transferred funds to pass automatically to the named beneficiary and without the necessity of the probate process.

Trust: A legal arrangement whereby property is transferred or set aside on behalf of another with the distribution of that property postponed or delayed by the grantor until some point in the future; used for a wide variety of purposes in estate and financial planning, but particularly to pass property to family members either during the grantor's lifetime (inter vivos) or at his or her death (testamentary).

Trustee: The legal owner of the property transferred into trust by the grantor; the trustee has a legal duty known as a "fiduciary duty" to act in the best interests of the trust beneficiary(ies) at all times.

U

Umbrella liability insurance: An alternative to increasing personal liability limits in either an automobile or homeowner's insurance policy; generally, the umbrella policy has high individual liability limits and can also protect the insured from personal risks, such as the risk of libel or slander, not typically covered under the underlying policies. A necessary part of protection planning for high net worth individuals.

V

Volatility: A commonly-used term to describe the daily movements of the financial markets. For example, if the market index averages are significantly different from the preceding day, the market is said to be extremely "volatile".

W

Wealth replacement trust: A type of irrevocable life insurance trust (ILIT) that is used to replace the value of property that is left to a qualified charity at the grantor's death, which would otherwise pass to an heir or family member of the grantor. In such trust, a life insurance policy is purchased on the life of the grantor with the family member named as the beneficiary.

www.ingramcontent.com/pod-product-compliance
Lightning Source LLC
Chambersburg PA
CBHW071353170526
45165CB00001B/22